Easy P

Upgrading

Robert Penfold

Bernard Babani (publishing) Ltd
The Grampians
Shepherds Bush Road
London W6 7NF
England
www.babanibooks.com

Please note

Although every care has been taken with the production of this book to ensure that any projects, designs, modifications, and/or programs, etc., contained herewith, operate in a correct and safe manner and also that any components specified are normally available in Great Britain, the Publisher and Author do not accept responsibility in any way for the failure (including fault in design) of any projects, design, modification, or program to work correctly or to cause damage to any equipment that it may be connected to or used in conjunction with, or in respect of any other damage or injury that may be caused, nor do the Publishers accept responsibility in any way for the failure to obtain specified components.

Notice is also given that if any equipment that is still under warranty is modified in any way or used or connected with home-built equipment then that warranty may be void.

© 2003 BERNARD BABANI (publishing) LTD

First Published - January 2003
Reprinted - November 2003
Reprinted - July 2004

British Library Cataloguing in Publication Data
A catalogue record for this book is available from the British Library

ISBN   0 85934 531 9

Cover Design by Gregor Arthur
Printed and bound in Great Britain by Cox and Wyman

Preface

Since its introduction in 1981 the IBM PC has undergone continuous changes and developments. IBM themselves led the way initially, but in recent times the various "clone" manufacturers have introduced some innovations of their own. Despite all the improvements that have been made, and the increased capabilities of modern PCs, a PC still remains very much a PC. Software and a fair percentage of add-ons for the original machines will still function perfectly well in a modern PC.

A factor that has certainly aided the popularity of PCs is their open architecture. IBM published the full specification of the PC expansion slots, making it easy for third party suppliers to produce and sell PC expansion cards of various types. This has led to numerous specialist add-ons for the PC being produced, as well as a good range of mainstream products. PCs and their interfaces have moved on over the years, but there are still countless add-ons available that enable PCs to work well in numerous everyday and specialist applications.

While expanding a PC is, in the main, a reasonably straightforward affair, there are inevitably a few complications to most aspects of PC upgrading. The main purpose this book is to first explain the basics of PC hardware, and to then help untangle the difficulties that can arise when undertaking the more popular of PC upgrades. The topics covered include floppy and hard disc drives, memory expansion, processor upgrades, CD-ROMs, ports, modems, and simple networking. The rate of change in the PC world is such that often the only way of upgrading the processor is to change the motherboard and memory as well. This type of upgrade is also given detailed coverage.

Do-it-yourself upgrading is a daunting task for those with little experience of dealing with PC hardware. However, most upgrading does not require much in the way of manual skills or tools. If you have a medium size cross point screwdriver you probably have all the tools needed for computer upgrading, but a pair of pliers might also come in useful. You need to be a reasonably practical person, but no real expertise is required. Provided you do not have a history of do-it-yourself disasters there should be no difficulty in undertaking PC upgrades. Many computer components are easily damaged, so you should make sure that you understand the simple handling precautions that are needed before undertaking any upgrading. Computer upgrading should then be reasonably problem free, and should cost much less than having the work done professionally.

Robert Penfold

Trademarks

Microsoft, Windows, Windows XP, Windows Me, Windows 98 and Windows 95 are either registered trademarks or trademarks of Microsoft Corporation.

Dreamweaver MX, Flash MX, and Fireworks MX are registered trademarks or trademarks of Macromedia Inc.

All other brand and product names used in this book are recognised trademarks, or registered trademarks of their respective companies. There is no intent to use any trademarks generically and readers should investigate ownership of a trademark before using it for any purpose.

Contents

1

PC overview 1

2

Upgrade basics 39

3

Adding ports 75

6

Adding drives 157

7

Memory upgrades 201

8

Major upgrades........................... 219

9

Modems 263

PC overview

Modular computer

The are many possible reasons for the unrivalled popularity of the IBM PCs and the numerous compatible machines, which have been the standard business microcomputer for many years now. There are also many millions of PCs in home use. One contributory factor is certainly their enormous expansion potential. The basic computer, or "system unit" as it is generally called, is unusable on its own. It requires the addition of disc drives, a monitor, a keyboard, and even such things as an add-on display generator before it will provide any useful function. This modular approach has been the cause of a certain amount of criticism, but in truth it is a very good way of doing things.

If all you require is a very basic computer with an inexpensive processor, a hard disc drive of modest capacity and a small monitor for text use, then you can buy a PC of that type. You do not need to spend money on expensive disc hard drives, up-market processors, or large monitors that you do not need or want. If, on the other hand, you are interested in graphics applications and require high-resolution true-colour graphics plus a large and fast hard disc drive, you will have a choice of several PC compatible systems that offer a suitable specification. With requirements for computer systems that fall somewhere between these two extremes you are likely to be spoiled for choice, with a vast number of suitable systems to choose from.

If you can not find something that exactly meets your requirements, then it is possible to buy a basic computer system and add in suitable peripherals yourself. Due to IBM's so-called "open architecture" policy (publishing full technical details of their microcomputers so that third party manufacturers can produce add-ons for them), the range of add-on boards and other peripherals for the PC series runs into many hundreds. Some PC suppliers will actually build a PC to your specifications.

In this book we will mainly be concerned with the hardware side of PC compatible computing. In this first chapter we will take a look at PC hardware in general, going into detail on some subjects, but considering others in a superficial manner. Subsequent chapters provide detailed information on several topics not fully discussed in this chapter (disc drives, memory, etc.). Those who are already familiar with the general principles of PC hardware and expansion will probably be familiar with some of the topics covered in chapter 1. Readers in this category might like to skip over some sections of this chapter.

Those who are not familiar with PC hardware should study this chapter in some detail before progressing to any of the other chapters that cover a topic of particular interest to them. Trying to expand a PC without understanding the differences between the various types of PC and their general make-up could easily lead to some costly mistakes.

You need to know where a PC fits into the overall scheme of things in order to judge whether or not it is feasible or worthwhile trying to upgrade it. On the face of it, the modular approach makes any PC fully upgradeable to the latest specification. In reality things do move on, and things such as expansion slots and the standard ports have evolved over the years. Upgrading some PCs to a modern specification would involve replacing virtually everything, and would produce what was virtually a new PC rather than an upgraded PC. You may feel that this is a viable approach, and it can certainly be an interesting exercise, but most people would probably prefer to buy a new PC and use the old one as a standby computer.

Software compatibility

The term "software compatibility" in a PC context originally referred to the ability (or lack of it) to run standard IBM PC software designed to operate under either the PC-DOS or MS-DOS operating systems. These two operating systems can for virtually all practical purposes be regarded as interchangeable. PC-DOS was the operating system produced by Microsoft for use with real IBM PCs, whereas MS-DOS is the version for compatibles. In theory, any software written to run under PC/MS-DOS should run on any computer that has either of these operating systems up and running properly. In practice there is a complication in that much software sometimes controls the computer's hardware by reading from it and writing to it directly, rather than going through the operating system.

The problem here is that any variations in the hardware are supposed to be handled by the operating system. If data is written to a printer port, the operating system should ensure that the data is sent to the right piece of hardware, and that the flow of data to the printer is controlled properly. If data sent direct to the hardware by the program, and it monitors the hardware directly to see if the printer is ready to receive data, there is a risk of incompatibility. In these circumstances the program will only run properly if the computer has the right peripheral components at the right places in the computer's input/output map. The operating system will not be involved in the exchange of data, and will not intervene to ensure that it all goes smoothly.

In days gone by quite a large number of programs relied on direct control of the hardware in order to achieve a suitably fast operating speed. This made it important to have hardware that accurately mimicked a genuine IBM PC. Of course, these days it is compatibility with Windows 95 through to XP that its of more importance and basic MS-DOS compatibility is something we now take for granted. Software drivers integrate hardware such as video boards and pointing devices with Windows (any version), and it is these drivers that ensure a modern PC is fully compatible. Odd incompatibility problems do still arise from time to time, but obtaining updated software drivers for the offending piece of hardware should sort things out. Bear in mind that PC hardware is useless unless suitable drivers are included in Windows, or the manufacturer supplies the appropriate drivers.

ROM BIOS

An important factor for good compatibility is the quality of the ROM BIOS. ROM stands for "read only memory", and it is a component (or two in the case of some older AT type computers) which contains a computer program. This program contains the BIOS, or "basic input/output system." The first function of the BIOS is to run a few diagnostic checks at switch-on to ensure that the computer is up and running properly. It then looks on the disc drives in search of the operating system, which it then loads into the computer's memory. The operating system then takes over, but the BIOS contains software routines that can be utilized by the operating system and applications programs.

You will often encounter the term "booting" or "booting-up", which refers to this process of the operating system being automatically loaded from disc and run. This term is derived from the fact that operating system appears to load itself into the computer's memory, which is akin to pulling one's self up by ones bootlaces. Of course, the operating system only appears to be loading and running itself. The truth of the matter is that routines in the ROM BIOS are carrying out this process.

The software in the BIOS, or "firmware" as programs in this form are often termed, must not be an exact copy of the IBM original due to copyright restrictions. Things have moved on anyway, and a modern BIOS has to deal with more hardware parameters than the original BIOS was designed to cope with. Several companies produce BIOS chips that do the same basic job as the IBM original, but by a different means so that copyright problems are avoided. Obviously this gives rise to the possibility of incompatibilities, but any modern BIOS should be well tried and tested. Again, I have used many IBM compatibles over the years, using BIOS chips from manufacturers including Phoenix, Award and AMI, and have yet to encounter any incompatibility problems.

Probably the most likely cause of software compatibility these days is simply not having a PC that is up to the task. The best modern PCs must be something like a thousand times faster than the originals, and have several hundred times more memory. Modern software mostly requires a PC that has a modern specification, and with the more demanding programs a very high specification is required. The much given advice of buy the software that suits your requirements first and then the buy hardware to suit it afterwards, remains as good as it ever was. It is as well to bear in mind that there is almost always a significant gap between new "improved" hardware arriving on the scene, and software being updated to take advantage of it. The widespread use of Windows has eased this problem, and new hardware should be supplied complete with Windows drivers. Even so, with the more advanced items of hardware there can still be a gap between its launch and the arrival of widespread software support.

PC versions

The PCs and compatibles have evolved over a period of several years, and the more up-market systems in use today have specifications that bear little resemblance to the original IBM PC, which was launched in 1981. The original had just 64k of memory, a monochrome text only display, and included a cassette port. The IBM compatible I am using to produce the text and illustrations for this book has 512 megabytes (524288k) of RAM, a colour graphics board and monitor that can handle up to 1600 by 1200 pixels with 16 million colours, plus a DVD drive, CD rewriter, and a 40 gigabyte fast hard disc. It also uses a microprocessor that renders it over a thousand times faster than the original PC. Despite this, it is still highly compatible with the original computer. It can almost certainly run any software that will run on the original version of the computer. It also has the standard parallel and serial ports that can be used with older peripherals. In common with most modern PCs though, it does lack compatibility with the original expansion cards and it will only take the modern PCI variety.

Compatibility between modern hardware and software and older PCs is less good. There is much software and a lot of expansion cards that will work in my PC, but are unusable with the original computer (and many of the more recent compatibles come to that). This factor produces the need to upgrade PCs or move on to newer and better ones. It is worth briefly considering basic details of the various versions of the IBM PC range. This is not just a matter of historical interest, but because it can be helpful to know how your particular machine fits into the overall scheme of things.

Original PCs

The "PC" in IBM PC merely stands for "personal computer". This is a possible cause of confusion since the IBM PCs and compatibles are often referred to simply as "PCs", but this is also a general term for any microcomputer which is primarily intended for business rather than home use. Anyway, in this book the term "PC" will only be used to refer to the IBM PC family of computers and the many compatible machines.

The original PC had relatively limited expansion potential. It had facilities for five full-length expansion slots, but this was not quite as good as it might at first appear. With a maximum of only 256k RAM on the main circuit board, (64k on the earliest PCs), and slots being required for disk controllers, serial and parallel ports, and the display card, some of these slots were required to provide essential functions. To ease the problem, several manufacturers produced multi-function cards, which gave such things as an extra 384k of memory, plus serial and parallel ports all on one card. This was more than a little helpful at the time, but with modern PCs this sort of thing is unnecessary, because the standard interfaces are included on the main board.

The main problem when trying to expand an early PC was often the power supply. This had a rating of 63.5 watts, which is low in comparison to the ratings of around 150 watts for the later versions, and 230 watts for a modern PC. 63.5 watts was actually quite a hefty power supply for a microcomputer of the time, but it nevertheless provided little more power than the basic system required, and little more than many modern microprocessors consume. Anything more than the addition of one or two low power cards required the fitting of a more beefy power supply unit, which usually meant a 150 watt type, as fitted to some later versions of the PC, and most early PC compatibles. Upgrading an early PC is not a worthwhile proposition these days, and the original PCs are now entering the realms of collector's items.

PC XT

IBM introduced the PC XT in 1983, and it is this model rather than the original PC that tends to be considered as the first "real" PC. The "XT" part of the name is an abbreviation for extended, incidentally. It was an improvement on the original design in a number of ways. One of the improvements was the ability to have up to 640k of socketed RAM on the main circuit board, or "motherboard" as it is usually termed. The original PCs had all the RAM chips soldered directly to the board, making it difficult and expensive to replace a faulty chip. With the ability to have 640k of RAM on the motherboard, which is the maximum that the design of the computer permits, there was no need to take up an expansion slot with a memory board if you need the full complement of RAM.

The expansion slot problem was eased anyway, by the inclusion of no less than eight slots on the motherboard. Even with slots occupied by disc controllers, serial and parallel ports, and a display board, there would still typically be four or five slots left for more exotic peripherals. Two of the slots are only suitable for short expansion boards. This is simply due to physical limitations, with a disc drive preventing full-length cards from being fitted into these two slots.

This was not a major drawback since many expansion cards were (and are) of the half-length variety. It was not inconceivable that users would wish to have seven or eight full-length boards in an XT, but this was a highly unlikely state of affairs. However, some compatibles were capable of taking eight full-length cards. The 135-watt fan cooled power supply (usually 150 watts on clones) enabled plenty of peripherals to be powered without any risk of overloading the supply unit. Originally the XT was supplied complete with a 10-megabyte hard disc drive, but this was later made an optional extra. A 20-megabyte hard drive option was also available

Turbo PCs

The computers in the IBM PC family are all based on microprocessors from the Intel 8086 series of microprocessors. The PC and PC XT computers are based on 8088, which is a slightly simplified version of the 8086. Whereas the 8086 processor has 16 pins which carry data into and out of the device, the 8088 has only eight pins for this purpose. This means that the 8088 has to take in and put out 16-bit chunks of data or program instructions as two 8-bit chunks ("bytes"), one after the other.

This is undesirable as it slows down the computer to a significant degree. Coupled with the relatively slow clock speed used in the PC and PC XT of just 4.77 megahertz, this meant that the standard PCs had little more computing power than the faster 8-bit computers of the time. It could be argued that the XT class PCs were in fact 8-bit computers and not "real" 16-bit types. By current standards they are very slow computers, and like the original PCs are now collector's items.

IBM never produced what could really be regarded as a "turbo" version of the PC or PC XT. Most PC clones were and are of this type, although modern PCs have developed to the point where the "turbo" name is no longer adequate to describe them. In the early days of "turbo" PCs there were three basic routes to obtaining increased speed. These could be used singly or in any combination. Details of the three methods are given below.

Increased clock speed

The most obvious way of obtaining increased operating speed is to use a higher clock frequency. It is an oversimplification to say that doubling the clock frequency of the processor doubles the speed of the computer, but in practice this is more or less what happens. In order to use a higher clock frequency successfully the microprocessor must obviously be able to run reliably at the higher frequency, as must the memory chips and other circuits in the computer. Alternatively, the processor can operate at full speed, with the other circuits operating more slowly. The processor has so-called "wait states" to slow things down and let the rest of the hardware catch up.

Using an 8086 Microprocessor

Using the 8086 with its 16-bit data bus might seem an obvious way of getting improved performance, but matters are not as simple as it might at first appear. The early PCs had 8-bit expansion slots, making it difficult to obtain full hardware compatibility with them if the 16-bit 8086 was used. This problem was not insurmountable, and some 8086-based compatibles (notably some Amstrad and Olivetti machines) were produced. This method of performance boosting was a relatively rare one though.

Using the NEC V20

The NEC V20 microprocessor was capable of undertaking all 8088 instructions, and was fully compatible with it. The point about the V20 is that compared with the 8088 it took fewer clock pulses to complete some instructions. This obviously gave a boost in speed, but not a vast one. From my experience and tests I would say that the increase was somewhere in the region of 20 percent to 30 percent. There was a V30 microprocessor, which was a streamlined version of the 8086. Although we are now used to PCs fitted with non-Intel processors, for many years the V20 and V30 were the only compatible processors available.

PC AT computers

Rather than trying to speed up the PC and PC XT, IBM produced what was effectively a completely new design, but one which largely maintained software and hardware compatibility with the PC and PC XT. This computer was the PC AT, and the "AT" part of the name stands for "advanced technology." This was based on the Intel 80286 microprocessor, which is an improved version of the 8086. Like the 8086 it has a 16-bit data bus, and the AT was therefore a true 16-bit computer. The AT achieves higher operating speeds than the PC and PC XT because it operates at a higher clock speed. The original AT operated at 6 megahertz, but the later versions had an 8 megahertz clock.

Comparing the speed of the PC and PC XT computers with the AT models is difficult since the 80286 takes fewer clock cycles per instruction than the 8086 or 8088. Thus, while it might seem as though a 10 megahertz XT compatible was faster than a 6 megahertz or 8 megahertz AT, this is not actually the case. Popular methods of speed testing generally put the AT many times faster than the original 4.77 megahertz PC and PC XT machines. If you take the clock speed of an AT in megahertz, then it is roughly that many times faster than a 4.77 megahertz XT, according to the popular speed test programs anyway.

The original IBM AT computers were fitted with 512k of RAM on the motherboard, but later compatible machines were able to take the full 640k on the motherboard. In fact most AT computers could take at least 1 megabyte of memory on the main circuit board, and many were equipped to take 4 or 8 megabytes. These large amounts of RAM are made possible by an extra operating mode of the 80286 which takes advantage of extra address lines on the chip. However, when running PC/MS-DOS software the 80286 can not directly use the RAM above the 640k limit. This is not to say that there is no point in having the extra RAM. Some programs can use it in slightly roundabout methods, such as using the RAM for a disc cache or a RAM disc. Also, operating systems such as OS/2 and Windows 95/98 can run programs in the mode that takes full advantage of the whole 16-megabyte address range.

16-bit slot

As it was a true 16-bit computer, in order to take full advantage of the 16-bit data bus the AT needed to have 16-bit expansion slots. This obviously raised possibilities of incompatibility between the AT and existing 8-bit PC expansion cards. In order to minimise these problems the 16-bit expansion slots of the AT and subsequent PCs are in the form of standard 8-bit slots plus a second connector which carries the extra lines needed by 16-bit expansion boards.

This means that any 8-bit card should work in an AT style computer, with the only exception of boards that are PC or PC XT specific for some other reason. The only common example of this that springs to mind are the PC and PC XT hard disc controller cards. These have their own BIOS, whereas an AT hard disc controller card makes use of routines in the main BIOS on the motherboard. This gives what is really a firmware compatibility problem, rather than what could strictly speaking be termed hardware incompatibility.

There were actually some boards, such as certain 16-bit VGA display cards, that would work in either type of computer. They sometimes achieved this by detecting electronically which type computer they were fitted in, and then configuring themselves accordingly. In other cases the user had to set a switch on the card to the appropriate position. In most cases though, 16-bit cards are incompatible with PC and PC XT machines.

AT computers, even those using the faster versions of the 80286 chip, are now well and truly obsolete. If still in good order they will quite happily run contemporary software, but there are no practical upgrades that will bring one of these computers up to a specification that is suitable for running modern software. So much of the original PC would have to be replaced that you would effectively be building a new computer.

80386 ATs

When Intel produced an improved version of the 80286 microprocessor, the 80386, it was inevitable that this device would soon be used in a new and faster generation of PCs. However, IBM never produced an 80386-based version of the PC. IBM has produced computers based on this microprocessor, but not in a straightforward PC guise. The IBM "PS/2" range used a different form of expansion bus, and it is discussed in more detail later on in this chapter. This lack of an IBM 80386-based PC to clone meant that the clone manufacturers were left without any standards to follow when producing 80386 PCs. Computers of this type are effectively AT clones, but using the 80386 plus its support chips instead of the 80286 and the relevant devices. Modern PCs are developments of the 80386 AT style computers. Although they have developed almost beyond recognition, modern PCs are still AT class PCs.

Using the 80386 in an AT style computer does have some advantages. The 80386 can operate with clock rates of up to 33 megahertz, or 40 megahertz for some 80386 compatible chips. I have often seen it stated that the 80386 performs instructions in fewer clock cycles than the 80286, giving a vast increase in performance. On the other hand, the results of speed tests on various 80286 and 80386 computers would seem to suggest that there is little to choose between the two types of computer when running at the same clock rate. The 80386 is a 32-bit microprocessor, which makes it potentially more powerful in maths intensive applications than the 16-bit 80286. However, to take advantage of this it is necessary to have software that is written specifically for the 32-bit 80386. These days we take 32-bit operating systems and applications software for granted, but when the 80386 first came along there was relatively little software that could fully exploit its potential.

Apart from its ability to access memory 32 bits at a time, the 80386 has other advantages in the way that it handles memory. For straightforward PC/MS-DOS applications it runs in the "real" mode (as does the 80286), and effectively just emulates the 8086. In the "protected virtual" mode (often just called "protected" mode) it is much like the 80286 in its mode which gives a 16 megabyte memory address range. It has some extensions in this mode though, including a memory management unit (MMU) which provides sophisticated memory paging and program switching capabilities. Perhaps of more immediate importance to most users, the 80386 can switch from the protected mode back to the real mode much more simply and quickly than the 80286 can manage. A program running in real mode, but making use of extended memory and protected mode via a RAM disc or whatever, will therefore operate more quickly when accessing the extended memory. This is not purely of academic importance, and some methods of using the extended memory on an 80386-based AT are not worthwhile when implemented on an 80286-based AT as they simply do not work fast enough.

The 80386 has a third mode of operation called "virtual real" mode. The 80286 has no equivalent of this mode. In essence it permits the memory to be split into several sections, with each one running its own operating system and an applications program. Each program is run entirely separately from the others, and if one program should crash then all the others should remain running normally. Only the crashed section of memory needs to have its operating system rebooted and the program reloaded. This solves what has tended to be a big problem with many multi-tasking computers, where programs tend to crash regularly due to one program interfering with another, and with one program crashed the whole system tends to follow suit. The amount of memory that the 80386 can handle is so large (4 gigabytes, or some 4000 megabytes in other words) that most of today's PCs can not actually take this much RAM.

There is a sort of cut-down version of the 80386, the 80386SX. This has a 16-bit bus like the 80286, but internally it has all the 80386 registers. This enables it to run 80386 specific software as well as standard PC software, albeit somewhat more slowly than on an 80386-based computer. The reduced speed is the result of the 32-bit pieces of data or instructions having to be loaded as two 16-bit chunks rather than being loaded simultaneously. 80386-based PCs are now well and truly out of date, and not really worthwhile candidates for upgrading.

PS/2 computers

When IBM ceased making the PC range of computers they were replaced with the PS/2 range. This should perhaps be considered as two ranges, since it consists of relatively simple machines that could reasonably be regarded as PC compatibles, and a more advanced range which are still basically PCs, but which depart from the previous standards in some quite radical ways.

The most basic of the PS/2 range were the Model 25 and the Model 30. These were 8 megahertz 8086-based computers which used standard ISA expansion slots of the 8-bit variety. They differed from earlier PCs in that they had a number of functions (such as the display generator circuitry) on the motherboard rather than requiring these functions to be provided by cards fitted in expansion slots. There was also a Model 30 286 computer, which was a 10 megahertz 80286-based computer having 16-bit ISA expansion slots. ISA (industry standard architecture) slots are the ordinary 8-bit and 16-bit PC expansion slots incidentally. The Model 25/30 and Model 30 286 computers were effectively more modern equivalents of the XT and AT computers, and PCs in the generally accepted sense of the term.

The Model 50, 60, 70, and 80 computers were more advanced computers which used a different form of expansion bus called "micro channel architecture", or just "MCA" as it is much better known. This is not really the place for a discussion of this expansion bus standard, since the subject of this book is the expansion of what for the want of a better term we will call the traditional PC. The subject of MCA will therefore not be considered any further here.

80486

The 80486DX is essentially a more efficient version of the 80386 that requires fewer clock cycles per instruction, and has some extra instructions. It departed from the 80386 and previous processors in this series by having the maths-coprocessor built-in, rather than as a separate chip. The maths-coprocessor is a microprocessor that is designed to handle complex mathematics, and is mainly intended as a means of speeding up floating-point calculations. Virtually all PCs using an 80386 or earlier processor had a socket on the motherboard for a maths-coprocessor, but it was normally an optional extra and not fitted as standard. Most software did not require the co-processor, and few PC users actually bothered to add one.

The 80486DX encouraged software authors to make use of the maths co-processor, which it turned into a standard feature where it had previously been an expensive add-on. The 80486DX version of the co-processor was more efficient than its predecessors, giving a useful increase in performance. There was a cut-down version of the 80486DX, the 80486SX, which lacked the built-in co-processor. Like the earlier PC processors, the maths co-processor was available as an optional extra.

The original 80486DX operated at a clock frequency of 33 megahertz, but some of the 80486SX chips were slower than this. Faster versions were developed over the years though, including some non-Intel alternatives to the 80486DX. I think I am right in stating that the fastest genuine Intel 80486DX operated at 100 megahertz, but non-Intel chips operating at up to about 133 megahertz were produced. The faster 80486DX-based PCs are powerful computers, but even if fitted with adequate RAM there is little modern software that they can handle adequately. There were processor upgrade kits that could be used to boost the performance of these PCs, but it is unlikely that anything of this type is still available. The boost in performance would not bring one of these PCs close to a modern level of performance anyway.

Pentiums

All modern PCs are based on an Intel Pentium processor, or a compatible processor from another manufacturer. Pentium processors have additional instructions, but are basically just faster and more efficient versions of the 80486DX. The original chips ran at 60 megahertz and 66 megahertz, and in most speed tests did not perform significantly better than the faster 80486 chips. Later versions used higher clock rates, fitted into a different socket, and had improved motherboards. This provided a boost in performance that gave much better results than any 80486DX PCs could achieve.

The clock frequencies for these "classic" Pentium processors are 75, 90, 100, 120, 133, 150, 166, and 200 megahertz. Figures 1.1 and 1.2 respectively show the top and underside of a Pentium 133 megahertz processor. Although

Fig.1.1 An Intel 133 megahertz Pentium processor

Fig.1.2 The underside of the chip

far more complicated, modern microprocessors for PCs do not look much different to the early Pentium designs, or the 80386 and 80486 processors come to that. Figure 1.3 shows a 2.4 gigahertz Pentium 4 processor in its protective packaging. Although far more complex than the 133 megahertz Socket 7 chip, its encapsulation is actually much smaller.

Although not exactly in the "antique" category, the early Pentium processors are now completely obsolete and have not been used in new PCs for some years.

Fig.1.3 This Pentium 4 does not look much different to its predecessors

Pentium processors with MMX (multimedia extension) technology replaced them. The MMX technology is actually an additional 57 processor instructions that are designed to speed up multimedia applications, but can also be used to good effect in other applications such as voice recognition. There were also some general improvements that produced an increase in performance of around 10 or 15 percent when using non-MMX specific software. These MMX Pentium processors were produced in 166, 200, and 233 megahertz versions.

Pentium II

These are now obsolete and were been replaced by Pentium II processors. Pentium II processors were produced with clock frequencies from 233 megahertz to around the 600 megahertz mark. The original Pentium processors fitted onto the motherboard via a conventional integrated circuit holder known as Socket 4. Those operating at 75 megahertz and above used an improved version called Socket 7. Pentium II processors look nothing like conventional processors, and in physical appearance they are like a cross between a videocassette and a memory module. They fit into a holder that is more like a PC expansion slot or holder for a memory module than an integrated circuit holder. Figure 1.4 shows an early Pentium II processor inside a PC, complete with its

Fig.1.4 The slot technology of the Pentium II is no longer used

massive heatsink. A Slot 1 motherboard is shown in Figure 1.5, and the processor fits into the slot in the upper right-hand section of the board.

One reason for this change in style is that it supposedly enables higher clock speeds to be utilized. However, the gigahertz processors of today manage to get by without the aid of slot technology. Probably the main reason for this change in style is that Pentium II chips were so complex that with the technology of the time it was not possible to put the processor and cache memory on the same chip. Cache memory is high-speed memory that is used to store recently processed data. It is likely that this data will need to be accessed again, and having it available in high-speed memory ensures that it can be processed very efficiently when it is needed. In virtually all practical applications this significantly speeds up the rate at which data can be processed.

Previous Pentium processors had some cache memory (typically 32k) on the chip, with a much larger cache of about 256 to 512k on the motherboard. These are known as level 1 and level 2 cache respectively. Level 1 cache is faster, but there are practical limits on the amount of cache memory that can be included in the processor. With the Pentium II chips it had to be omitted altogether, but a "piggy-back" memory chip included in the processor module provides a 512k cache.

Fig.1.5 An ATX motherboard for Slot 1 processors

The Pentium II is really a development of the Pentium Pro processor. This relatively unsuccessful processor was an improved version of the "classic" Pentium design, but when running Windows 95 software it often failed to provide much improvement over an ordinary Pentium chip. The Pentium Pro became overshadowed by the MMX Pentium processors, which proved to be an immediate hit with PC buyers. The Pentium II has the additional MMX instructions, and slightly improved performance compared to an ordinary MMX Pentium processor. The faster versions are designed to operate on motherboards that operate at a 100 megahertz clock frequency and use fast memory modules. The slower Pentium processors operate with 66 megahertz motherboards and relatively slow RAM. This gives the 350 and 400 megahertz chips a greater speed advantage over the slower versions than a comparison of the clock frequencies would suggest.

Although they are now getting "long in the tooth", the better Pentium II based PCs are quite powerful and with sufficient memory can run most modern software. The older Pentium II PCs are perhaps a bit low in speed and nearing their "use by" date, so expensive upgrades to one of these is perhaps not such a good idea. It would probably be better to put the money towards a new PC instead.

Fig.1.6 Socket 7 motherboards like this one were in production for many years

Celeron

The Intel processor for entry-level PCs is the Celeron, but at the time of writing it seems likely that this will be phased out in the very near future. The original Celeron was basically just a Pentium II with the add-on cache omitted. This saved on manufacturing costs but clearly gave a reduction in performance. The original Celeron did not exactly receive universal praise from the reviewers, and the absence of any on-board cache gave it a tough time keeping up with the latest budget processors from other manufacturers. Its performance was actually quite respectable, being around 15 to 30 percent faster than an Intel 233 megahertz MMX Pentium chip, depending on the type of software being run. This was still well short of full 266 megahertz Pentium II performance though.

Later versions of the Celeron were equipped with 128k of on-chip cache. Although the 128k is only one quarter of the cache fitted to a Pentium II, the fact that it is on the same chip as the processor (and therefore very fast) to some extent makes up for the smaller amount of cache. The Celeron cache runs at the same speed as the processor, while that of the Pentium II runs at half the processor's clock rate. Numerous faster versions of the Celeron were produced, and the original slot design was abandoned in favour of a return to conventional socket design. This was possible with the Celeron as it did not require the so-called "piggy-back" memory chip.

These Celerons use a different socket to the original Pentium chips, and it is called Socket 370 because there are 370 pins on the processor. Confusingly, there are two versions of Socket 370 that are physically much the same but use slightly different methods of connections. Figure 1.6 shows a Socket 370 motherboard which takes the original socket 370 chips. The second type is known as the FC-PGA (flip chip pin grid array) or just plain "flip-chip" version. Celerons around the 500 megahertz mark were made in both versions. The latest Celeron processors either fit the FC-PGA version of Socket 370 or the newer 478-pin socket. The FC-PGA chips have been produced with various clock frequencies up to 1.4 gigahertz (1400 megahertz). Faster clock rates of up to 1.8 gigahertz are available with the 478-pin versions.

The Celeron has been in use for several years and there are numerous versions of the chip. Clearly the latest versions are very powerful and the PCs that use them can run any current PC software. PCs that use the original version are very much slower and will have been in use for several years. Spending more than small amounts on upgrading an early Celeron-based PC does not make good economic sense, but the middle period chips at around the 500 megahertz mark still offer quite good performance and are mostly worthy of some expenditure to modernise them. These Celeron chips actually gave Pentium II chips of the same clock frequency a good "run for their money" and should not be underestimated.

Xeon

The Xeon is a form of Pentium II processor, and it is available with various cache options and clock speeds of 400 megahertz and upwards. Some previous Pentium processors can be used in dual processor systems, which, with the right software support, give significantly higher performance than equivalent single processor systems. The Xeon takes things further, and can be used in four-processor systems, with eight-processor computers planned for the future. It uses Slot 2 technology, and is therefore physically and electrically incompatible with Slot 1 motherboards. With its larger and faster cache than earlier Pentium processors, together with a 100 megahertz system bus, this processor is substantially faster than ordinary Pentium II chips. It is really intended for use in expensive network servers and not desktop PCs. It is beyond the budgets of most PC users and is not a processor that we will consider further in this book.

Pentium III

The Pentium II chips were followed by the Pentium III. Originally this processor required Slot 1 motherboards and these chips are similar in general appearance to the Pentium II. Most of the later Slot 1 motherboards can be used with Pentium II or Pentium III processors. The Pentium III has SIMD (single-instruction multiple data) technology, which is 70 new instructions designed to speed up certain types of software. These instructions are mainly aimed at high-speed 3D graphics and applications that include voice recognition. They are only of use with software that is written to take advantage of them.

Like the Pentium II processors, the early Pentium III has 512k of cache memory running at half the clock speed. Later versions have 256k of one-chip cache running at the full clock speed, and could reasonably be regarded as upgraded Celerons rather than a natural successor to the earlier Pentium III devices. These later Pentium IIIs use the same FC-PGA version of Socket 370 as some Celerons. The Pentium III has been produced with clock frequencies of one gigahertz and beyond. The Pentium III is a powerful processor, and PCs based on any version of this chip are well worth expanding and keeping up to date.

Pentium 4

At the time of writing this, the Pentium III has virtually disappeared from the new PC market and it has been replaced by the Pentium 4. This is by no means a new chip, and it has been on offer as an up-market alternative to the Pentium III for some time. The original Pentium 4 processors required Socket 423 motherboards, but the current ones are of the Socket 478 variety. This processor is basically a faster version of the Pentium III, but the most recent versions have extra instructions and 512k of on-chip cache. With clock frequencies of up to 2.8 gigahertz (2800 megahertz), Pentium 4-based PCs are clearly very powerful computers that can handle any PC software. They are certainly worthy of expansion, should it prove necessary.

Non-Intel Inside

The manufacturers of compatible processors were reluctant to shift over to Slot 1 technology or their own version of slot technology. In the main they have instead opted to develop Socket 7 and socket technology as far as possible. Since Intel eventually abandoned slot technology, this would seem to have been a wise move. The front runners in compatible chips are AMD and Cyrix. Cyrix was been sold by National Semiconductors and is now owned by VIA, the PC support chip manufacturer. Development of these processors should therefore continue, but in recent times their market share in the PC world has been quite small.

The first AMD processor for PCs was the K5, which was produced in 75, 90, 133, 150, and 166 megahertz versions. This chip was an alternative to the "classic" Pentium processor. It was replaced by the K6, which has the MMX instructions, and clock frequencies of 166, 200, 233, 266, and 300 megahertz. This was replaced by the K6-2, which was in turn superseded by the K6-2 3D Now! chip. This is a Pentium-style processor that includes the MMX instructions, but it also has its own set of instructions that, together with the later versions of Microsoft's Direct X system, enable 3-D games to run at increased speeds. This processor requires a motherboard that can operate at 100 megahertz and fast memory modules. It was available with clock speeds of up to 550 megahertz.

Fig.1.7 This early Athlon processor uses Slot A technology

The K6-2 was joined by the K6-3, which is basically just a K6-2 with 256k of on-chip cache operating at the full processor clock speed. The cache on the motherboard operates as a level three cache incidentally. Versions having clock speeds of 400, 450, 500 and 550 megahertz were available. With a substantial amount of on-chip cache memory running at the full clock speed the K6-3 provides a high level of performance. Of course, it is no longer the fastest AMD processor and that title goes to the Athlon (formerly known as the K7). The original Athlon used a slot rather than a socket and looks similar to a Slot 1 Pentium II or III (Figure 1.7), but it does not utilize Intel's Slot 1 technology. Instead it uses what AMD have dubbed Slot A technology. The early Athlon processors were available with clock speeds of 500, 550, and 600 megahertz, had 512k of level two cache, and operated with a system bus frequency of 200 megahertz.

Cyrix M*

The Cyrix equivalent of the AMD K6 is the 6X86 processor. This was produced in 90, 120, 133, 150, 166, and 200 megahertz versions. These chips cause a certain amount of confusion, because their speed ratings are not their actual clock frequencies. For instance, a 200 megahertz 6X86 processor is a 200 megahertz chip in the sense that it offers performance that is broadly similar to an Intel 200 megahertz Pentium. The actual clock frequency is somewhat less, and is actually 166 megahertz in this case. It has to be pointed out that how well (or otherwise) one make of processor compares to another depends on the type of software being run. Intel chips traditionally do well on floating point mathematics, but perform less well in other areas. If you are running a reasonably wide range of applications software, overall you are unlikely to notice much difference between equivalent chips from different manufacturers.

The original Cyrix processors are now long obsolete. They were replaced by processors that have the MMX instructions and these are the M2 series. These have nominal clock frequencies of 166, 200, 233, 266, 300, and 333 megahertz. Like the 6X86 processors, the speed ratings of M2 chips are their equivalent clock frequencies, and the actual clock frequencies are lower (225 megahertz or 233 megahertz for the 300 megahertz chip for example). Figure 1.8 shows an old 200 megahertz Cyrix chip next to a Socket 7 holder, but all the Socket 7 and 370 chips look much the same, as do the sockets. There have been some further developments in the Cyrix chips, but they have only been suitable for use in budget PCs and there has not been anything to rival the modern Intel and AMD offerings. The PCs based on the more recent Cyrix chips are probably worth keeping up to date, but the early PCs based on these processors are probably too old to be worthy of much expense.

Fig.1.8 A Cyrix 686MX processor next to a Socket 7 holder

Winchip

IDT and its Winchip are relative latecomers to the world of PC processors. The Winchip was intended to be a low cost processor for entry level PCs. It has the MMX instructions, and is produced in 150, 180, 200, 225, and 240 megahertz versions. I think that I am correct in saying that the Winchip was bought by VIA, and some of its technology may have been used in the later Cyrix chips. The Winchip as such was not developed further though. PCs using the Winchips are now quite old and are probably not worthwhile candidates for anything other than the most simple of upgrades.

Modern Athlon

Like the recent Pentiums, modern AMD Athlon chips use conventional sockets (Socket A), and they remain physically and electrically incompatible with the Pentium processors. A modern PC motherboard is designed to take one type of processor or the other, and although the two types of socket may look similar, they are totally incompatible. The normal Athlon chips have been produced with clock frequencies of up to 1.4 gigahertz, but there are now faster versions. It is the Athlon XP that is normally used in desktop PCs, and the fastest at the time of writing is the Athlon XP2600+. Faster versions are expected in the near future.

Like some earlier processors, the speed ratings of Athlon XP processors refer to their equivalent Pentium speed. An XP1900+ for example, is supposedly slightly faster than a Pentium 4 running at more than 1.9 gigahertz, and this claim is probably justified. The actual clock frequency of this chip is 1.6 gigahertz. The non-XP Athlons were mostly made in two versions for system frequencies of 200 megahertz or 266 megahertz, but there are no 200 megahertz versions of the Athlon XP. Clearly the faster Athlon and Athlon XP based PCs are powerful PCs that are worthy of upgrades for some time to come.

Duron

The Duron processor is AMD's equivalent to the Celeron, and it is essentially a simplified Athlon with less cache. Although the Duron is less potent that the Athlon, like the Celeron it has achieved good popularity. At one time a PC with a Duron operating at about 800 megahertz was the standard choice for a business PC, and these computers are still more than capable of running standard business applications. In fact speed is not the issue that it once was, and Duron-based PCs are still good workhorse PCs that can run most applications. The later Durons with clock speeds of a gigahertz and beyond were perhaps less popular than their predecessors, but they had less price advantage over the Athlons at the cheaper end of the range. These later Duron based PCs are, of course, well worth expanding and keeping as up to date as possible.

Non-standard

There are other PC processors, but these are non-standard devices that integrate functions such as video and sound onto the processor chip. These require special motherboards that do not seem to be generally available. Some of these chips are intended for use in low cost PCs, but others are for use in embedded applications. In other words, for use in household gadgets, etc., that include a basic PC for Internet connection, or something of this type. This includes things like Internet television sets and the well-publicized Internet connected "smart fridge".

Repair upgrade

With the possible exceptions of the very early computers, it should be possible to repair a PC based on a Pentium class processor. It should be possible to effect most repairs quite easily and at reasonable cost. Unless something pretty catastrophic happens, such as dropping the PC from a second floor window, it should be economic and worthwhile repairing this type of PC. Rather than opting for a straightforward repair you may decide to undertake a major upgrade instead. This will probably cost more than simply replacing the faulty part with a new one, but for the extra money you may well obtain a vast improvement in performance. Some spare parts for older PCs have quite high prices, so it is conceivable that an upgrade will sometimes be cheaper than a straightforward repair.

The best choice depends on the particular PC you have, and how badly (or otherwise) you require an increase in performance. It also depends on the nature of the fault. There is little point in opting for a major upgrade if a replacement floppy drive is all that is needed. On the other hand, if a motherboard becomes faulty it would probably be worthwhile replacing the processor and memory as well, to bring the PC up to a more modern specification.

System make-up

A traditional PC is a so-called three-unit style computer. These three separate units are the keyboard, the main computer unit and the monitor. They are connected together by cables, although wireless connections are sometimes used for the keyboard and peripherals. The three-unit arrangement is a convenient one in that it makes it easy to accommodate everything on practically any computer desk. Bear in mind though, that PCs are mostly quite large and heavy, and likely to prove both too big and too heavy for a low-cost computer desk designed for a small home computer or a laptop.

The main unit is comprised of several sub-units. The main ones are the case, power supply unit, motherboard, and one or more disc drives. Additionally, certain expansion cards must be present on the main board for the system to function. In the past it was necessary to have a hard/floppy disc controller card, plus a card or cards to provide standard interfaces such as serial and parallel ports. The current practice is for these functions to be provided by the motherboard, and the only essential expansion card is a video type to drive the monitor.

In fact it is now quite common for motherboards to have an on-board display generator as well, but this is not a standard feature. Although a sound card is not essential, a sound card and speakers has become a standard PC feature. The sound card usually includes a game port for joysticks, etc., although many games controllers now use a USB interface.

The game port doubles as a MIDI port that enables the PC to be connected to synthesisers and other musical instruments or gadgets that have a MIDI port. A basic multimedia PC would consist of something like the following list of main parts.

Keyboard and mouse

Case

Motherboard fitted with BIOS and memory nodules

17 inch colour monitor

SVGA display card with 16 megabytes of RAM

Floppy disc drive

Hard disc drive

CD-ROM writer

Sound card and speakers

A more up-market PC might have the following set of main components.

Keyboard and mouse

Case

Motherboard fitted with BIOS and memory modules

19 inch colour monitor

2-D/3-D display card with 64/128 megabytes of RAM

Floppy disc drive

Hard disc drive

DVD drive

CD-ROM writer

Sound card and speakers

Modem for Internet connection

Some of these constituent parts, plus more specialised forms of expansion are discussed in later chapters, but there are a few aspects of these main parts that we will take the opportunity to discuss here.

Keyboards

The original PC keyboard was an 83 key type. At least, it was in its native (U.S.A.) form. The U.K. version had a slightly different layout plus an extra key in order to accommodate the pound sign ("£"), which was absent on the U.S.A. keyboard. The U.K. version was therefore generally known as the 84 key layout PC keyboard. This had ten function keys in two vertical rows of five, positioned to the left of the main QWERTY keys, and is now obsolete. 83/84 key keyboards were replaced by the enhanced layout that was introduced by IBM in 1986.

This has 101 keys in its original U.S.A. version, or 102 keys in the case of the U.K. version. Twelve function keys on the enhanced layout replace the ten function keys of the original design. These keys are relocated to a single row above the main QWERTY keyboard (which is where the "Esc" key is also to be found). The numeric keypad/cursor key arrangement is retained, but only for those who are used to the original scheme of things and wish to go on using it. This keypad is moved over to the right in order to make room for a separate cursor cluster, etc.

The102 key layout has now been replaced by the 105 key Windows 95/98 layout. This is basically the same as the 102 key layout, but there are three additional keys next to the spacebar. These bring up Windows 95/98 menus, and two of the keys have the same effect as operating the "Start" button on the Windows desktop. The third is equivalent to right "clicking" the mouse. As the additional keys are simply duplicating functions provided by the mouse, it is not essential to have a 105 key keyboard in order to use Windows 95/98. All current standard keyboards seem to have the 105 key layout. Of course, there are also fancy keyboards having all sorts of additional functions available.

Ergonomic

If you look at the keyboards in a computer shop you can not miss the "ergonomic" variety, which have the two sides of the keyboard at different angles. They are designed to make touch-typing easier and less fatiguing, and seem to be liked by many touch-typists. Two-finger typists should stick to the traditional style PC keyboard.

The enhanced keyboards retain the original method of interfacing, and it is quite possible, for instance, to use a 105 key keyboard as a replacement for a 102 key, or even an old 84 key type type. This will not necessarily give perfect results though, since the BIOS in the computer may not be equipped to deal with a modern keyboard. Although most of the keys are merely duplicating those of the old 83/84 key layout, there are obviously a few additional ones that might have no effect when used with an old PC, or could produce the wrong characters. Any problems when using a new keyboard on an old PC are usually quite minor, and most users can live with them. Note that XT class PCs have the same type of keyboard connector as later PCs, but are nevertheless incompatible with modern PC keyboards. If you have an "antique" XT class PC and its keyboard fails, it must be replaced with a proper XT keyboard and not a modern one.

A PC keyboard is a quite sophisticated piece of electronics in its own right, and is actually based on an 8048 single chip microprocessor (or "microcontroller" as these devices are alternatively known). This controller provides "debouncing", which prevents multiple characters being generated if the keyboard switches open and close something less than completely cleanly (which is always the case in practice). The keyboard controller also performs simple diagnostic tests, and can detect a key that is stuck in the "on" position for example. It also contains a 20 byte buffer, which is simply a small amount of memory that is used to store characters if one key is pressed before the character from the previous one has been read by the computer.

Rollover

The keyboard also has multi-character rollover. In other words, if you press one key, and then another while still holding down the first one, the second key will be read correctly. In fact you can hold down several keys and the next one that is operated will still be read correctly. I do not know how many keys can be pressed before this system breaks down, but attempts to overload the keyboard on my computers proved to be fruitless. Of course, like most computer keyboards and electric typewriters, the keyboard includes an auto-repeat function (i.e. holding down any character key results in that character being produced once initially, and then after a short delay it is repeated for as long as the key is pressed).

Connection to the computer is used to be via a 5-way cable fitted with a 5-way 180-degree DIN plug. These days most PCs have a keyboard connector of the PS/2 variety, which is a sort of miniature version of the standard type. Figure 1.9 shows both types of keyboard connector. When buying a new keyboard for an old computer it is necessary to check the type of connector used, and ensure that a suitably equipped keyboard

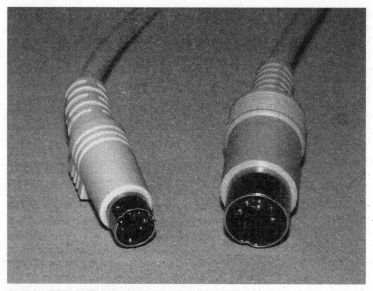

Fig.1.9 PS/2 (left) and DIN keyboard connectors

is obtained. Keyboards having the older style connector are becoming more difficult to track down, but some have both types. Also, it is possible to obtain adapters that permit old style keyboard connectors to be used with modern PCs (Figure 1.10) and modern keyboards to be used with PCs having the old DIN connector.

Motherboards

Unless you get into DIY PC assembly or undertake large scale upgrades you may not need to know too much about motherboards, although background information of this type often proves to be invaluable from time to time. At one time there were two main motherboard categories: the PC/PC XT type, and the AT type. However, these are now well and truly obsolete, although modern motherboards are actually developments of the AT layout. I suppose that if you look at things in broad terms there are still two forms of motherboard, which are the AT and ATX varieties. The AT boards use what is basically the original AT layout, although modern AT boards are generally much smaller than the original design. Hence they are sometimes referred to as "baby AT" boards. You are unlikely to find any new AT style motherboards or PCs that use them, but these boards were quite common until relatively recently.

They have been gradually replaced by ATX boards. ATX motherboards have a modified layout that puts the processor to one side of the expansion slots. Modern processors, when complete with

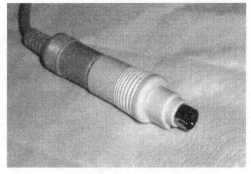

Fig.1.10 A DIN to PS/2 keyboard adapter

heatsinks and cooling fans, tend to be quite tall and can obstruct several of the expansion slots. This prevents the slots from being used with the longer expansion cards. By moving the processor to one side this problem is avoided, and it is possible to use long expansion cards in any of the expansion slots. However, unless the board layout is well designed there can be problems with large heatsinks being obstructed by the power supply unit or one of the drives.

There are other differences between the two types of board, such as the different power supply requirements and the on-board serial and parallel port connectors of ATX boards. The practical consequence of these is that the two types of board require different styles of power supply and case. When replacing a motherboard you must therefore be careful to replace it with one that has the same form factor. It is actually possible to use some AT motherboards with an ATX case and power supply. Unfortunately, it is more likely that you would need to use an ATX motherboard with an AT case and power supply, which is not possible.

AT and ATX boards can be further subdivided according to the processors that they support. When buying a replacement motherboard you must therefore make sure that it has the correct form factor and that it supports the processor you are using. Obtaining a motherboard to suit an early Pentium processor or any pre-Pentium processor can be difficult and expensive. Similarly, obtaining a replacement for an early Pentium processor or an 80X86 series processor can be time consuming and costly. If a fault occurs in the motherboard or processor of a PC that is something less than up-to-date it is often better to upgrade it to a more modern specification rather than try to do a straightforward repair job.

Chipsets

When looking at the specifications for Pentium-based PCs and Pentium motherboards you will inevitably come across references to chipsets. These are the integrated circuits that provide various essential functions that are not included in the processor itself. In the original PCs these functions were provided by dozens of ordinary logic integrated circuits. Even though a modern PC requires much more help from the supporting electronics, there are normally just two support chips. Some budget boards using a single support chip have been produced. Intel has manufactured various Pentium support chipsets, and these seem to be used on most motherboards. However, other manufacturers make Pentium support chips. Here are brief details of the main Intel chipsets.

FX   Early and basic Pentium chipset.

HX   Early chipset that is in many ways basic but is also fast. Provides dual processor support. Used for both Socket 7 and early Slot 1 motherboards.

VX   Early and basic chipset for Socket 7 motherboards giving SDRAM support.

TX   Improved chipset for Socket 7 motherboards which provides support for SDRAM, USB, and UDMA33 hard disc interface.

LX   First chipset specifically for Pentium II processors and Slot 1 motherboards. Provides dual processor, SDRAM, USB, UDMA33 and AGP support. Maximum memory of 512MB SDRAM, or 1GB EDO RAM.

BX   Effectively an improved LX chipset that supports 100 megahertz system bus and fast SDRAM. Up to 1GB or SDRAM or EDO RAM. Also supports 66 megahertz system bus for compatibility with 333 megahertz and slower Pentium II processors.

EX   Optimised for Celeron processor. Up to 256MB of SDRAM or EDO RAM. No dual processor support.

GX Optimised for the Pentium II Xeon processors (i.e. 100 megahertz system bus processors) with no support or 66 megahertz bus.

NX Support for up to four Pentium II Xeon processors and 8GB of SDRAM or EDO RAM. No AGP support.

810E Designed for use with Pentium III and Celeron processors, it incorporates a graphics system.

815 There are a number of versions of this Pentium II/III chipset, which incorporates graphics and audio in addition to the usual input/output functions.

850 Pentium 4 chipset that supports fast but expensive RDRAM, but not cheaper types of memory. This made Pentium 4 PCs of the period an expensive option.

850E A version of the 850 chipset that supports a system bus frequency of 533 megahertz as opposed to the 400 megahertz of the standard 850 set.

845 Optimised for the Pentium 4 processors, it supports DDR (double data rate) RAM at 200 or 266 megahertz in addition to ordinary PC133 SDRAM.

845E Updated 845 that supports Pentium 4 processors with 533 megahertz FSB, more types of memory, and USB 2.0.

845G Effectively an 845E but with built-in graphics adapter. Also supports a 4X AGP slot that can be used with the on-chip graphics disabled. The 845GL is a budget version with 400 megahertz FSB, intended primarily for Celeron based systems.

860 For Xeon based systems.

North and south

This list does not include every Intel support chip and variation, and it is only half the story because the processors from AMD use different support chips. The full list of support chips produced over the last few years is vast. When looking at the descriptions of motherboards you will inevitably encounter the terms "North bridge" and "South bridge". Most chipsets consist of two chips, which have been given these two generic names. The "bridge" part of the name presumably refers to the fact that the chips provide a bridge between the processor and other parts of the system such as the hard disc and the memory.

The North bridge chip is responsible for handling the memory and the AGP graphics port. The South bridge chip handles things like the IDE ports for the drives, USB ports, and so-called legacy ports such as the standard serial and parallel types. In fact the South bridge chip handles all input and output functions apart from memory and the graphics card. The North and South bridge chips are linked via a high-speed interface that usually operates at 266 megahertz or more in modern PCs. Although most PCs are based on North and South bridge chips from the same manufacturer, this is not invariably the case. The PC I am using to produce this book has one support chip from AMD and one from VIA.

Configuration

For the computer to function properly it must know a few basic facts about itself, such as the type of display card and amount of memory fitted. This ensures that it produces an initial display properly, that it does not try to access memory it does not have, or ignore memory that it does have available. On the original PCs some switches on the motherboard were used for configuration purposes. AT class computers, from the originals to the latest super-fast PCs, have some low power CMOS memory that is powered from a battery when the main power source is switched off.

This memory circuit is actually part of a built-in clock/calendar circuit, which the operating system uses to set its clock and calendar during the booting process. It is also used by applications software, such as a word processor when it automatically adds the date into a letter or other document. If a PC keeps failing to boot-up correctly, and takes you into the BIOS Setup program instead, it is likely that the back-up battery for the CMOS memory has failed. Most modern motherboards have a lithium battery that should last about five years, so this problem mainly afflicts "antique" computers.

In the past motherboards often had a rechargeable battery that was trickle-charged while the computer is switched on. I have not seen this method used in PCs for some time, and it often had a major flaw. If the computer was not used for a week or two it was quite normal for the battery to run flat. The computer then had to be reconfigured using the BIOS Setup program and left running for a few hours to recharge the battery. It would then boot-up properly and run normally again. Configuring motherboards and using the BIOS Setup program is dealt with in the final two chapters of this book which deal with major PC upgrades and DIY PCs. Therefore, we will not consider this subject further here.

Maths co-processor

The maths co-processor used to be an integrated circuit which looked very much like the main microprocessor in most cases. It was normally fitted into a special socket on the motherboard. Any PC processor from the full 80486DX onwards has the maths co-processor built-in, and not as an add-on chip. Therefore, unless you are using a very old PC it should be able to run any software that requires a maths co-processor without having to resort to an upgrade. If you have an old PC that requires a maths co-processor upgrade you are probably out of luck, because these chips are now obsolete.

Ports

In order to be of any practical value it is normally necessary for a PC to connect to other devices such as printers, modems, and scanners. The original PCs had serial and parallel ports provided by expansion cards. With modern PCs two serial ports and one parallel type are normally included on the motherboard, but additional ports can be provided via expansion cards. Parallel ports were originally used to output data from the PC, and were mainly used with printers. Data is exchanged in the form of complete bytes, making this type of interface relatively fast. Modern printer ports are bidirectional and even faster than the originals, widening their usefulness. Data can be sent or received at a respectable maximum rate of about two megabytes per second.

Serial ports can simultaneously sent and receive data, but they are relatively slow. The fact that data is sent one bit at a time further reduces the rata at which data can be transferred. Even when used in "turbo" modes, most serial ports can only swap data at a rate of about 11 kilobytes (0.011 megabytes) per second. This greatly reduces their usefulness, and they have mainly been used with external telephone modems, mice, and other pointing devices.

Parallel and serial ports are perhaps less straightforward to use than might be the case, and this led to the development of the USB 1.1 and USB 2.0 ports. These are high-speed and very high-speed serial ports that are largely compatible with each other, but not with ordinary serial ports. After one or two "teething" problems USB ports have started to take over from serial and parallel ports. The old types of PC port will presumably become totally obsolete in the coming years. The next chapter covers PC ports in greater detail.

Digitising tablets

Digitising tablets are absolute pointing devices, rather than relative types (like mice). In other words, whereas a mouse can only be used to indicate movement in a certain direction, a digitising tablet deals in definite screen positions. If you lift a mouse from its mat, move it to a new position, and then replace it on the mat, the on-screen pointer will not move. With a digitising tablet, if you raise the "pen" or puck from the tablet, and then move it, the on-screen pointer will not move. However, as soon as you lower the "pen" or puck down onto the tablet the pointer will immediately jump to the appropriate point on the screen.

Most software is no easier to use with a digitising tablet, and they then offer no real advantages. As they are several times more expensive than a mouse, this has led to them being far less popular. Where a program does properly support a digitising tablet, it might be well worthwhile paying the extra money for one. Some CAD programs only use part of the digitiser for controlling the on-screen pointer, with the rest being given over to menus that are used instead of on-screen menus. This leaves virtually the whole screen free to act as the drawing area. Usually the digitising tablet can accommodate a large number of menus, and user defined menus incorporating macros (a series of commands) can be used. This enables quite complex tasks to be performed with a minimum of effort, and is one of the most efficient ways of working.

A tablet is very useful for use with illustration programs, etc., where it is often necessary to trace existing artwork into the computer, and to do free-hand drawing work. The ability of a tablet to operate using a "pen", or "stylus" as it is more correctly termed, makes it more suitable for applications where free-hand drawing is involved. Most people, even after gaining much experience with a mouse, find it difficult to use for free-hand drawing. A stylus is much better for this type of thing, being very much like using an ordinary pen or pencil. Modern tablets are quite sophisticated, often using a lead-free stylus, and offering pressure sensitivity when used with suitable software.

Pressure sensitivity is very useful when a tablet is used with software such as paint and photo-editing programs. The pressure of the stylus can be used to control line width, colour strength, etc., making it possible to accurately simulate real painting and drawing media. With the increasing use of PCs in graphics applications, digitising tablets are becoming more and more popular.

In the past there could be difficulties in using graphics tablets due to a lack of support in the applications programs. This problem has been eased to a large extent by the popularity of Windows 95 and later versions of Windows. Any graphics tablet should be supplied complete with drivers for 32-bit versions of Windows. With the appropriate drivers installed the tablet will operate as the pointing device for Windows itself and any Windows application. Support for pressure sensitivity is not guaranteed, but this feature is supported by many Windows graphics applications.

With most graphics tablets you can also have a mouse connected to the computer, and can move freely from one to the other. This is a useful feature, because some software is difficult to control using a tablet and stylus. Of course, you will need separate ports for the mouse and the tablet, but as most PCs have two serial ports and a mouse port this should not be a problem. Some recent graphics tablets are supplied complete with a mouse that can be used in place of the stylus. In fact there might be a choice of several pointing implements for use with the tablet.

Soundcards

PCs have a built-in loudspeaker, but this is driven by some very basic hardware that is really intended to do nothing more than produce a few simple "beep" sounds. For anything more than this a proper sound card and a pair of active speakers is needed. Most soundcards do actually have built-in amplifiers, but they only provide low output powers and generally provide quite modest volume levels when used with passive speakers (i.e. speakers that do not have built-in amplifiers). The simplest soundcards only offer synthesised sounds, almost invariably produced using FM (frequency modulation) synthesis.

This gives adequate sound quality for many purposes, but wavetable synthesis is better for music making. This method uses standard analogue synthesis techniques, but the basic sounds are short bursts of recorded instrument sounds rather than simple waveforms from oscillator circuits. This gives much more realistic results, although all wavetable sound cards seem to produce variable results. There are usually a few hundred different sounds available, and I suppose it is inevitable that some will sound more convincing than others. Modern soundcards can typically produce 32 or 64 different sounds at once, and they are capable of reproducing quite complex music sequences. Even the cheapest cards have the ability to record and play back in high quality stereo, and to play back pre-recorded sound samples (.WAV files).

The audio section of PCs is an aspect that has become ever more complex over the years. Surround sound is now commonplace and there are up-market PC sound systems that are suitable for recording and editing to professional standards. There has been a strong trend towards integrated audio systems where the audio circuits are included on the motherboard. Some of these integrated sound facilities are now quite sophisticated, and even the basic ones are adequate for most purposes. If you need the latest thing in PC soundcards it is usually possible to disable the built-in audio circuits so that a high-quality soundcard can be added via an expansion slot.

Apart from three or four audio input and output sockets, soundcards normally have a 15-way connector that is a combined MIDI port and game port (Figure 1.11). When used as a game port it takes standard PC joysticks and similar devices. Most of the current games controllers connect to the PC by way of a USB port rather than the game type, but it is still useful to have this port if you still have old games controllers. When used as a MIDI port it enables music programs to operate with MIDI synthesisers, keyboards, sound modules, etc. However, note that standard MIDI cables have 5-way (180 degree) DIN plugs at both ends, and are therefore incompatible with the 15-way D connector of a PC soundcard. A special MIDI cable/adapter is needed to connect a PC soundcard to MIDI devices.

In the past PC soundcards were often equipped with an interface for a CD-ROM drive. The reason for this is simply that many people added a CD-ROM drive to their PC at the same time as they added a soundcard, since both of these items are required in order to run multimedia applications. Several CD-ROM interfaces have been used in the past, but only the ATAPI interface is currently used for low cost internal drives (the SCSI interface is used for some up-market CD-ROM drives). The

Fig.1.11 The game port is the large connector on the left

ATAPI interface is the same as the IDE interface used for normal PC hard disc drives, and modern motherboards have at least two ports of this type, each of which is capable of supporting two drives. Any IDE port fitted on a soundcard is therefore of no value when the card is used in a reasonably modern PC, and if possible it should be switched off. Otherwise it is simply ignored.

Specification

People who ask for advice about upgrading their PC tend to assume that all PCs are much the same, and that an upgrade for one will be suitable for all other PCs. This is clearly far from the truth. PCs have changed quite quickly and radically in recent years. A good upgrade for one PC might be totally inappropriate for most others. Before you try to upgrade a PC it is essential to find out as much as you can about its specification. You can learn a great deal by simply looking at the ports and connectors on the outside of the computer, and more can be gleaned by looking inside the case. Are there any spare expansion slots, and if so what type or types are these slots?

The manual for the PC or its motherboard should provide plenty of detailed information about compatible processors and memory modules, the BIOS, and just about everything you need to know. It is normal for the BIOS to produce various screens of information just after the computer is started, and these can be useful if information is difficult to obtain. Modern PCs do not spend much time in this pre-boot testing period, so you may have to reboot the PC a few times in order to extract all the available information. There are system analyser and testing programs available, and these can provide some useful information about the installed hardware.

Do not commence upgrading a PC until you are sure of its current configuration, and the suitability of the proposed upgrade components. Modern PC components cost "peanuts" in comparison to the prices of a few years ago, but it would be easy to waste a great deal of money by obtaining parts without checking their compatibility first.

Points to remember

You do not require a vast toolkit in order to upgrade PCs. In most cases it is unnecessary to have anything more than a medium size cross point screwdriver. It can also be useful to have a pair of tweezers. These are good for recovering any screws that fall deep into the interior of the PC.

It is not necessary to have a range of manual skills in order to upgrade PCs. Most of the skill is in knowing what to buy and how to set it up correctly. Actually fitting the components can be a bit fiddly, but it does not require much skill. You do need to be a reasonably practical person and not someone with a track record of DIY disasters.

The modular construction used for PCs makes it easy to upgrade practically any part of the system. You can customise a PC so that it exactly meets your requirements.

With an older PC you have to carefully consider its suitability for anything more than a simple and inexpensive upgrade. It is probably possible to bring any PC up to a modern specification, but with older PCs practically every component would have to be replaced. Simply building or buying a new PC would seem to make more sense

PCs have evolved very rapidly over recent years, and this has seriously complicated anything more than a very simple upgrade. Always check the suitability of upgrade components very carefully before buying them.

Upgrade
basics

Ad infinitum

In this chapter some general points will be addressed, so that they only have to be covered here, and not over and over again as they crop up throughout the book. You could skip this chapter and refer back to it each time a relevant reference is encountered in the later chapters. However, I would definitely not recommend doing things this way. Modern computer components are easily damaged and simply taking some components out of their wrapping can be sufficient to ruin them if you do not know what you are doing. Although modern computers are relatively inexpensive, learning from your mistakes could still prove to be a costly business. The information in this first part of this chapter will enable you to avoid costly and unnecessary damage to components.

The subsequent sections also contain useful background information that it is better to learn sooner rather than later. In particular, there is a substantial section dealing with the BIOS and the BIOS Setup program. With more and more aspects of a PC controlled via the BIOS this is no longer an aspect that can be largely ignored when upgrading PCs. A lot of problems can be solved or avoided in the first place if you have a reasonable understanding of the BIOS.

Shocking truth

When dealing with modern electronic components it is not just a matter of handling the components carefully to avoid physical damage. There are hidden dangers that can cause a lot of expensive damage if you do not take suitable precautions. Those readers who are used to dealing with electronic components will no doubt be aware that many modern semiconductors are vulnerable to damage by static electricity, as is any equipment that incorporates these devices. They will also be used to handling static-sensitive components and taking the necessary precautions to protect them from damage. Probably most readers are not familiar with these precautions, and I will therefore outline the basic steps necessary to ensure that no components are accidentally "zapped".

I think it is worth making the point that it does not take a large static charge complete with sparks and "cracking" sounds to damage sensitive electronic components. Large static discharges of that type are sufficient to damage most modern semiconductor components, and not just the more sensitive ones. Many of the components used in computing are so sensitive to static charges that they can be damage by relatively small voltages. In this context "small" still means a potential of perhaps a hundred volts or so, but by static standards this is not particularly large. Charges of this order will not generate noticeable sparks or make your hair stand on end, but they are nevertheless harmful to many electronic components. Hence you can "zap" these components simply by touching them, and in most cases would not be aware that anything had happened.

Health warning

I think it is also worth making the point that it is not just the processor and memory modules that are vulnerable. Completed circuit boards such as video and soundcards are often vulnerable to static damage, as is the motherboard itself. In fact most modern expansion cards and all motherboards are vulnerable to damage from static charges. Even components such as the hard disc drive and CD-ROM drive can be damaged by static charges. Anything that contains a static-sensitive component has to be regarded as vulnerable. The case and power supply assembly plus any heatsinks and cooling fans represent the only major components that you can assume to be zap-proof. Everything else should be regarded as potentially at risk and handled accordingly.

When handling any vulnerable computer components you should always keep well away from any known or likely sources of static electricity. These includes such things as computer monitors, television sets, any carpets or furnishings that are known to be prone to static generation, and even any pets that are known to get charged-up fur coats. Also avoid wearing any clothes that are known to give problems with static charges. This seems to be less of a problem than it once was, because few clothes these days are made from a cloth that consists entirely of man-made fibres. There is normally a significant content of natural fibres, and this seems to be sufficient to prevent any significant build-up of

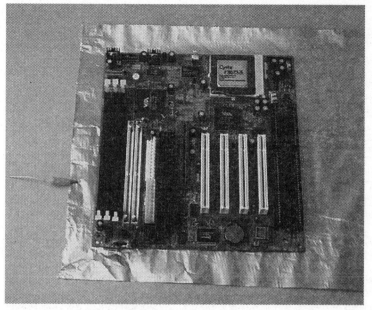

Fig.2.1 An improvised conductive work surface

static charges. However, if you should have any garments that might give problems, make sure that you do not wear them when handling any computer equipment or components.

Anti-static equipment

Electronics and computing professionals often use quite expensive equipment to ensure that static charges are kept at bay. Most of these are not practical propositions for amateur computer enthusiasts or those who only deal with computers professionally on a very part-time basis. If you will only be working on computers from time to time, some very simple anti-static equipment is all that you need to ensure that there are no expensive accidents.

Unless you opt for a massive upgrade it is unlikely that it will be necessary to remove the motherboard from the case. However, if you do replace a motherboard or have to remove the existing one to work on it, make sure that suitable precautions are taken. The motherboard itself is quite

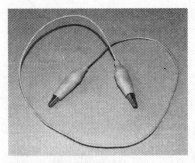

Fig.2.2 A crocodile clip lead

expensive, and the potential loss is much greater if it is fitted with memory and (or) a processor. When working on a motherboard it is essential to have some form of conductive worktop that is earthed. These can be purchased from the larger electronic component suppliers, but something as basic as a large sheet of aluminium cooking foil laid out on the workbench will do the job very well (Figure 2.1).

The only slight problem is that some way of earthing the foil must be devised. The method I generally adopt is to connect the foil to the metal chassis of a computer using a crocodile clip lead (Figure 2.2). Crocodile clips are available from electronic component suppliers, as are sets of made-up leads. The ready-made leads are often quite short, but when necessary several can be clipped together to make up a longer lead. Anyway, it should not be difficult to improvise a connection to the foil. The computer that acts as the earth must be plugged into the mains supply so that it is earthed via the mains earth lead. The computer should be switched off, and the supply should also be switched off at the mains socket. The earth lead is never switched, and the case will remain earthed even when it is switched off.

Wristbands

If you wish to make quite sure that your body remains static-free, you can earth yourself to the computer by way of a proper earthing wristband. This is basically just a wristband made from electrically conductive material that connects to the earth via a lead and a high-value resistor. The lead is terminated in a clip that permits easy connection to the chassis of the computer. The resistor does not prevent any static build-up in your body from leaking away to earth, but it will protect you from a significant shock if a fault should result in the earthing point becoming "live". A variation on this system has a special mains plug that enables the wristband to be safely earthed to the mains supply. Earthing wristbands are available from some of the larger computer component suppliers, and from electronics component retailers.

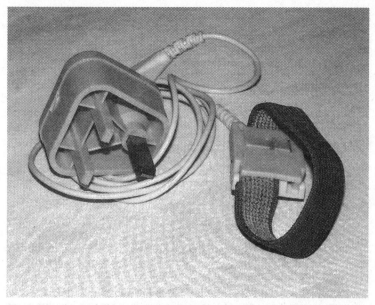

Fig.2.3 An earthing wristband complete with special mains plug

A typical wristband, complete with lead and special earthing plug, is shown in Figure 2.3. Note that these are sometimes sold together as a kit, but they are also sold as separate items. Make sure you know what you are buying before you part with your money. The wristband on its own is about as much good as a monitor without the rest of the PC. It is possible to buy disposable wristband kits, but if you are likely to do a fair amount of PC upgrading from time to time it is probably worthwhile obtaining one of the cheaper non-disposable types. With intermittent use one of these should last many years.

Keeping in touch

If you do not want to go to the expense of buying a wristband, a simple but effective alternative is to touch the conductive worktop or the metal chassis of the computer from time to time. This will leak away any gradual build-up of static electricity before it has time to reach dangerous proportions. Again, the computer must be connected to the mains supply, but it should be switched off and the mains supply should be switched

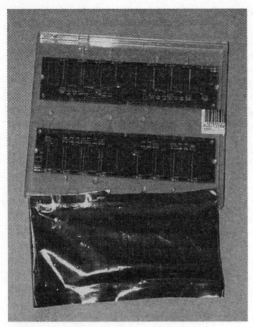

Fig.2.4 Two forms of anti-static packing

off at the mains outlet. The more frequently you touch the computer or other earthed object the lower the likelihood of static build-up in your body. Before removing any component from its anti-static packing, touch the earthed chassis while holding the component and its packing.

That is really all there is to it. Simply having a large chunk of earthed metal (in the form of the computer case) near the work area helps to discourage the build-up of any static charges in the first place. The few simple precautions outlined previously are then sufficient to ensure that there is no significant risk to the components.

Do not be tempted to simply ignore the dangers of static electricity when handling computer components. When building electronic gadgets I often ignore static precautions, but I am dealing with components that cost a matter of pence each. If one or two of the components should be zapped by a static charge, no great harm is done. The cost would be minimal and I have plenty of spares available. The same is not true when dealing with computer components, some of which could cost in excess of a hundred pounds. Also, the computer would remain out of commission until a suitable replacement spare part was obtained.

Anti-static packing

One final point is that any static sensitive components will be supplied in some form of anti-static packaging. This is usually nothing more than a plastic bag that is made from a special plastic that is slightly conductive. Processors and memory modules are often supplied in something more elaborate, such as conductive plastic clips and boxes. There is quite a range of anti-static packaging currently in use, and Figure 2.4 shows a couple of examples. Some packing effectively short circuits the pins or connectors of the protected components so that no significant voltage can build up between them. Others are designed to electrically insulate the components from the outside world so that stray static charges can not get to them. Both methods should provide complete protection from normal static charges.

Although it is tempting to remove the components from the packing to have a good look at them, try to keep this type of thing to a minimum. Ideally it should be completely avoided. I think it is worth reiterating the point that due care must be taken when you do remove a component from its packing. Always make sure that both you and the plastic bag or other packing is earthed before the component is removed. As explained previously, simply touching the earthed chassis of a computer while holding the component in its bag should ensure that everything is charge-free. Make sure that you always handle the components in an environment that is free from any likely sources of static charges. Check for any likely sources of static before you start handling sensitive components. There will then be a minimal risk of any damage occurring.

It is worthwhile keeping some of the anti-static packing that you get with spare parts or components bought for upgrading. Repairing or upgrading a PC often involves partially dismantling the base unit, and it is useful to have some anti-static packing to keep components safe until they are reinstalled in the computer. Some types of anti-static packing are available from some of the larger electronic component retailers incidentally.

Cracking it

It is possible to greatly expand a PC system by adding peripherals to the standard ports, but before too long you will probably need to delve inside to add extra memory, fit an expansion card, or something of this type. Gaining entry to the interior of a PC is straightforward provided it uses a conventional case. Older PCs often have an AT style case, and these almost invariably have the two sides and top panel as a single piece.

Four or six screws on the rear of the PC are removed and then the outer casing can be pulled free and completely removed from the chassis (Figure 2.5). For reasons I have never understood, the smaller cases

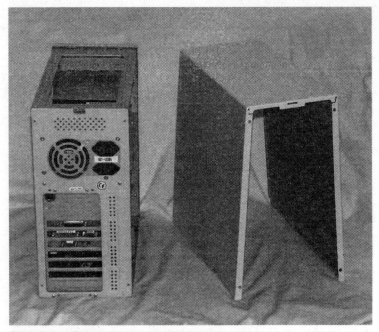

Fig.2.5 An AT case has a one-piece outer casing

usually have six fixing screws while the larger ones have just four. Anyway, look carefully at the rear of the PC to determine which screws must be removed. There will usually be other screws of about the same size that hold the power supply unit in place of fix the pieces of the case together, so do not simply remove all the screws.

The outer casing of an AT case is often a bit reluctant to pull free, especially if the case has not been opened up for many months. Some cases have grips to help you pull the outer casing backwards, but this useful feature is usually lacking. The "hammer and tongs" approach is not the correct one with computers. Always proceed carefully and patiently using the minimum of force. If the outer casing is proving to be very stubborn, a small screwdriver blade can be inserted between the back of the main casing and flange at the rear of the outer casing. Some leverage can then be used to prise the two sections of the case apart.

With most cases it is only necessary to pull the outer casing back by about 10 to 20 millimetres and it can then be lifted free. Computer cases

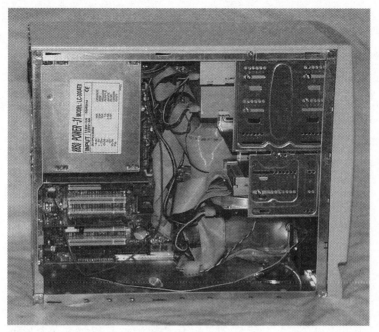

Fig.2.6 An ATX case has removable panels

often have edges and corners that are sharper than they should be, so be careful not to hurt yourself (or the furniture) once the outer cover has been removed. Speaking from bitter experience, store the cover safely where no one will trip over it, sit on it, or otherwise do anything silly.

ATX cases

ATX cases look much the same as the AT variety, but in general they are slightly wider (tower cases) or higher (desktop models). Taking tower cases first, the top panel might be removable, but it is usually left in place when working on the interior of the PC. The two side panels are removable, and it is these that give access to the interior of the unit. As viewed from the front, it is usually the left-hand side panel that has to be removed when working on the interior of a PC (Figure 2.6). This gives access to the expansion slots, memory, the cabling, etc. It also gives access to the drives, but in some instances it is necessary to remove the other side panel in order to obtain full access to the drive bays. This is normally only necessary when fitting or removing a drive, and many cases now permit drives to be added or removed with only the right-hand panel in place.

The situation is much the same with desktop cases, but it is the top panel that is removed in order to gain access to the main components. It might be necessary to remove the base panel when dealing with some components. In the world of PCs there is probably no such thing as a true standard, and manufacturers tend to "do their own thing" for the slightest excuse. Cases seem to have more than their fair share of variations with the PC manufacturers trying to make their particular models stand out from the crowd. Consequently, it might be necessary to study the outer casing of your PC very carefully in order to discover how to "crack" it. Some of the desktop cases are the most difficult to deal with.

There can be further complications with the low-profile desktop cases which have insufficient height to accommodate expansion cards. The usual solution is to have a vertical daughterboard that plugs into the motherboard, and the expansion cards then fit horizontally into the daughterboard. In addition to its awkwardness, this system has the drawback that there are usually only two expansion slots. With most of the hardware integrated with the motherboard on modern PCs this is less of a drawback than was once the case. On the other hand, it does limit the upgrade potential of the PC, especially if one slot is already used by (say) a modem. Low-profile cases are not the only non-standard type in use, and with any of these imaginative cases you have to do some careful investigation in order to get them apart. You then have to do some further delving in order to find where everything is situated inside the case.

Fitting cards

Although there has been a trend towards the use of USB wherever possible for upgrades, much expansion still requires an expansion card to be fitted inside the case. Physically fitting the card is much the same regardless of whether it is a PCI, ISA, AGP, or AMR type. Once the case is open you have an obvious problem in that the expansion slot you wish to use will be blocked by a metal bracket at the rear of the PC's casing. There are three main types of blanking plate. The original type is held in place by a single screw that fixes the bracket to the rear of the case. A bracket of this type is shown on the right in Figure 2.7. If you undo the screw using a largish cross-point screwdriver the bracket should pull free without any difficulty. It is advisable to keep the bracket so the hole

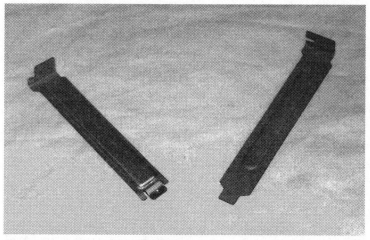

Fig.2.7 Two types of blanking plate

in the rear of the case can be blocked up again if you remove the expansion card at some later date. The bracket's fixing screw will be needed to hold the expansion card in place.

Some modern PC cases still use this method of fixing the brackets in place, but it is mainly the more upmarket cases that retain this method. Probably the most popular kind of bracket these days is the type that is semi cut out from the rear of the case. In order to remove one of these it is necessary to twist it to and fro until the thin pieces of metal connecting it to the main casing fatigue and break. Figure 2.8(a) shows the rear of a new ATX case with all of the brackets in place. In Figure 2.8(b) two of the brackets have been twisted round slightly to show how they can be broken away from the main casing. There is little point in keeping this type of bracket since it can not be fitted back in place again. A third method has brackets that clip into the screw holes in the main case. A bracket of this type is shown on the left in Figure 2.7. These can be twisted slightly and pulled free, and the process is reversible. It is therefore worthwhile keeping these brackets as they can be fitted into the case again should the need arise.

Softly, softly

With the metal bracket removed, the expansion card can be removed from its anti-static packing and pushed into position on the motherboard.

Fig.2.8(a) A new case with a full set of blanking plates

Some cards and slots fit together quite easily while other combinations are less accommodating. Never try the brute force method of fitting expansion cards into place. Using plenty of force is virtually always the wrong approach when dealing with PCs, but it is certainly asking for trouble when applied to expansion cards. Apart from the risk of damage to the card itself there is also a likelihood of writing off the motherboard.

If a card seems to be reluctant to fit into place, start by checking that the metal bracket is slotting correctly into place between the case and the motherboard. With some PCs the bottom end of the bracket has to be bent away from the circuit board slightly as it otherwise tends to hit the motherboard rather than fitting just behind it. Look carefully at the connector on the card and the expansion slot. It can be quite dim inside a PC, so if necessary, get some additional light inside the PC using something like a spotlamp or a powerful torch.

Probably the most common problem is the card being slightly too far forward or back. This is the same problem with the metal bracket, but manifesting itself in a different manner. The bracket is fitting into place correctly, but the rest of the card is then out of alignment. If the

Fig.2.8(b) The plates can be twisted and eventually broken free

misalignment is only slight, you should be able to ease the card backwards or forwards slightly and then into place.

Where there is a large error it will be necessary to form the bracket slightly in order to get the card to fit properly. In one or two cases where all else has failed, slightly loosening the screws that fix the motherboard to the chassis has provided the solution. Presumably in these cases the motherboard has been bolted in place when it is fractionally out of position. Loosening the mounting bolts and then fitting the expansion card shifts it into the correct position. The mounting bolts are then retightened, and fitting further expansion cards should be perfectly straightforward.

Down and out

Sometimes everything appears to be in position correctly, but when the PC is switched on and booted into Windows there is no response from the card. Windows seems to be oblivious to its presence in the computer. Alternatively, with the new card installed the computer refuses to do

Fig.2.9 This expansion card is fully fitted into place

anything when it is switched on. It could be that the card is genuinely faulty, but in most cases it is simply that the card has not been pushed down into the expansion slot correctly.

Look inside the computer and check that the card is parallel to the slot and not raised slightly at one end. With the card in the expansion slot at an angle it is possible for the connector on the card to short circuit the terminals on the connector in the expansion slot. This will be detected by the power supply at power-up, and it then refuses to switch on as a safety measure. Hence there is no response from the PC when it is switched on. Getting the card pushed right down into the expansion slot should cure the problem.

If the computer boots into Windows correctly but ignores the card, the most likely cause is that the card is simply not pushed down into the slot correctly at either end. In consequence, all or most of the terminals on the card's connector are failing to make contact with their counterparts on the expansion slot. Windows fails to recognise the card because it is effectively absent from the PC and is not contactable. Shut down Windows and switch off the computer before trying to rectify the problem.

Fig.2.10 Here the card has only partially slotted into place

Look carefully at the card, which should have little or nothing of the connector showing if it is fitted into the expansion slot correctly (Figure 2.9). It is probably not properly inserted into the expansion slot if the copper "fingers" of the edge connector are still clearly visible (Figure 2.10).

Remove the fixing screw so that the card can be manoeuvred easily, and the try gently pushing the card right down into the slot using a rocking motion. Do not force it into position as this could damage the motherboard, and should not be necessary. The front to back alignment is incorrect if the board will not go down into the slot. Correct this problem and it should fit into place without too much difficulty.

All change

In the event that the card seems to be fitted correctly but it is failing to work properly or stalling the computer at start-up, it is worth trying the card in a different expansion slot. In theory the expansion slots are all the same, but in practice it sometimes happens that a card that fails in one slot works perfectly well when installed in a different one. There is no problem in using a different slot provided the computer actually has a spare slot. If it does not, you could still try swapping the new card with an existing one. Alternatively, try removing the card and reinstalling it. In the case of an AGP slot there will only be one, and removing and reinstalling the card will be the only option.

It is by no means certain why using a card in a different slot will often cure the problem. Perhaps there are minor physical differences between the slots giving better compatibility between some slots and certain cards. Inserting a card into a slot and removing tends to clean the card's connector and the one in the slot, possibly producing more reliable connections between the two. This could explain why removing and reinstalling a card sometimes brings results. Perhaps some cards appear to be properly installed but are not quite into the expansion slot correctly. Removing and reinstalling the card could then result in it fitting that little bit further into place the second time. Whatever the reasons, it does sometimes work, and it is certainly worth a try when dealing with troublesome expansion cards.

On the level?

Probably the most common card installation problem with current PCs is that of the expansion card tending to ride up at the rear. Sometimes this happens as soon as the card is bolted into place, but it does sometimes happen that the card is all right for a while and then it pops up out of place. This usually manifests itself in the form of the card working perfectly until the outer casing is replaced, whereupon it refuses to work or the computer will not power-up.

The usual cause of the problem is the mounting bracket not having the proper right-angle fold at the top. Initially the card fits down into the slot correctly, as in the upper diagram of Figure 2.11, but when the fixing bolt is tightened the card tends to go out of alignment, as in the lower diagram of Figure 2.11. With the expansion card in the slot at an angle, the terminals of the slot tend to be short-circuited by the expansion card, bringing the whole computer to a halt. A visual inspection of the expansion cards will usually reveal this problem. It is also worthwhile pressing on the expansion cards to see if any of them will push down further into the expansion slots. If a card pushes further into place but almost immediately pops back up again, there is almost certainly a problem with the mounting bracket. The cure is to carefully bend the mounting bracket to the correct shape.

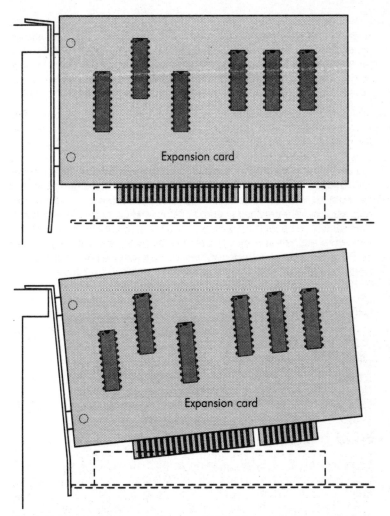

Fig.2.11 A mounting bracket can cause problems if it does not have the correct right-angled bend

Which slot?

I am often asked if it matters which expansion slot is used when adding a new one. Apart from fussy cards that work well in one slot but refuse to work in another, it does not matter which slot is used provided it is the correct type for the card. Some people prefer to use the slots nearest the processor first, working on the basis that inductance and capacitance in the board's copper connecting tracks will have less effect on the slots nearest the processor, giving greater reliability. I do not know of any testing that has proven this theory, but I suppose that working methodically away from the processor is as good a way of doing things as any other.

The BIOS

The BIOS is something that most PC users never need to get involved with, but for anyone undertaking PC servicing it is likely that some involvement will be needed from time to time. Even if you do not undertake work that requires some of the settings to be altered, it will occasionally be necessary to check that the existing settings are correct. Things like memory and disc failures can be due to incorrect settings in the BIOS. In days gone by it was necessary to have a utility program to make changes to the BIOS settings, but this program is built into a modern PC BIOS. A modern BIOS Setup program enables dozens of parameters to be controlled, many of which are highly technical. This tends to make the BIOS intimidating for those who are new to PC servicing, and even to those who have some experience of dealing with PC problems. However, most of the BIOS settings are not the type of thing the user will need to bother with. In general it is only the standard settings that control the disc drives that you will need to check, plus settings that relate to the type of memory used, and possibly one or two others. It is these parameters that we will consider here.

BIOS basics

Before looking at the BIOS Setup program, it would perhaps be as well to consider the function of the BIOS. BIOS is a acronym and it stands for basic input/out system. Its primary function is to help the operating system handle the input and output devices, such as the drives, and ports, and also the memory circuits. It is a program that is stored in a ROM on the motherboard. These days the chip is usually quite small and sports a holographic label to prove that it is the genuine article (Figure 2.12). The old style ROM is a standard ROM chip, as in Figure 2.13. Either way its function is the same. Because the BIOS program is in a ROM on the motherboard it can be run immediately at start-up without the need for any form of booting process.

Fig.2.12 The BIOS is a program stored in a ROM chip

The BIOS can provide software routines that help the operating system to utilize the hardware effectively, and it can also store information about the hardware for use by the operating system, and possibly other software. It is this second role that makes it necessary to have the Setup program. The BIOS can actually detect much of the system hardware and store the relevant technical information in memory. Also, a modern BIOS is customised to suit the particular hardware it is dealing with, and the defaults should be sensible ones for the hardware on the motherboard. However, some parameters have to be set manually, such as the time and date, and the user may wish to override some of the default settings.

The Setup program enables the user to control the settings that the BIOS stores away in its memory. A backup battery powers this memory when the PC is switched off, so its contents are available each time the PC is turned on. Once the correct parameters have been set it should not be necessary to change them unless the hardware is altered, such as a new floppy drive being added or the hard disc being upgraded. In practice the BIOS settings can sometimes be scrambled by a software or hardware glitch, although this is not a common problem with modern

Fig.2.13 An older style BIOS ROM chip

PCs. If the settings do become corrupted, there is no option but to use the BIOS Setup program to put things right again.

Entry

In the past there has been several common means of getting into the BIOS Setup program, but with modern motherboards there is only one method in common use. This is to press the Delete key at the appropriate point during the initial testing phase just after switch-on. The BIOS will display a message, usually in the bottom left-hand corner of the screen, telling you to press the "Del" key to enter the Setup program. The instruction manual should provide details if the motherboard you are using has a different method of entering the Setup program. The most common alternative is to press the "Escape" key rather than the "Del" key, but numerous alternatives have been used over the years, and several are still in use today.

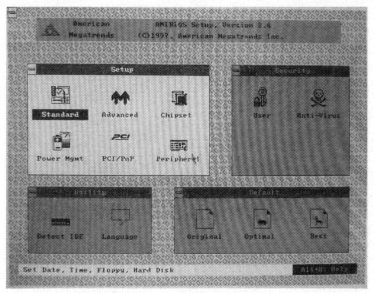

Fig.2.14 The AMI BIOS has a WIMP environment

Every PC should be supplied with a manual that has a section dealing with the BIOS. Actually a lot of PCs are supplied with only a very simple "Getting Started" style manual, but this is usually augmented by the manufacturers' manuals for the main components. It is then the motherboard manual that will deal with the BIOS. It is worth looking through the BIOS section to determine which features can be controlled via the BIOS.

Unfortunately, most motherboard instruction manuals assume the user is familiar with all the BIOS features, and there will be few detailed explanations. In fact there will probably just be a list of the available options and no real explanations at all. However, a quick read through this section of the manual will give you a good idea of what the BIOS is all about. Surprisingly large numbers of PC users who are quite expert in other aspects of PC operation have no real idea what the BIOS and the BIOS Setup program actually do. If you fall into this category the section of the manual that deals with the BIOS should definitely be given at least a quick read through.

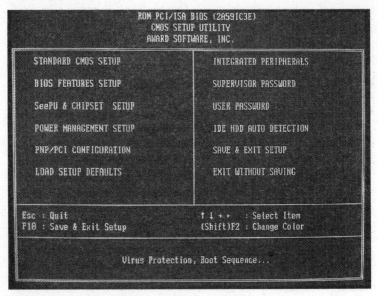

Fig.2.15 The Award BIOS is more conventional

There are several BIOS manufacturers and their BIOS Setup programs each work in a slightly different fashion. The Award BIOS and AMI BIOS are two common examples, and although they control the same basic functions, they are organised in somewhat different ways. A modern AMI BIOS has a Setup program that will detect any reasonably standard mouse connected to the PC, and offers a simple form of WIMP environment (Figure 2.14). It can still be controlled via the keyboard if preferred, or if the BIOS does not operate with the mouse you are using. The Award BIOS is probably the most common (Figure 2.15), and as far as I am aware it only uses keyboard control.

Apart from variations in the BIOS due to different manufacturers, the BIOS will vary slightly from one motherboard to another. This is simply due to the fact that features available on one motherboard may be absent or different on another motherboard. Also, the world of PCs in general is developing at an amazing rate, and this is reflected in frequent BIOS updates. The description of the BIOS provided here has to be a representative one, and the BIOS in your PC will inevitably be slightly different. In particular, if you are servicing an old PC there will be a much more limited range of parameters that can be controlled via the BIOS

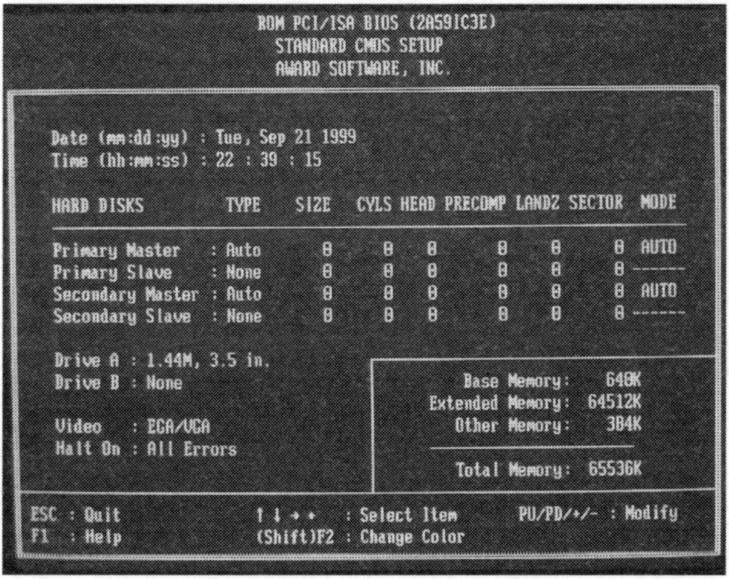

```
                    ROM PCI/ISA BIOS (2A59IC3E)
                       STANDARD CMOS SETUP
                       AWARD SOFTWARE, INC.

   Date (mm:dd:yy) : Tue, Sep 21 1999
   Time (hh:mm:ss) : 22 : 39 : 15

   HARD DISKS         TYPE   SIZE   CYLS HEAD PRECOMP LANDZ SECTOR  MODE

   Primary Master   : Auto     0      0    0      0      0      0  AUTO
   Primary Slave    : None     0      0    0      0      0      0  -----
   Secondary Master : Auto     0      0    0      0      0      0  AUTO
   Secondary Slave  : None     0      0    0      0      0      0  -----

   Drive A : 1.44M, 3.5 in.
   Drive B : None                          Base Memory:     640K
                                        Extended Memory:  64512K
   Video   : EGA/VGA                       Other Memory:     384K
   Halt On : All Errors
                                           Total Memory:  65536K

 ESC : Quit              ↑↓→← : Select Item      PU/PD/+/- : Modify
 F1  : Help             (Shift)F2 : Change Color
```

Fig.2.16 An example of a Standard CMOS Setup screen

Setup program. The important features should be present in any BIOS, and it is only the more minor and obscure features that are likely to be different. The motherboard's instruction manual should at the least give some basic information on setting up and using any unusual features.

Standard CMOS

There are so many parameters that can be controlled via the BIOS Setup program that they are normally divided into half a dozen or so groups. The most important of these is the "Standard CMOS Setup" (Figure 2.16), which is basically the same as the BIOS Setup in the original AT style PCs. The first parameters in the list are the time and date. These can usually be set via an operating system utility these days, but you can alter them via the Setup program if you prefer. There are on-screen instructions that tell you how to alter and select options. One slight oddity to watch out for is that you often have to use the Page Up key to decrement values, and the Page Down key to increment them.

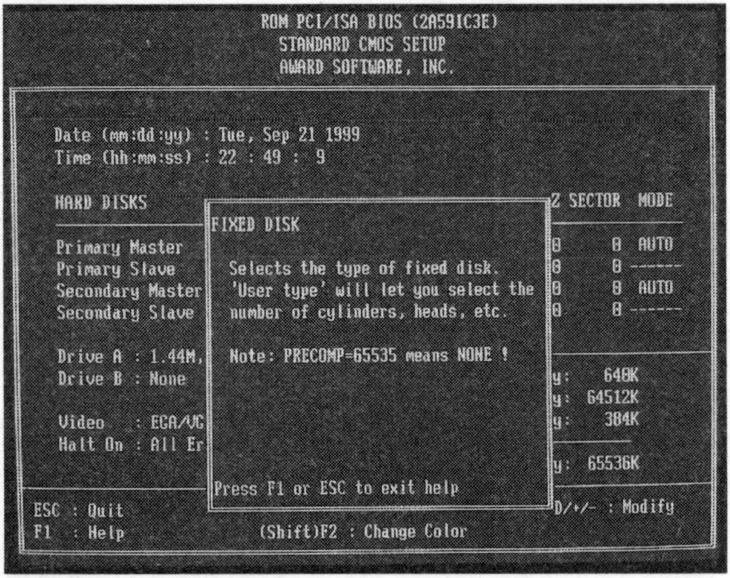

Fig.2.17 Pressing F1 will usually bring up a help screen

With virtually any modern BIOS a help screen can be brought up by pressing F1, and this will usually be context sensitive (Figure 2.17). In other words, if the cursor is in the section that deals with the hard drives, the help screen produced by pressing F1 will tell you about the hard disc parameters. It would be unreasonable to expect long explanations from a simple on-line help system, and a couple of brief and to the point sentences are all that will normally be provided.

Drive settings

The next section is used to set the operating parameters for the devices on the IDE ports. The hard disc is normally the master device on the primary IDE channel (IDE1), and the CD-ROM is usually the master device on the secondary IDE channel (IDE2). However, to avoid the need for a second data cable the CD-ROM drive is sometimes the slave device on the primary IDE interface. In the early days there were about 40 standard types of hard disc drive, and it was just a matter of selecting the appropriate type number for the drive in use. The BIOS would then supply the appropriate parameters for that drive. This system was unable

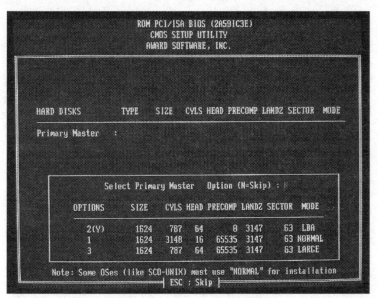

Fig.2.18 An IDE automatic detection screen in action

to cope with the ever increasing range of drives available, and something more flexible had to be devised. The original 40 plus preset drive settings are normally still available from a modern BIOS, but there is an additional option that enables the drive parameters to be specified by the user. This is the method used with all modern PCs and their high capacity hard disc drives.

The drive table parameters basically just tell the operating system the size of drive, and the way that the disc is organised. Although we refer to a hard disc as a singular disc, most of these units use both sides of two or more discs. Each side of the disc is divided into cylinders (tracks), and each cylinder is subdivided into several sectors. There are usually other parameters that enable the operating system to use the disc quickly and efficiently. You do not really need to understand these parameters, and just need to check that the correct figures are present. The manual for the hard drive should provide the correct figures for the BIOS. If you do not have the manual, it can probably be downloaded from the disc manufacturer's web site.

A modern BIOS makes life easy for you by offering an "Auto" option. If this is selected, the BIOS examines the hardware during the start-up routine and enters the correct figures automatically. This usually works very well, but with some drives it can take a while, which extends the boot-up time. If the PC has been set up with this option enabled, the drive table will be blank. There is an alternative method of automatic detection that avoids the boot-up delay, and any reasonably modern BIOS should have this facility.

If you go back to the initial menu you will find a section called "IDE HDD Auto Detection" (Figure 2.18), and this offers a similar auto-detection facility. When this option is selected the Setup program examines the hardware on each IDE channel, and offers suggested settings for each of the four possible IDE devices. If you accept the suggested settings for the hard disc drive (or drives) they will be entered into the CMOS RAM. There may actually be several alternatives offered per IDE device, but the default suggestion is almost invariably the correct one. If you do not know the correct settings for a drive, this facility should find them for you.

It is perhaps worth mentioning that with an IDE drive the figures in the drive table do not usually have to match the drive's physical characteristics. Indeed, they rarely if ever do so. The electronics in the drive enable it to mimic any valid physical arrangement that does not exceed the capacity of the drive. In practice it is advisable to use the figures recommended by the drive manufacturer, as these are tried and tested, and should guarantee perfect results. Other figures can sometimes give odd problems such as unreliable booting, even though they are within the acceptable limits.

The last parameter for each IDE drive is usually something like Auto, Normal, LBA (large block addressing), and Large. Normal is for drives under 528MB, while LBA and Large are alternative modes for drives having a capacity of more than 528MB. Modern drives have capacities of well in excess of 528MB, and mostly require the LBA mode. The manual for the hard drive should give the correct setting, but everything should work fine with "Auto" selected.

Some users get confused because they think a hard drive that will be partitioned should have separate entries in the BIOS for each partition. This is not the case, and as far as the BIOS is concerned each physical hard disc is a single drive, and has just one entry in the CMOS RAM table. The partitioning of hard discs is handled by the operating system, and so is the assignment of drive letters. The BIOS is only concerned with the physical characteristics of the drives, and not how data will be arranged and stored on the discs.

Floppy drives

The next section in the "Standard CMOS Setup" is used to select the floppy disc drive type or types. Provided the PC is not a virtual museum piece, all the normal types of floppy drive should be supported, from the old 5.25 inch 360k drives to the rare 2.88M 3.5 inch type. You simply check that the appropriate type is set for drives A and B. "None" should be selected for drive B if the computer has only one floppy drive. This bottom section of the screen also deals with the amount of memory fitted to the motherboard. In days gone by you had to enter the amount of memory fitted, but a modern BIOS automatically detects the memory and enters the correct figures into the CMOS RAM. The "Standard CMOS Setup" screen will report the amount of memory fitted, and will display something like Figure 2.19.

Note that there is no way of altering the memory settings if they are wrong. If the BIOS reports the wrong amount of RAM there is a fault in the memory circuits, and the correct amount will be reported if the fault is rectified. Sometimes what appears to be an error is just the way the amount of memory is reported by the BIOS. For those who are new to computing the way in which the amount of memory is reported can seem rather strange. It should look very familiar to those who can remember the early days of IBM compatible PCs. The original PCs had relatively simple processors that could only address one megabyte of RAM, but only the lower 640k of the address range were actually used for RAM.

The upper 384k of the address range was used for the BIOS ROM, video ROM, and that sort of thing.

Modern PCs can address hundreds of megabytes of RAM, but the lowest one megabyte is still arranged in much the same way that it was in the original PCs. The BIOS therefore reports that there is 640k of normal (base) memory, so many

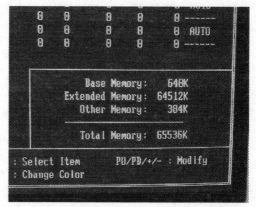

Fig.2.19 The Bios reports the memory it finds. The user can not alter these settings

kilobytes of RAM above the original one megabyte of RAM (extended memory), and 384k of other memory. This "other" memory is the RAM in the address space used by the BIOS, etc.

The final section of the standard set-up enables the type of video card to be specified, and the degree of error trapping to be selected. The BIOS will probably detect the video card and set the appropriate type, which for a modern PC will presumably be a EGA/VGA type. It is possible to select the old CGA and mono adapters, but these are obsolete and not used in modern PCs. The error trapping controls the way in which the computer responds to errors that are found during the BIOS self-testing routine at switch-on.

The default of halt on all errors is probably the best choice, particularly when you are having problems with the PC. Once the PC has been fully serviced and is running properly again you may prefer to alter this setting, but I would not bother. You can alter this setting if you wish to have the computer continue with the start-up routine despite a major error being detected by the BIOS. In theory this might enable the nature of the fault to be investigated more thoroughly, but in practice the PC might simply crash during the start-up routine, or on exiting it.

The BIOS, especially if it is a modern type, is likely to have several pages of additional parameters that can be adjusted. Most of these are not of any great relevance when faultfinding, and "playing" around with most of these settings is likely to do more harm than good. There may be some settings that govern the memory timing, and these will often be found in the section called something like Chipset Setup. If the PC is suffering from a general lack of reliability, with things occasionally coming to an abrupt halt, it is certainly worthwhile checking the memory settings.

The memory speed shown in the BIOS Setup program must match that of the memory fitted on the motherboard, and where appropriate the memory type must also match. If the BIOS gives the memory as 60ns EDO DRAM and the board is fitted with 80ns fast page DRAM, it is unlikely that the PC will work properly. In some cases there is more than one set of timing values given for each type of memory. The choice is usually between a relatively slow but safe option, and one that is faster but may not give good reliability. If the computer lacks good reliability and the faster memory timing is set, it makes sense to use the more conservative setting. In this context larger figures normally correspond to slower memory timing.

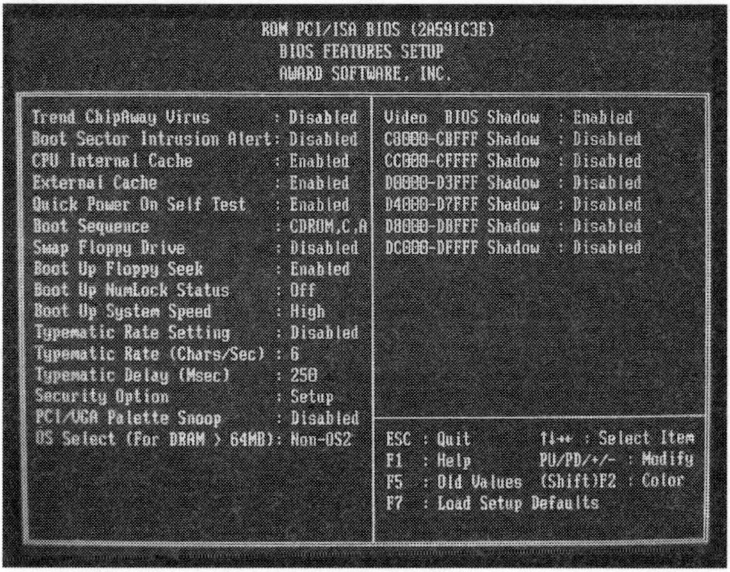

```
                    ROM PCI/ISA BIOS (2A59IC3E)
                        BIOS FEATURES SETUP
                        AWARD SOFTWARE, INC.

 Trend ChipAway Virus      : Disabled    Video  BIOS Shadow  : Enabled
 Boot Sector Intrusion Alert: Disabled   C8000-CBFFF Shadow  : Disabled
 CPU Internal Cache        : Enabled     CC000-CFFFF Shadow  : Disabled
 External Cache            : Enabled     D0000-D3FFF Shadow  : Disabled
 Quick Power On Self Test  : Enabled     D4000-D7FFF Shadow  : Disabled
 Boot Sequence             : CDROM,C,A   D8000-DBFFF Shadow  : Disabled
 Swap Floppy Drive         : Disabled    DC000-DFFFF Shadow  : Disabled
 Boot Up Floppy Seek       : Enabled
 Boot Up NumLock Status    : Off
 Boot Up System Speed      : High
 Typematic Rate Setting    : Disabled
 Typematic Rate (Chars/Sec) : 6
 Typematic Delay (Msec)    : 250
 Security Option           : Setup
 PCI/VGA Palette Snoop     : Disabled
 OS Select (For DRAM > 64MB): Non-OS2    ESC : Quit        ↑↓→← : Select Item
                                         F1  : Help        PU/PD/+/- : Modify
                                         F5  : Old Values  (Shift)F2 : Color
                                         F7  : Load Setup Defaults
```

Fig.2.20 A screen for controlling BIOS features

Integrated ports

Some of the standard ports are integrated with the motherboard of any reasonably modern PC. Typically there are two serial ports, one parallel type, and two USB ports on the motherboard. There will be a page in the BIOS Setup program that deals with these ports, and this will normally be under a heading called something like Integrated Peripherals. If there are problems with one of the built-in ports it clearly makes sense to look at the relevant BIOS settings to ensure that the faulty port is actually switched on, and that any other settings are correct. With modern PCs the CPU settings are often controlled via the BIOS rather than using jumpers or DIP switches. If a PC is proving troublesome it will not do any harm to check the CPU settings, but if the correct CPU is reported during the start-up routine, it is unlikely that any errors will be found here.

In one of the BIOS Setup screens you should be able to choose between various boot options (Figure 2.20). In other words, it should be possible to select which drives the computer tries to boot from, and the order in which it tries them. With some PCs you can select any drive as the first, second, and third boot drives. Others are less accommodating and you have to select from a list of available boot options. This is an important part of the BIOS when servicing PCs, because it is often necessary to change the boot options.

For example, you may need to reinstall the operating system by booting from a CD-ROM, but by default most PCs are not set to use this method of booting. You may need to boot from a floppy disc drive to run anti-virus software or a disc-partitioning program. By default a modern PC may not be set to boot from the floppy disc. It is worthwhile looking at this part of the BIOS Setup program to see what the current settings are, and determine what alternatives are available. Ideally when booting from a floppy disc or CD-ROM drive, that drive should be set as the first boot drive. If the BIOS checks for an operating system on the hard disc drive first, and it finds a faulty operating system, it might bring things to a halt there rather than proceeding to other boot drives.

It is worth noting that no settings are actually altered unless you select the Save and exit option from the main menu. If you accidentally change some settings and do not know how to restore the correct ones, simply exiting without saving the new settings will leave everything untouched. You can then enter the Setup program again and have another try. It is also worth noting that the main menu usually has a couple of useful options such as reverting to the previously saved settings, or loading the Setup defaults. If disaster should strike, it might therefore be possible to go back one step to some workable settings, or to simply use the defaults and then do any necessary "fine tuning".

There has been a trend towards using the BIOS to control as many settings as possible, with little or nothing configured via jumpers or DIP-switches on the motherboard. This has resulted in a steady increase in the number of sections and subsections in the BIOS Setup program. Particularly if you are dealing with a modern PC, it is likely that there will be more sections in its BIOS Setup program than are featured here. These extra sections generally cover the more obscure aspects of the hardware, and you may never have to use them. It is still a good idea to look through the instruction manual for the motherboard to determine which aspects of the hardware are controlled via the BIOS. Alternatively, look through each section of the Setup program, but do not play around with settings that you do not understand.

Switches and jumpers

Although many settings have been transferred to the BIOS over the years, I have yet to encounter a PC that lacks any configuration jumpers or switches. In fact some PCs still have large numbers of them, although in some cases they are optional and the BIOS can be used for most settings if preferred. Anyway, in order to deal with a PC, ancient or modern, it is certainly necessary to understand the use of configuration switches and jumpers. What parameters are likely to be set via switches or jumpers?

With Socket 7 motherboards and some later ones it is necessary to set the correct clock multiplier for the processor. This is less common but not unknown with later boards. With more recent boards it is more likely to be the motherboard's bus frequency that is set via jumpers or switches. The multiplier is usually set automatically so that the processor can not be overclocked by setting a higher than normal multiplier value.

With Socket 7 motherboards it is usually necessary to set the processor core voltage. Conventionally logic circuits operate from a 5-volt supply, but in order to get the highest possible performance it is common practice for other supply voltages to be used in parts of the computer. Memory circuits and some sections of the processor often operate at 3.3 volts, and the main processor circuits often work at a somewhat lower voltage. It is this second voltage, or core voltage that is set via the jumpers or DIP-switches. The instruction manual for the motherboard should give the correct settings for all the usable processors. It is common for the correct core voltage to be marked on the top surface of the processor, particularly with non-Intel devices. If the marked core voltage is different to the one indicated on the chip itself, set up the motherboard to provide the voltage indicated on the chip.

Clear CMOS

There may be other settings to make, but these additional parameters vary a lot from one motherboard to another. One virtually standard feature is a jumper that enables the CMOS memory to be disconnected from the backup battery. By default this should be set so the board functions normally, with the backup battery ensuring that the BIOS is free from amnesia, with the correct drive parameters, etc., being used each time the computer is switched on. Setting this jumper to the "off" position for a few minutes wipes the CMOS memory of all its contents. With the jumper restored to the "on" setting the computer is able to function again, but it is a matter of starting "from scratch" with the CMOS memory settings.

In effect, this jumper provides a means of resetting the CMOS memory. This would be probably only be necessary if someone started to use the

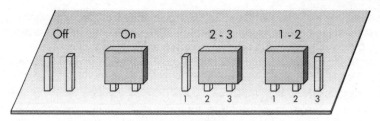

Fig.2.21 The two types of jumper normally used on motherboards

password facility and then forgot his or her password. The only way of getting the computer to boot if this happens is to clear the current set-up from memory. The next time the computer is started it uses the default settings, which means that it starts up without implementing the password facility. Unless there is a good reason to do so, it is best not to use any BIOS password facility. Note that it is not usually necessary to clear the CMOS memory in this way if you manage to make a complete mess of the BIOS settings. From within the BIOS Setup program it is usually possible to revert to one or two sets of default settings, and then do any necessary "fine tuning". It would only be necessary to clear the CMOS memory if a bad setting prevented the PC from starting up.

There can be other jumpers or DIP-switches to set such things as the supply voltage for the memory modules, to disable the built-in audio system, and this type of thing. You really have to read the manual for the motherboard to determine what jumpers or DIP-switches have to be set up correctly, if any. As pointed out previously, the modern trend is towards

as much as possible being set using auto-detection methods, or via the BIOS Setup program. Older motherboards often have numerous switches or jumpers, but many modern motherboards only have one switch or jumper that can be used to power-down the CMOS memory.

Fig.2.22 The "ON" marking on a DIP-switch

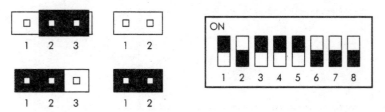

Fig.2.23 Some switch and jumper diagrams are clearer than others

Setting up

Actually setting any jumpers or switches should not give any major problems. There are two types of jumper, which are the straightforward on/off type and the two-way variety. The on/off type has two pins and you fit the jumper over the pins to connect them together ("on") or do not fit the jumper at all ("off"). This simple scheme of things is shown in the left-hand section Figure 2.21. It is common practice to fit the jumper on one of the pins to provide the "off" setting. If you should need to change the setting at a later time you then know exactly where to find the jumper. The jumpers are minute and are likely to get lost if you store them somewhere other than on the motherboard.

The second type of jumper block has three pins, and the jumper is used to connect the middle pin to one of the outer pins, as in the right-hand section of Figure 2.21. The jumper is connecting together two pins, as before, and the jumpers are exactly the same whether they are used on a two-pin block or a three-pin type.

DIP-switches are normally in blocks of four or eight switches, but not all the switches in a block will necessarily be utilized. They are a form of slider switch, and are more or less a miniature version of the switches

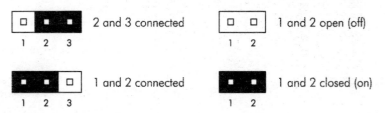

Fig.2.24 An explanatory diagram for jumper settings

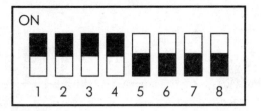

Fig.2.25 An explanatory diagram for DIP-switches

often used in small electronic gadgets such as cassette recorders and personal stereo units. The block of switches is marked with "on" and (or) "off" legends (Figure 2.22) to make it clear which setting is which.

The motherboard's instruction manual normally includes a diagram showing the correct switch or jumper settings for a given processor. There is a slight problem here in that these diagrams are open to misinterpretation. In the two examples of Figure 2.23, which pins do the jumpers connect and which switches are in the "on" position. My guess would be that the black blocks represent the jumpers and the control knobs on the switches, but there is no way of telling for sure without some further assistance. The manual should provide this assistance in the form of another diagram showing exactly how the switch or jumper setting diagrams should be interpreted. These diagrams will be something like Figure 2.24 and 2.25. Never rely on guesswork when setting jumpers and DIP-switches. Mistakes are unlikely to result in any damage, but it is not worth taking the risk. Carefully study the instruction manual for the motherboard and get things right first time.

Points to remember

Although the risk of damaging computer components with static charges is perhaps not as great as the manufacturer' warnings would suggest, it is a very real risk. It is certainly not worth taking risks when dealing with even the cheaper computer components.

Static-sensitive components are supplied in some form of packing to protect then against static charges. Leave them in this packing until it is time to fit them into the computer. Avoid the temptation to remove the components from the packing just to have a good look at them.

Some expensive anti-static equipment is available, but due care and some improvised equipment will suffice. However, it is worth investing in an anti-static wristband and earthing plug or clip if you will be undertaking a lot of computer upgrades.

Most expansion cards fit into place without too much difficulty. Do not use brute force when a card is reluctant to fit into place. This is unlikely to damage the expansion card but does run a real risk of damaging the motherboard.

If a card will not fit into its slot, look carefully to see what is obstructing it. Sometimes the metal mounting bracket needs to be bent into shape, or it might be necessary to reposition the motherboard slightly. The card will fit into place properly provided everything is aligned properly.

Do not be intimidated by the BIOS. The huge range of settings in a modern BIOS can be rather daunting even for those with plenty of experience at dealing with this aspect of PCs. However, there is no need to get involved with most settings as they will be set at suitable defaults. In all probability you will only have to deal with the Standard CMOS settings and a few others.

Do not be intimidated by the BIOS, but do not be gung-ho about it either. It is unlikely that incorrect settings would cause any damage, but this possibility can not be totally ruled out. If the worst comes to the worst, the CMOS memory can be cleared and the standard defaults can be selected on re-entering the BIOS Setup program.

Make sure that you understand configuration diagrams for jumpers and DIP-switches. If the diagrams are ambiguous there might be explanatory diagrams or a settings chart that clarifies matters. Do not simply take a guess as this could result in something being damaged.

Adding ports

Communicating

While it is not inconceivable that a computer could be put to good use without the aid of printers, modems, and other peripheral devices, few people can utilize one in this way. Unless you are using a computer for an application where there will be no need to produce any hard copy, or transfer data via means other than swapping floppy discs, at least one parallel, serial, or USB port will be required. Modern PCs have two serial ports and a parallel port built-in, with the necessary hardware (including the connectors) fitted on the motherboard.

There are usually two or more USB ports as well. The standard arrangement is to have two USB connectors included on the motherboard with the other ports, with any additional USB ports on a bracket at the rear of the PC. Some PCs have the additional ports on the front panel, often behind some sort of hinged or sliding cover. This feature is useful if you will use the ports with peripherals like mice and digital cameras.

All the port connectors on the motherboard are accessed via cut-outs in the rear of the case, rather like the keyboard connector of an old-style motherboard and case. These old-style motherboards and cases are of the AT variety incidentally. The motherboards that include the port connectors are ATX boards, and the same name is used for the cases that take them.

With older PCs connection to the outside world is via sockets mounted on the rear of the casing (most cases have holes for standard D type connectors ready cut), or mounted on expansion slot blanking plates. AT cases and motherboards have not been used in new PCs for some time now, and will gradually fade into history over the next few years. However, at the present time there must be millions of these PCs still in everyday use.

More ports?

Probably for many users the serial and parallel ports supplied as standard with the PC will suffice. Most computers are connected to a printer, usually via a parallel port. This is the only parallel port peripheral used with many computer systems although parallel port scanners have been quite popular in the past, as have various types of external add-on disc drive such as Zip drives. These normally have a connector for a printer so that you can use one printer port to drive both a printer and a scanner or drive. Newer scanners, printers, and external drives have USB ports, which has reduced the need for parallel ports. However, if you should need an extra printer port, it is just a matter of adding a printer port card into one of the expansion slots. ISA and PCI parallel port cards are available.

A mouse (or other pointing device such as a digitising tablet or tracker ball) is now a standard PC peripheral, and these can be of either the mouse port (PS/2), serial, or USB varieties. There is also a third type known as a bus mouse, which is supplied complete with an expansion card that interfaces the mouse to the computer. However, the built-in mouse port of most modern PCs has led to the demise of this type of mouse. A serial mouse connects to a standard serial port, and on the face of it a mouse-port mouse is the better option, as it leaves the serial port free for other purposes. In practice there is a slight risk of a mouse-port mouse conflicting with other hardware, but it should be possible to sort out any hardware conflict that occurs.

Even with a printer and a serial mouse connected to the computer, the ports supplied as part of the standard system will almost certainly suffice. It is only if you need to add a second printer, a plotter, a modem, or some more exotic piece of equipment that further ports might be needed. Even then, with the increasing use of USB ports there might be no need for additional serial and parallel types.

On the face of it, making use of the existing ports is better than choosing peripherals that necessitate additional ports. In practice it might be better to opt for USB peripherals even if this means adding further USB ports. The cost of the upgrade is unlikely to be very great, and the USB option is better future-proofed. Serial and parallel port peripherals might fit your current PC without the need for any add-ons, but there is a slight risk that they will be difficult to use or unusable with your next PC.

Limited expansion

You need to bear in mind that there is a limit to the number of serial and parallel ports that can be added to a PC. You can have up to three parallel ports ("LPT1" to "LPT3"), and up to four serial ports ("COM1" to "COM4"). Software supports for anything beyond LPT2 and COM2, used to be something less than universal. In fact some software, rather unhelpfully, seems reluctant to recognise anything beyond LPT1 and (possibly) COM1. Windows has eased this problem, and if Windows recognises a serial or parallel port it should be usable with any Windows applications software.

When buying parallel and serial port cards you need to ensure that the card will provide the particular port you require. Most cards of this type now have configuration switches or jumper blocks so that they can be set to act as at least port 1 or port 2, and possibly as port 3 or 4. You may still find some cards that have the port number or numbers preset. This is most common with single parallel and serial port cards, where the port is often preset as port 1. With twin serial port cards you sometimes find that the port is preset at port 1, with some optional components providing a second port that acts as port 2. However, with most modern serial and parallel port cards you have a large amount of control over the port numbering.

When expanding a system, what you will almost certainly need is a card to provide port 2 or beyond. Expansion cards that do not allow you to set the port number via configuration switches or jumper blocks are probably best avoided. Although you might be able to reconfigure one of the existing ports to operate as port 2, so that the new port can operate as port 1, these older types often lack the capabilities of modern cards.

For example, modern parallel ports have bi-directional modes that enable them to receive parallel data as well as send it. This capability is exploited by many modern peripherals that utilize a parallel port, including printers, scanners, and external disc drives of various types. Where possible it is preferable to leave the existing ports operating under their original numbers, and to have any new ports as port 2, port 3, or whatever. If you do need to reconfigure the built-in ports, it will be necessary to do so via the BIOS Setup program.

When configuring serial and parallel ports you do not normally set them as LPT1, COM2, or whatever. Instead you set the port base address and the operating system assigns the port numbers and in the case of a parallel port (and possibly a serial port) an interrupt number as well.

Port addressing works much like ordinary memory addressing, and it enables the processor to "talk" to the appropriate register in a selected piece of hardware. A hardware interrupt is where a peripheral device or a piece of built in hardware activates an input line of the processor to indicate that it has produced data that requires processing. Every time you move the mouse, for instance, it generates an interrupt. The processor then fetches and processes the new data, moves the cursor to the appropriate new screen position, and then carries on where it left off. This avoids having the processor waste large amounts of time repeatedly monitoring hardware devices that are idle.

This table shows the usual addresses and (where appropriate) interrupt numbers for COM1 to COM4, LPT1 and LPT2 (the addresses are in hexadecimal and are the base addresses. If a parallel port has a base address of 3BC (interrupt 7) it will probably be set as LPT1 by the operating system, and the other printer ports are moved one number higher.

PORT	ADDRESS	INTERRUPT
LPT1	378/3BC	IRQ7
LPT2	278	IRQ5
COM1	3F8	IRQ4
COM2	2F8	IRQ3
COM3	3E8	
COM4	2E8	

Automatic numbering

As pointed out previously, the operating system automatically assigns serial and parallel port numbers. Although you can not control the port numbers directly, it is possible to set a port to the required number if the port addresses are under manual control. These days it is unlikely that it would be necessary to do so, but this ability is there should it be needed. This automatic allocation system can be confusing because adding a new port can result in the number of an existing one being changed. The method of numbering used for serial and parallel ports is to have the one at the highest address as port one, the port at the next lowest address as port two, and so one.

Suppose that the existing parallel port is at address 378 and you add a new port at 278. As the only port, the original port at 378 would have been set as port one. With the new port added it is still at the higher address, and it remains as port one. The new parallel port at address 278 becomes port two. However, if the new port was set to address 3BC, it would be at the higher address, and would become port one. The original parallel port would then have its number shifted to port two. This can cause problems if the operating system still looks for (say) a printer on port one when it is connected to what is now port two. This is not a major problem since it can be corrected by either altering the printer's port setting in Windows or simply switching the printer to the new printer port one.

In the original PCs there was no parallel port at address 3BC. There were only two addresses available at 278 and 378. The 3BC address was apparently introduced with the Hercules monochrome graphics card which was a popular choice with buyers of the early PCs. Although this address may seem to be of no relevance to modern PCs, it is supported by most printer port cards and it can also be used for the built-in port of many PCs. In fact some PCs use this as the default address for the built-in printer port, so do not assume that the 378 address will be used. I suppose that 3BC is actually the better choice for the built-in port, since it ensures that any additional ports are port two and port three, with the original port always remaining as port one.

BIOS configuration

Some general information about the BIOS was provided in the previous chapter, and here we will look specifically at the sections that deal with the built-in ports. Note that any ports provided by expansion cards will be configured via jumpers or DIP-switches on the expansion card itself. The BIOS only controls ports provided by the motherboard. It is usually possible to switch ports on and off, and where appropriate the port addresses and IRQ settings can be altered.

If you are using a PC that is something less than the latest thing in PC technology, the BIOS Setup program will be relatively simple, and there should be no difficulty in finding the menu that deals with the integral ports. A modern BIOS is too complex to have all the settings in a single menu, so the initial screen is effectively a menu of the available menus. There should be an option called something like "Integrated Peripherals", and this is the one where the port settings are controlled. Figure 3.1 shows a typical Integrated Peripherals menu.

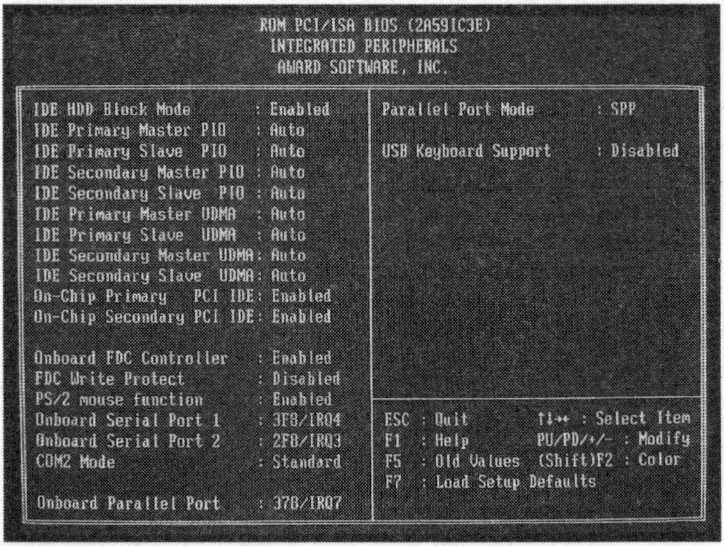

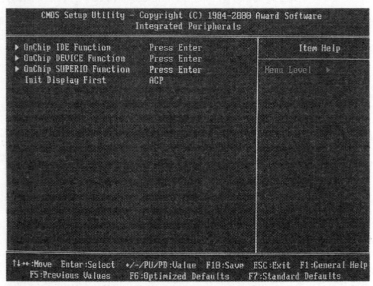

Fig.3.1　The Integrated Peripherals section of a BIOS

Fig.3.2　There will be a submenu in a modern BIOS

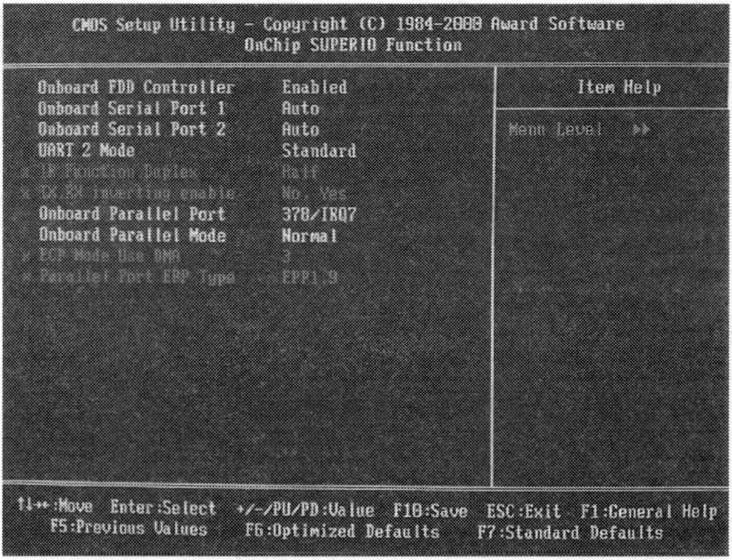

Fig.3.3 The SUPERIO section controls the ports

With a modern BIOS it can be more difficult to find the appropriate menu. There are so many settings that can be altered via the BIOS Setup program that some of the menus have several submenus. Having access to a detailed instruction manual for the PC or the manual for the motherboard makes life much easier with a BIOS of this type. However, it should still be possible to find the required settings without the aid of an instruction manual. As before, there should be a menu called something like Integrated Peripherals, but selecting this option will not give direct access to the port settings. Instead, a menu offering a few submenus will appear (Figure 3.2). If in doubt, select each menu in turn until you find the one that deals with the parallel port. In this example, the OnChip Device Function and OnChip SUPERIO Function seem to be the most likely candidates. In fact, the latter controls the port settings (Figure 3.3).

PCI or ISA

Serial and parallel port expansion cards are produced in PCI (Figure 3.4) and ISA (Figure 3.5) versions. Since many modern PCs lack any ISA slots there may be no choice but to opt for a PCI card. In general it

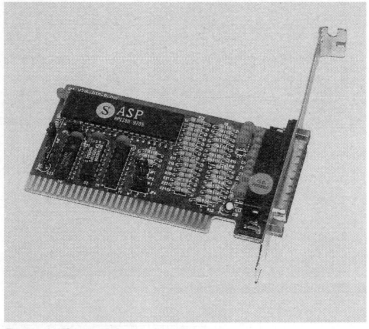

Fig.3.4 An ISA parallel port expansion card

is better to opt for PCI rather than ISA expansion cards whenever you have a choice. You may well need to use the expansion card in a new PC in the future, but it is unlikely that this will be possible if you choose an ISA type. Also, PCI cards are generally less troublesome than the ISA variety. PCI cards are better at sharing system resources, and problems with hardware conflicts should be avoided if the PCI option is taken. They also provide better Plug and Play support. On the other hand, there are a few ifs, buts, and maybes when using serial and parallel ports provided by a PCI expansion card.

It is important to realise that ISA and PCI cards provide two rather different types of serial/parallel port. The advantage of an ISA type is that the card connects direct to the processor's buses, and it provides traditional ports that have the usual base addresses. In other words, you can use the serial and parallel ports on ISA cards in exactly the same manner as the ones on the motherboard. After all, the original PCs had the standard ports provided by ISA expansion cards. They could be regarded as more standard than the built-in ports.

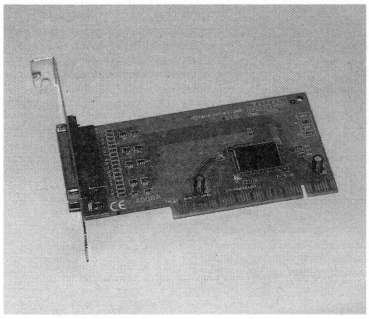

Fig.3.5 A PCI parallel port card

PCI cards have their advantages, but there is a price to pay for them. The PCI bus is really a form of input/output port, and devices on the PCI bus can not fit into the input/output map in the normal way. On the face of it, this is unimportant because PCI port cards are supplied with a disc containing a suitable device driver. This enables Windows to use the card much as if it was an ISA type providing ports at the usual input/output addresses. Provided all the software does things "by the book" and only contacts the ports via the operating system, everything should work fine.

Unfortunately, real-world software does not always do things this way, and it might try to directly control the port's hardware. This will not work at all, because the port's hardware will not be at the usual addresses in the input/output map. It can only be accessed indirectly via the PCI bus, using relatively complex routines. In general, the more common peripherals such as printers and modems are contacted via the usual channels and should not give any problems with a PCI port card. Many devices are less accommodating though, and parallel port scanners and

Zip drives mostly use the direct access method. It is therefore better to use the more "run of the mill" devices on PCI port cards, and the more specialised peripherals on the PC's built-in ports. With luck, this will avoid any problems.

Re-mapping

The expansion card might be supplied with a software solution in the form of a re-mapping program. This tries to intercept instructions that are directed at the standard port addresses. It then substitutes an appropriate routine to drive the PCI card. There is no guarantee that this type of thing will work properly, but it usually works well enough. One potential problem is that software often controls the hardware directly in order to obtain greater speed. This method of intercepting instructions and substituting appropriate routines might slow things down to an unacceptable degree. This does not seem to be a significant problem in practice, probably due to serial and parallel ports being quite slow in relation to the rest of the PC.

Note that a PCI card is unlikely to use the re-mapping facility by default. The card's device driver should have a properties window that enables the re-mapping to be enabled. This might be available by double clicking on the port's entry in Device Manager, but this often gives access to a cut down version of the properties window. Where this is the case, look for another entry for the card in Device Manager, in amongst the main categories. Double clicking on this entry should give access to the full properties window.

If a re-mapping facility is provided, there should be a Configuration section or something similar (Figure 3.6). In this example, the re-mapping can be enabled by ticking the appropriate checkbox, and base addresses of H278 and H378 can be selected for the parallel port. Of course, the address selected must not be in use by another port. Where necessary, check the properties windows for the other ports to determine their base addresses, so that address conflicts can be avoided.

Adapters

Over the years a vast number of adapters have been produced, enabling virtually any type of port to be adapted to suit practically any other type. Most of these are now obsolete, and many of these adapters were too approximate to be of much use. There are still a few adapters produced, and the ones that permit serial or parallel port devices to be used with a

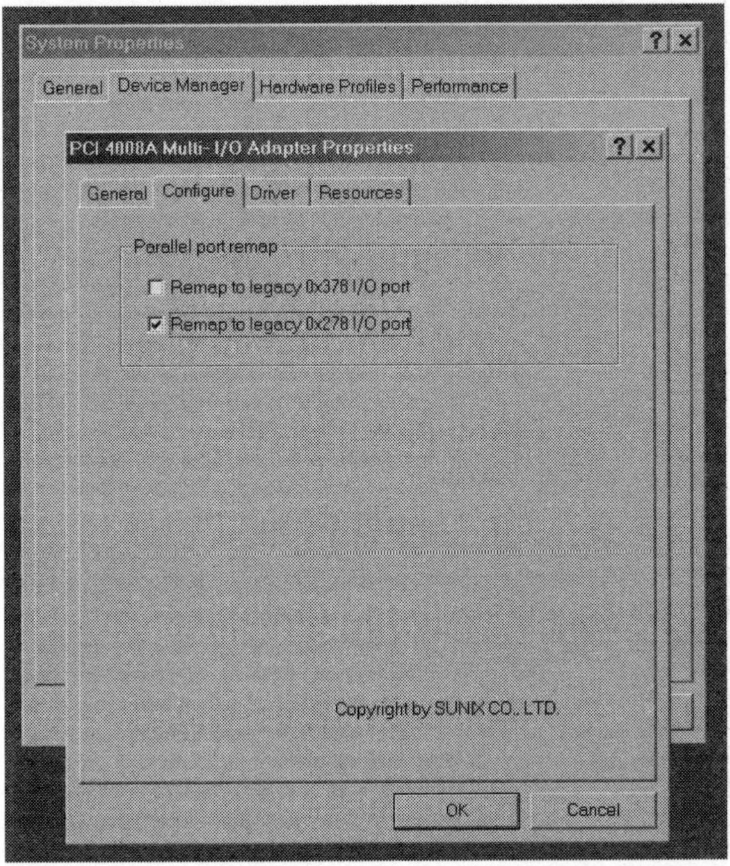

Fig.3.6 Any re-mapping facility will probably not be used by default, and it will have to be activated via Device Manager

USB port are by far the most popular. They mostly look like an ordinary lead, as does the USB to printer port adapter shown in Figure 3.7. However, there is some sophisticated electronics in the larger of the connectors.

These adapters are not really intended as a means of adding more ports to a standard PC, where an expansion card is the normal solution. They can be used in this way if you would prefer not to delve into the interior of your PC, but they are primarily intended for use with Macintosh computers and laptop PCs that only have a USB port.

Fig.3.7 A USB to parallel port adapter

When using these adapters with a PC you have to bear in mind that, like PCI serial and parallel cards, the port hardware is not at its normal place in the PC's input/output map. This factor could give problems with awkward peripherals. The parallel adapters almost invariably have a Centronics connector at the parallel end, rather than a female D connector. This makes it easier to use the adapters with a parallel printer, since the Centronics connector will plug straight into the printer's input port. It deliberately discourages people from trying to use the adapter with anything other than a printer. Most of these adapters only provide a basic printer port, and do not support any form of bi-directional operation. This renders them unsuitable for many non-printer applications.

Port sharing

Gadgets that permit more than one device to be connected to a parallel or RS232C serial port were quite popular at one time, but they seem to be used less widely these days. If you contemplate this type of port expansion it is important to bear in mind that only one of the peripheral devices can be connected to the PC at any one time. These units are simply switches that permit the port to be connected to one of two or

Fig.3.8   A manual two-way switching unit

more peripheral devices. This is fine if you will only need to connect one device or another to the port at any one time, but additional ports are needed if it will be necessary to use any of the peripherals simultaneously.

The simplest unit is a two-way type that has manual switching (Figure 3.8). There are three 25-way D connectors on the rear panel (Figure 3.9), and there are two ways of using the unit. In order to use two peripherals with one printer port, the INPUT/OUTPUT socket is connected to the PC's printer port. Sockets A and B then connect to the two peripherals. The alternative is to connect sockets A and B to ports on different PCs. The INPUT/OUTPUT socket then connects to a peripheral that is shared by the two PCs.

Switching units of this type are primarily intended for use with parallel ports and printers, but all 25 input/output terminals are switched, and they will therefore work with serial ports and with any serial or parallel peripheral. When used with a parallel port or ports, a 25-way cable having a male D connector at each end is required to connect the switching unit

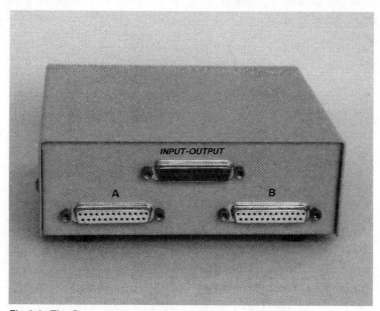

Fig.3.9 The D connectors on the rear of the switching unit

to a PC. This standard cable should be available from the same shop as the switching unit. Parallel peripherals connect to the switch box using whatever cable would be used for direct connection to the PC's parallel port.

Things are more awkward when these units are used with an RS232C port. It might be possible to obtain a lead that will connect the switching unit to a 9-pin PC serial port, but it would probably be a matter of making a custom cable. The two ports on the switching unit will be non-standard, having female instead of male D connectors. It is possible to obtain adapters called "gender benders" that correct this type of problem. However, be warned that these adapters often provide the required "sex change", but do not provide the necessary "mirroring" of the pin numbers in the process. What should be pin 1 is pin 13, what should be pin 2 is pin 12, and so on. Seeking out a switching unit that is specifically designed for use with serial ports could save a lot of hassle.

Peripheral sharing

Utilising one peripheral with two PCs is a relatively safe way of using a switching unit. Using two peripherals with one port is more risky. In the days of MS/DOS there was no major problem, because each program had its own driver software for use with each output device. This greatly reduced the risk of one driver interfering with another, because there would normally be just one driver program in operation at any one time. The situation is very different with Windows, where device drivers for both peripherals would have to be installed, and might be left running in the background. This can result in one device driver interfering with the other. It is safer to install more ports and operate on the basis of one peripheral per port, although this clearly increases the risk of hardware conflicts.

Manual switching units do not have a good reputation for reliability. There is inevitably a large number of switch contacts in a unit of this type, and over a period, there is inevitably some build up of dirt and corrosion on the contacts. The switches used in these units are normally sealed in an attempt to keep dirt at bay. Unfortunately, this makes it virtually impossible to use switch cleaner when the contacts do succumb to dirt and corrosion. Repeatedly switching the unit backwards and forwards will often clean the contacts sufficiently to restore normal operation. It will probably be necessary to repeat this process periodically.

The problem is not always due to faulty contacts, and this is unlikely to be the cause if the switch unit is nearly new. It is more probable that the switching from one unit to another is getting the PC or a peripheral confused. Mechanical switches do not operate "cleanly", and tend to produce spurious signals during the changeover. The usual solution is to switch off the peripheral before switching from one PC to another, or switch off both peripherals when switching from one to the other, as appropriate.

Automatic sharing

Printer sharers that provide automatic switching used to be quite expensive, but like most other computer gadgets they can now be obtained at surprisingly low prices. There no need to manually select the computer that you wish to use with the printer when using a device of this type. You just start printing, and the switching unit automatically couples the appropriate computer through to the printer. The obvious restriction is that you must not attempt to print from both computers at once. Trying to do so is unlikely to have dire consequences, and most units will simply continue to use whichever computer activated the printer first. This results in a timeout error from the other PC when it fails to contact the printer after the allotted waiting period.

I have occasionally been asked for assistance with an automatic printer sharer that sometimes works, but frequently refuses to couple the signals through to the printer. This problem is not usually due to a fault in the equipment. The normal cause of the problem is that the printer sharer will only work if both PCs are switched on. In fairness to the manufacturers, this point is usually made clear in the instruction manual, and is not omitted or hidden in the "fine print". Unfortunately, few people ever bother to read the instruction manuals.

The problem occurs because the printer sharer monitors certain output lines of the printer ports on the PCs, and reacts to certain levels on these outputs. The outputs of a port go to logic 0 when the PC is switched off, and the printer sharer erroneously interprets these levels as the computer trying to print. Unfortunately, there is no easy way around this problem. A manual switching unit is a more practical proposition if you do not wish to have both PCs running when only one of them is actually in use.

USB, etc.

Although USB ports have been around for some time, and most modern motherboards include at least two of them, until recently they have not been used a great deal in practice due to a lack of proper support from the Windows operating system. This was rectified with the release of Windows 98, and USB seems likely to play an increasingly important role in the PC world. USB is a form of serial interface, but it is much faster than a conventional RS232C serial port. An ordinary PC serial port can, at best, operate up to about 115000 bits per second, whereas a USB port can operate at more than 10 million bits per second. In fact a USB port is potentially faster than a standard parallel port. Another advantage of a USB port is its ability to operate with more than peripheral device.

USB (universal serial bus) was designed to address the problems with the existing computer interfaces used with Macintosh computers and PCs. A lack of proper standardisation caused problems with most of these interfaces, but particularly problematic with the SCSI and RS232C varieties. A parallel system such as SCSI offers very high data transfer rates, but the cables tend to be bulky and expensive. A high-speed serial port offers reasonably fast data transfers, and can use relatively simple and inexpensive cables. A serial system was therefore adopted, and after a few "teething" problems USB 1.1 was launched, and finally worked properly.

USB 1.1 has a maximum data transfer rate of 12 megabits per second, but this is not quite as good as it seems because any one device in the system can only utilise half of the bandwidth. Even so, data can be uploaded or downloaded at a rate of over 600,000 bytes per second, which is sufficient for most purposes. It is certainly high enough for printers, external modems, digital cameras, scanners, and most other popular peripherals. After a slow start, USB interfaces are now a common feature on computer peripherals. In order to broaden the usefulness of USB ports, version 2.0 was devised and it is now starting to appear in real-world devices. It is backward compatible with USB 1.1, and offers a much higher maximum transfer rate of 480 megabits per second. This is more than adequate for virtually all peripherals, including fast disc drives and video devices.

USB advantages

USB was designed to have advantages over the alternative types of port, and it has been successful to a high degree. These are the main advantages:

Built-in

USB has the advantage of being built-in to a PC, unlike the main alternatives of SCSI and Firewire. Apart from the greater convenience, this avoids the cost of an expansion card, and the problems that can arise when trying to install the card.

Speed

Like an RS232C interface, a USB type provides two-way operation, but with much faster transfer rates. A modern parallel port can provide fast two-way operation, but requires the use of bulky and expensive cables.

Expandability

PC parallel and serial ports are only intended for use with one device per port. With the aid of switching units it is possible to use more than one device on each port, but only in a relatively crude and inconvenient fashion. USB is designed to handle numerous devices, and in theory at any rate, up to 127 peripherals can be connected to a PC via this interface.

Power

A few serial and parallel ports have power supply outputs, but this is not a standard feature and it is something that is not supported by PC versions of these ports. A USB port has a +5-volt supply output, and a version 1.1 port can supply up to 0.5 amps. This works out at only 2.5 watts, and large peripherals still require their own power supply. However, it is sufficient for smaller devices, such as joysticks and modems.

Plug and Play

USB properly supports the Windows Plug and Play feature. With some of the more simple devices, Windows will detect their presence at boot-up and automatically load the necessary device driver. It is necessary to go through the usual installation process when dealing with units that are more complex. A disc containing the device drivers should then be supplied with the peripheral. Either way, the new device should always be detected properly provided there are no hardware faults. Using other ports, Plug and Play tends to be a bit iffy, or even non-existent.

Standardised

The slow speed of an ordinary serial port is a major drawback, but the lack of standardisation and built-in complexities make it difficult to use. There can be problems when using a serial interface with a modem, but the likelihood of problems are many times greater when it is used for other peripherals. In fairness, the RS232C standard was only designed for use with communications devices such as modems, and it was never intended for printers, etc. A USB port is suitable for non-technical users because it requires no setting up of baud rates or word formats. All data is handled using the same system.

Simple cables

A USB link uses a four-way cable, and two of the wires carry the ground and +5-volt connections. The other two wires form what is termed a "twisted pair", and they carry the data. There are no handshake lines to deal with, and it should never be necessary to make a custom cable. The complexities of a USB link are handled in the software rather than by having numerous connections between the two units. For example, a system of addressing is used so that the computer can send data to the appropriate device when there are two or more peripherals connected to the same USB port. A system of coding is used so that the peripherals treat received data in the correct way. This complexity is handled by the device drivers and the firmware in the peripherals. Users just plug everything in, load the device drivers where appropriate, and then start using the equipment.

Plugging/unplugging

Connecting any device to a computer while either of the units is switched on is not normally to be recommended. Disconnecting devices under the same circumstances is usually discouraged as well. There is a real risk of damage to the computer and the peripheral if you simply plug in and unplug things as the fancy takes you. However, USB is designed for connection and disconnection "on the fly", thus removing the need to switch everything off before adding a USB device to or removing it from the system.

Conflicts

USB makes it easy for peripherals to share system resources. In theory at any rate, it is possible to add dozens of peripherals to the USB ports without any risk of problems with hardware conflicts.

USB 2.0

Although USB 1.1 has many advantages over the older PC interfaces, it is still not fast enough for some applications. In particular, downloading large amounts of video information in real-time is beyond USB 1.1 unless the resolution and quality are quite low. Even downloading high resolution still images can be time consuming using an ordinary USB interface. The speed of external USB drives such as CR-RW types is relatively low due to the limitations of ordinary USB ports.

USB 2.0 ports operate properly with USB 1.1 equipment, but only at the normal data transfer rate. In theory anyway, faster overall operation can be obtained when using several USB 1.1 devices with a USB 2.0 port. Note that connecting a USB 2.0 device to a USB 1.1 port is not permitted. When a USB 2.0 port is used with USB 2.0 equipment the data transfer rate is very high at a theoretical maximum of 480 megabits per second. This equates to something in the region of 50 megabytes per second, which is fast enough for video, fast external drives, or any current application. In practice such a high data transfer rate might not be achieved, and it is probably beyond the capabilities of many PCs. It still provides much greater speed than USB 1.1 though, and opens up new possibilities.

The maximum number of devices per port remains the same at 127, but with USB 1.1 this figure was rather theoretical. The relatively limited bandwidth of the system made it impossible to use the full number of peripherals. It is unlikely that USB 2.0 could actually handle 127 devices properly, but its wider bandwidth means that the realistic maximum number is raised to something close to this figure. USB 2.0 should certainly be able to handle more devices than most users will ever need to connect to their PC.

USB hubs

If you PC already has a couple of USB ports and you wish to add some more, it is not necessary to add a USB card to the PC. In fact this is definitely not the way to go about things. It is possible to use the chain method of connection with USB peripherals, where each device has a USB output that can be connected to the next device in the chain. This approach never seemed to catch on, and I have yet to encounter a USB device having an output port.

The usual way of using more than one device per USB port is to use a device called a hub. This is a box having two or more USB ports on the front, and a cable at the rear that connects to a USB port on the PC. The simplest USB hubs are non-powered devices that have two ports (Figure 3.10). With most PCs the USB ports are in the cluster of connectors at the rear of the PC where they are difficult to get at. Some PCs have one or two more USB ports in a concealed compartment on the front panel. This is a more convenient place when the ports are used with gadgets such as USB microphones and pointing devices. It is now quite common for monitors to have a built-in USB hub that also gives easy access to two or more ports. If your system lacks these facilities, a simple two-port hub is useful if you need a couple of easily accessible USB ports.

The larger USB hubs have four or more ports and have their own power supply. The USB hubs built into monitors are normally of this type. The practical significance of the hub being powered is that the full 0.5 amps of current should be available from each port. With a non-powered hub only 0.5 amps can be drawn in total, since that is all that is available from the PC port to which the hub is connected. In order to be certain of satisfactory results, only one device that draws power from the USB port should be used with this type of hub. In practice, it is likely that there will be no problem if two low-power devices are used, such as a USB mouse and a microphone. However, there is no guarantee that both devices

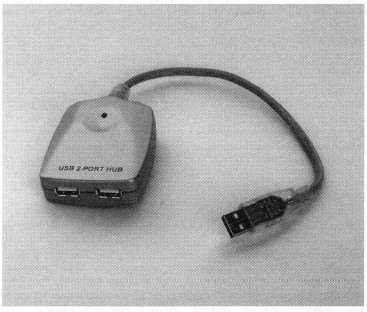

Fig.3.10 A simple twin port USB hub

will work with a non-powered hub. Note that the hub should be of the same type (USB 1.1 or 2.0) as the port it is driven from.

USB cards

There are two reasons for using an expansion card to add USB ports to a PC. One is simply that the PC does not have any built-in USB ports, and a hub is not an option. Some older PCs do actually have the necessary hardware on the motherboard, but were not supplied with the connectors to permit the hardware to be connected to the outside world. This may seem to be a strange state of affairs, but the USB hardware was around for a year or two before proper support was available from the operating system. PC manufacturers were reluctant to sell PCs complete with ports that were not fully operational. Hence the hardware on the motherboard was not made available to users.

All that is needed to get these ports working is a metal blanking plate fitted with the appropriate connectors and leads. A spare expansion slot is needed so that an existing blanking plate can be removed and the new one can be added. The leads from the new blanking plate are connected to the USB ports on the motherboard.

In practice there is a major complication in that each motherboard manufacturer tended to use a different connector on the motherboard, or the same connector wired in a different manner. This is a viable way of adding USB ports if a suitable blanking plate assembly can be obtained, but it is easy to end up buying the wrong thing. The odd economics of the electronics industry mean that it is unlikely to cost much more to use a USB expansion card instead. This is the safer method, since it is guaranteed to work.

USB 2.0 cards

The second reason for adding a USB expansion card is that you need to use USB 2.0 peripherals with a PC that only has USB 1.1 ports. As USB 2.0 is relatively new, very few PCs are equipped with this type of port. Fortunately, USB 2.0 cards are not very expensive, so abandoning the built-in ports will not cost the proverbial "arm and leg". The fact that most USB 2.0 cards have at least four ports, like the one shown in Figure 3.11, makes this upgrade more attractive. Most PCs only have two built-in USB 1.1 ports. Remember that the new USB 2.0 ports are fully compatible with USB 1.1 peripherals, so any existing peripherals should work at least as well with the new ports.

A USB expansion card is usually in the form of a small PCI card that is added in the usual way. The new card might work with the existing ports enabled, but before fitting the new card it is advisable to go into the BIOS Setup program and disable the USB hardware on the motherboard. The Plug and Play feature will operate when the PC is booted into Windows with the new card installed. It is advisable to carefully read through the installation instructions supplied with the card, as some cards have to be installed in Windows without using the Plug and Play facility. Also, the installation method tends to vary somewhat from one version of Windows to another. Any necessary software drivers should be supplied with the card.

Note that USB ports can not be used with Windows 95 or earlier versions or Windows. Support for USB 2.0 is built into Windows XP but it is not supported by earlier versions of Windows such as Windows 98 and NT. This does not mean that USB 2.0 cards are unusable with Windows 98, etc., but it does mean that third-party software is needed in order to get

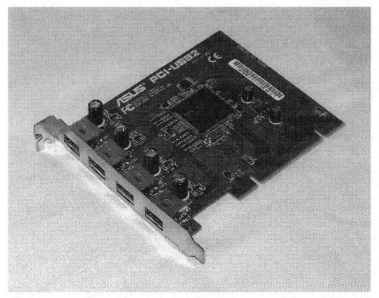

Fig.3.11 This USB 2.0 expansion card provides four ports

the card working properly. This should all be taken care of by the driver software supplied with the card, but with a USB 2.0 card it is best to check that it is usable with the appropriate version of Windows prior to buying it.

Device Manager

Before testing the new card it is advisable to go to Device Manager and check that the driver software has installed correctly. In fact it is a good idea to check the drivers have been installed properly for any new hardware. In Windows 98 and ME the first step is to launch the Control Panel by going to the Start menu and selecting Settings followed by Control Panel. This will produce a screen like the one in Figure 3.12. Double-clicking the System icon brings up the System Properties window (Figure 3.13) and operating the Device Manager tab produces the screen of Figure 3.14. Here there are categories that cover all the installed hardware. In standard Explorer fashion, the categories can be expanded by left-clicking on the "+" symbols (Figure 3.15).

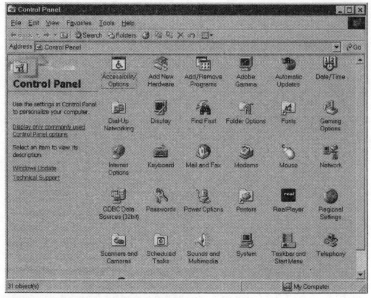

Fig.3.12 The Windows Control Panel

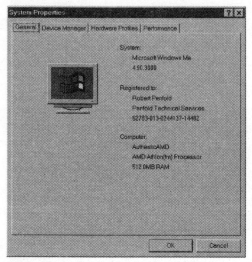

Fig.3.13 The System Properties window

In Windows XP the Control Panel can be accessed direct from the Start menu (Figure 3.16). It looks much the same as the Windows 98/ME version if the "classic" view is used (Figure 3.17). Double-clicking the System icon produces the System Properties window (Figure 3.18). Next the Hardware tab is operated, and in the new version of the System Properties window (Figure 3.19)

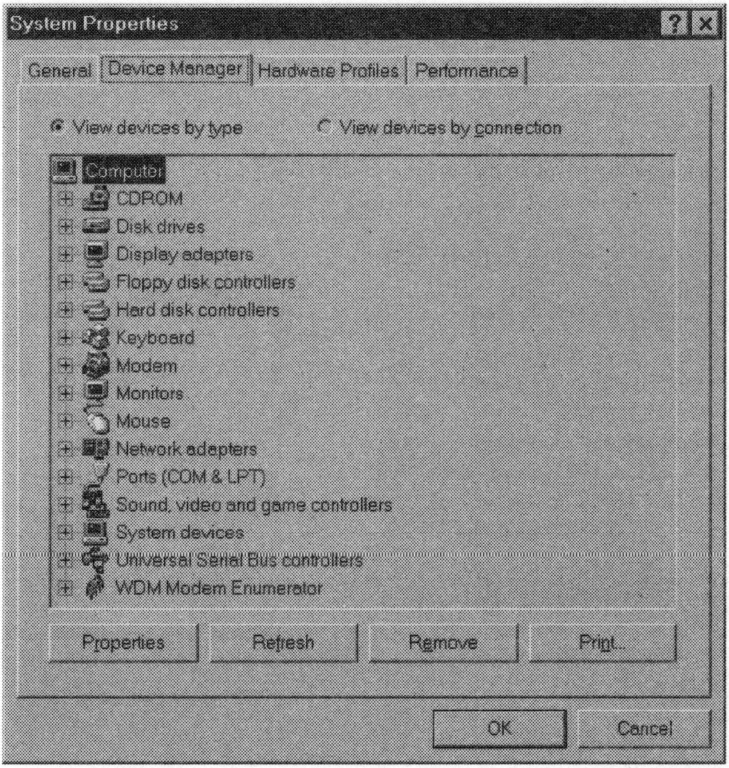

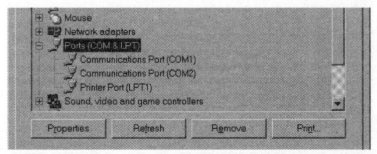

Fig.3.14 Device Manager has categories for all the installed hardware

Fig.3.15 Each category can be expanded in standard Explorer fashion

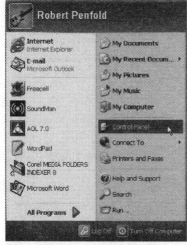

Fig.3.16 Launching the Control Panel in Windows XP

the Device Manager button is operated. This launches the Control Panel (Figure 3.20), which looks similar to the Windows 98/ME version.

In this example there is a yellow question mark against the Other Devices entry, which has automatically expanded to show the device that is giving the problem. This is a USB controller. Yellow question marks and exclamation marks are used by Device Manager to indicate that there is a possible problem or that something seems to be seriously amiss. Fortunately, in this case the suspected problem is caused

Fig.3.17 The Windows XP version of the Control Panel

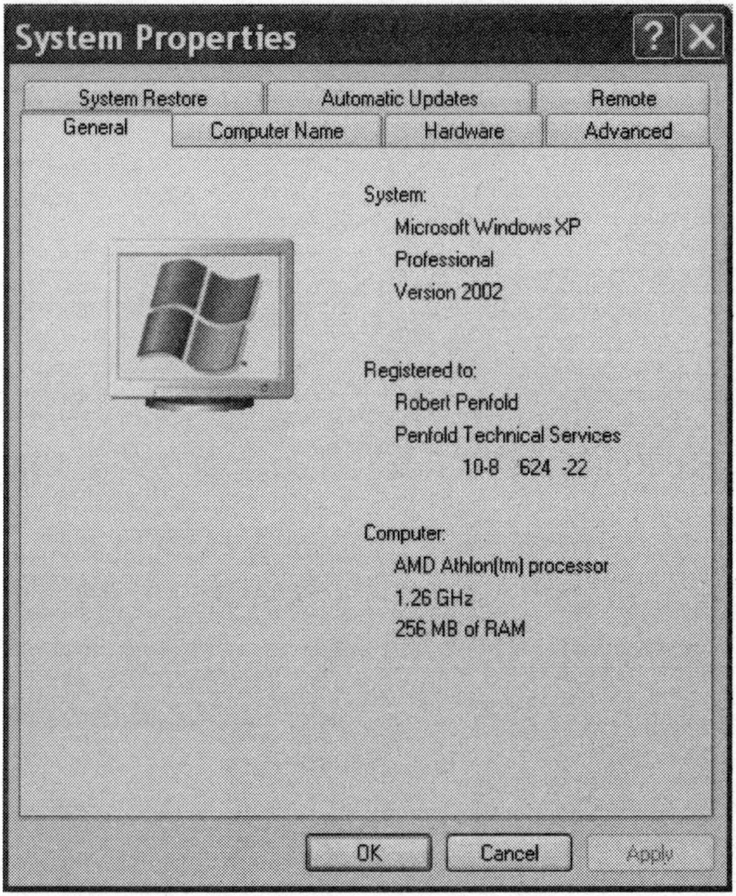

Fig.3.18 Operating the Hardware tab is the next step

by the USB ports on the motherboard that have been disabled in the BIOS. The drivers are still present, and Windows is puzzled by the lack of hardware for these drivers.

The computer should still work properly, but it is best to tidy things up by removing any drivers for hardware that has been removed or switched off. This is just a matter of right-clicking on the relevant entry and selecting Delete from the popup menu (Figure 3.21). Note that it is not possible to remove a complete category in this way, and that only individual device

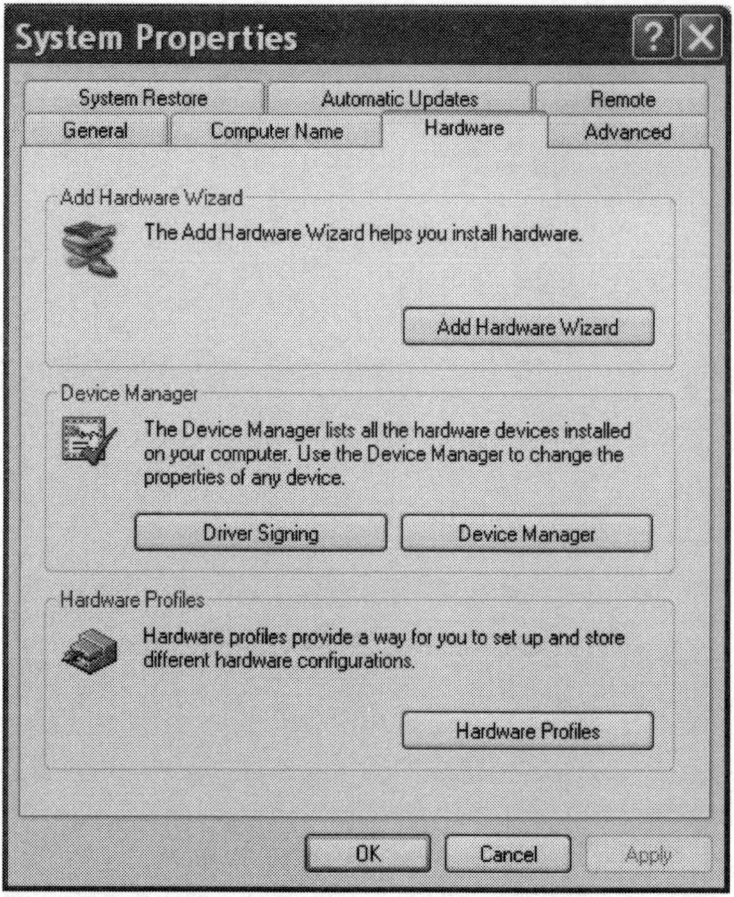

Fig.3.19 Finally, operating the Device Manager button launches this utility program

entries can be deleted. However, a category will be automatically deleted once it no longer contains any entries. No problems remain once the offending device driver has been deleted (Figure 3.22). The entry for the new USB 2.0 card is the one at the bottom of the list.

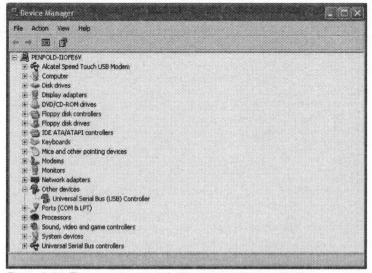

Figure 3.20 The question mark indicates a problem with the
corresponding piece of hardware

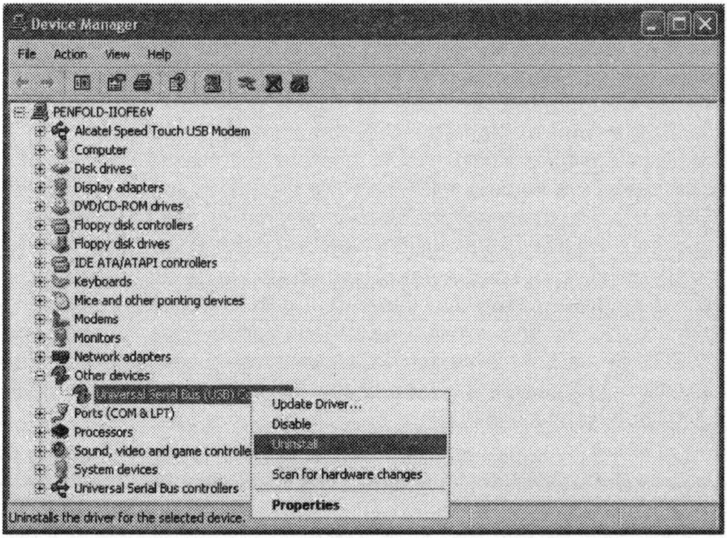

Fig.3.21 The unwanted drivers can be deleted via the popup menu

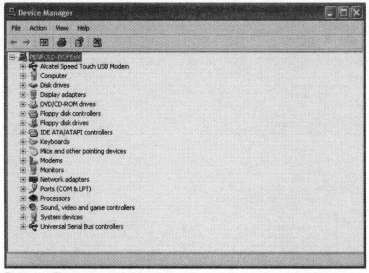

Fig.3.22 The unwanted drivers have been removed and there are no further problems reported

SCSI and Firewire

Some scanners and other devices interface to the computer via a SCSI port (small computers systems interface and pronounced "scuzzy"), which is a form of high-speed bi-directional parallel port. A few motherboards have a built-in SCSI interface, but this is something of a rarity. There are numerous ISA and PCI expansion cards that provide SCSI ports, and many peripherals that require this type of interface are supplied complete with a suitable card and connecting cable (or they are offered as an optional extra). The card should be supplied with any necessary driver software to integrate it with the common operating systems. SCSI is sometimes used for high performance hard disc and CD-ROM drives, but with modern PCs having high speed (UDMA33, etc.) hard disc interfaces built-in, it is probably not worth bothering with SCSI drives for a stand-alone PC.

Firewire is a high-speed serial link, similar in some respects to USB 2.0. It has a maximum data transfer rate of 400 megabits per second, so it is not quite as fast as USB 2.0. Whether it actually manages to produce faster data transfers in a real world situation is another matter. It has been used for up-market scanners and digital cameras, but it is mainly used with digital camcorders. It is so well established in this field that it is unlikely to be displaced by USB 2.0 in the near future.

There are other types of input and output port that can be fitted to a PC, such as analogue types. These are only needed for specialist applications such as scientific and medical research. Being specialised items they do not operate under any true standards. Most hardware of this type is fitted into the part of the input/output map reserved for "prototype cards". The exact address range is sometimes adjustable so that more than one card of this type can be used in the computer. However, when purchasing this type of hardware you need to make detailed enquiries in order to ensure that it will fulfil your requirements. You need to be especially careful that it is compatible with any software you will wish to use with it, or that any information you need in order to exploit the interface with your own software is provided by the vendor.

All these ports are added in much the same way as USB ports provided by an expansion card. Switch off the computer, remove the outer cover, add the card into a vacant expansion slot, replace the cover, and switch on the computer. Go through the Plug and Play routine or use a different method if advised accordingly by the installation booklet. Finally, use Device Manager to check that the device drivers have been installed correctly, and if all is well the new ports are ready for testing.

Try and try again

These days the vast majority of cards install into Windows at the first attempt. Many ISA expansion cards were troublesome, but these have now been largely replaced by PCI cards. In fact many PCs now only take PCI expansion cards. Use Device Manager to delete the drivers if they fail to install properly, and then reboot the PC and try the installation process again. If necessary, try this a few times.

Where the Plug and Play system is failing to install the drivers correctly it might be better to keep hitting the Cancel button to skip this procedure. Once the PC has booted into Windows you can use the Add/Remove Hardware facility of the control panel to install the drivers. Rather than letting Windows install the drivers automatically, try doing things manually and direct Windows to the drivers on the installation disc. Hardware is often supplied with a different device driver for each version of Windows. Make sure that you are using the correct driver for the version of Windows in use.

It is not unknown for hardware to be supplied with faulty drivers, so it is worthwhile going to the manufacturer's web site to look for updated drivers. Even if the supplied drivers do install properly, it is still a good idea to check for updated drivers from time to time. There will occasionally be new drivers that cure minor bugs or add new features.

Points to remember

You do not set a serial port as port one, port two, etc. The port numbering is done by the operating system, and it uses the port at the highest address as port one, the port at the next highest address is port two, and so one. It is therefore possible to indirectly control the port numbering via the port addresses.

Serial and parallel ports provided by ISA expansion cards are normal ports that should work with any software. The same is not true if the ports are provided via a PCI card. Software that tries to directly access the ports will not work with ports on a PCI card unless an effective remapping facility is available.

It is not necessary to add more USB ports via an expansion card if you need more of these ports. Connecting one or both of the existing ports to an external hub will provide more ports. Use a powered hub if you need to use peripherals that are powered from the USB ports.

USB 2.0 is a much faster version of USB 1.1, and it is in fact some 40 times faster. USB 2.0 ports can be added to a PC using a PCI expansion card, but it is advisable to disable any existing USB ports.

USB 1.1 peripherals are fully compatible with USB 2.0 ports, but it is not a good idea to connect USB 2.0 peripherals to a USB 1.1 port.

If USB ports are added via an expansion card it is advisable to disable any built-in USB ports. This might be achieved via jumpers or switches on the motherboard but in most cases the built-in ports are controlled by way of the BIOS Setup program.

Go to Device Manager once installation has been completed and check for problems. Yellow question marks or exclamation marks indicate that Windows has detected a problem. It is unlikely that the hardware will work properly with a problem indicated in Device Manager. Deleting the drivers and reinstalling them might clear the problem.

Go to the manufacturer's web site and look for improved drivers if a port card will not install in Windows correctly. It is possible that there is a hardware fault but it is far more likely that there is a problem with the device drivers.

Power
supplies

Why upgrade?

On the face of it, one computer power supply is very much like another, and there is no point in upgrading. In reality there are PC power supplies of various shapes and sizes, and there are a couple of reasons that could warrant an upgrade. The less likely reason is noise, and here I am talking in terms of noise in the sound sense, rather than electrical noise on the outputs of the supply. Modern PCs have more powerful processors than those of the past, more memory, more ports, and more of just about everything in fact. Although advances in modern electronics have reduced the power consumed by each transistor, the number of transistors in a PC's integrated circuits has mushroomed over the years.

Gone are the days when a PC had a 200 watt power supply and actually required only about half that power. A modern PC power supply is likely to be rated at around 300 to 400 watts, and in use it will probably have little spare capacity. Modern power supplies are quite efficient, but the higher the rating of the supply, the more power that is wasted. This wasted power manifests itself in the form of heat, and this is removed from the PC using metal cooling fins and a fan. In electronic circles the cooling fins are known as a heatsink. In order to get rid of the excess heat the cooling fans have become more powerful over the years, and this is reflected in generally higher sound levels. This noise is unwelcome in most environments, but it is particularly unhelpful if the PC is being used for multimedia applications.

Quiet power supplies are produced, and they are becoming quite popular despite their relatively high prices. It is only fair to point out that a quiet power supply will not render a PC silent. There are other sources of noise, such as the hard disc and the processor's cooling fan. However, in most cases the fan in the power supply is the main culprit. Replacing it with a quiet unit will usually give a very noticeable reduction in the noise level, especially if the original power supply unit is one of the more noisy types.

It might seem better to simply replace the cooling fan in the power supply with a quieter unit. This is possible, but is not the approved way of doing things. Delving into the interior of a PC power supply is something that should only be undertaken by those having the necessary experience. Another problem is that the replacement fan might be much quieter, but it could also be less efficient. You will have the ultimate in quiet PCs if the power supply starts to overheat and shuts down!

Power mad

The more common reason for upgrading a power supply is that so many upgrades have been added that the original supply can no longer cope. Adding more drives, a bigger and better video card, more memory, a faster processor, or just about any internal upgrade, results in greater loading on the power supply unit. Particularly with older PCs, where the original power supply is likely to be rated at about 180 to 230 watts, more than a modest amount of upgrading can result in the supply being "caught short".

I have heard of people upgrading a power supply because the original unit lacked sufficient power connectors to accommodate newly added drives. Possibly those concerned have assumed that the power supply does not have the wherewithal to operate more than one drive per connector. Actually, a supply is quite capable of powering two drives from one connector with the aid of a suitable adapter. The main proviso is that the additional drive must not result in the current drain from any of the supply's various outputs being exceeded.

Obviously the supply might have been operating "at the edge" prior to the new drive being added, and a power supply having a higher rating will then be required. On the other hand, there is a good chance that the original supply will have sufficient spare capacity to accommodate the new drive. The cost of a PC power supply of reasonable quality is not particularly high, but I would certainly opt for a supply splitter first. It could turn out to be a waste of money, but these adapters are quite cheap. They can often be picked up at computer fairs for pence rather than pounds. If the adapter does not have the desired result, it is a useful gadget to have in the spares box. It may well prove useful at some later date.

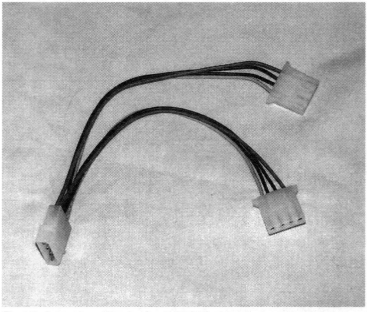

Fig.4.1 A supply splitter having 5.25-inch drive power connectors

There are various power supply adapters available, so it is necessary to make sure that you obtain a suitable type. Most PC power supplies have two power connectors for 3.5-inch floppy drives. These connectors are only used for 3.5-inch floppy drives, with 3.5-inch hard drives, CD-ROMS, etc., using the larger power connector. Most PCs only have one floppy disc drive. This leaves a spare 3.5-inch power connector, which can be connected to a CD-ROM drive, etc., via the appropriate adapter. The alternative is to use a splitter cable that enables two drives to be powered from one of the larger power connectors. Figure 4.1 shows an adapter of this type. The power supply's connector fits into the female connector of the adapter. The other two connectors of the adapter supply power to the two disc drives.

AT or ATX supply

The power supply for an ATX case and motherboard is different to that for an AT type. You therefore have to determine which type your PC uses before a more powerful or quieter unit can be obtained. One way is

Fig.4.2 AT motherboard power connectors

to measure the size of the power supply's case. An ATX case should be approximately 150 by 140 by 84 millimetres. If it is slightly smaller on one or more of these dimensions it is almost certainly an AT power supply.

You definitely have problems if the supply is not reasonably close to these dimensions, as it is a non-standard type.

One or two manufacturers have gone their own way with power supplies, and many Dell PCs have non-standard supply units. In other instances a case of unusual design requires an equally unconventional power supply unit. The manufacturer of the computer might be able to sell you a power supply that suits your requirements. If not, it will probably not be possible upgrade the power supply unit.

Fig.4.3 A single power connector is used for ATX motherboards

The most reliable method of differentiating between an AT power supply and an ATX type is to look at the connectors that supply power to the motherboard. If there are two of them side by side, as in Figure 4.2, the supply is an AT type. An ATX supply unit uses one large connector, as in Figure 4.3. Replacing a power supply is much the same whether it is an AT or ATX type, and it is an ATX type that will be used for this example.

Out with the old

Clearly the first task is to remove the original power supply, and this should not be difficult. First you must disconnect the PC from the mains supply and unplug the power lead from the supply unit. If the monitor is powered via the PC, its power lead must also be disconnected from the supply unit. In fact it is a good idea to disconnect everything from the PC, since it is difficult to work on a unit that has leads connecting to a variety of peripherals.

Next the supply is disconnected from the motherboard and drives. The larger drive connectors are notoriously stiff, and they are unlikely to pull free without a bit of a struggle. Do not disconnect one by pulling on the leads. Get a firm grip on the plug and wiggle it free of the socket. If there are any cooling fans or other gadgets that are powered from one of the drive connectors via an adapter, these should also be disconnected at this stage. Make a note of how everything fits together so that you can reassemble everything correctly when the new supply has been installed.

The motherboard connectors usually have a simple locking mechanism, so it is necessary to press the unlocking lever and then pull the plug free. If you have a close look at the connectors it is fairly obvious how the locking mechanism functions. If some of the connectors are inaccessible with the power supply in place, and the motherboard connectors may well fit into this category, they can be disconnected once the supply unit has been removed from the case.

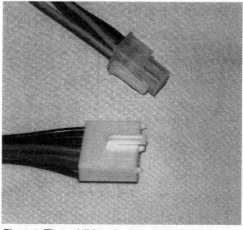

Fig.4.4 The additional connectors for a Pentium 4 motherboard

Fig.4.5 Four screws hold the power supply in place

Extra connectors

Most ATX supplies only have one connector to carry power to the motherboard. Some have one or two extra connectors (Figure 4.4) to carry additional power to motherboards that require it. Most motherboards do not require the additional connectors, but some Pentium 4 motherboards will not function unless one or other of them is implemented. Check for the extra connections to the motherboard before ordering a new power supply, and where appropriate make sure that you buy a power supply that has them. These supplies are usually described as something like "Pentium 4 ready" or "Pentium 4 equipped" supplies. The additional connectors are locking types, rather like miniature versions of the main ATX motherboard connector. Accordingly, the unlocking lever must be operated before the connector will pull free from the motherboard.

Most AT and ATX power supplies are only secured to the case by four screws. These fix the supply to the rear panel of the case, and they can be seen in Figure 4.5. Some ATX cases are bolted to the top or side of

Fig.4.6 Some ATX power supplies also have a mounting bracket

the case via a right-angle bracket. This bracket and fixing screw can be seen in Figure 4.6, and Figure 4.7 shows a clearer view of the bracket. Check for the additional bracket and fixing screw, and remove the screw if they are present. Then remove the four main fixing screws, being careful to support the supply unit so that it can not drop into the PC when the last fixing has been removed. Carefully manoeuvre the supply out of the case, and disconnect any leads if necessary.

It is then just a matter of reversing the

Fig.4.7 The bracket can be seen more clearly here

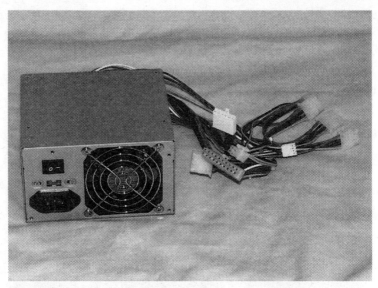

Fig.4.8 The replacement power supply is an ultra-quiet type

process to install the new supply. In this example the new supply unit
(Figure 4.8) looks much like the original, and has the same power rating
of 300 watts. It is an ultra quiet power supply though, and should help to
make the PC much quieter in use. It is unlikely that the new supply will
be fitted with a mounting bracket, and it was certainly absent from the
new supply unit in this case.

However, the new supply should have mounting holes that permit a
mounting bracket to be fitted. Therefore, if necessary, remove the bracket
from the old supply and fit it to the new one. If the power connectors on
the motherboard will be obscured when the supply is in place, connect
the supply to the motherboard before fitting it in place. It is best to fit all
the mounting bolts loosely at first, and then tighten them once they are
all in place. This avoids fitting one in place and finding that the others
can not be fitted because the mounting holes are out of alignment.

The larger drive connectors can only be fitted to the drives the right way
around, and it usually requires quite firm pressure to fully push them into
place. In theory it is not possible to connect the power to a 3.5-inch
floppy drive incorrectly, but in practice many drives have a slightly too
minimalist version of the connector. It might be possible to fit the

Fig.4.9 The replacement power supply installed in the PC

connector with the terminals one row out of alignment or even with it upside down. The broader, slightly concave surface is the one that goes down against the floppy drive, and the smaller convex surface faces upwards. Make sure that the five pins on the drive's connector are in proper alignment with the power connector. A mistake here could destroy the drive.

Figure 4.9 shows an external view of the new power supply bolted in place, and Figure 4.10 shows an internal view. The size of an ATX supply is well standardised, and although it is a tight fit inside the case, the new one fits in just like the original. The right-angle bracket has also fitted in perfectly with the new supply. The exterior view shows that the new supply has a space for a voltage selector switch, but no switch is actually fitted. It is unusual for a modern PC power supply to have one of these switches, and most supplies will automatically adjust to suit mains voltages from about 90 to 250 volts. However, it is a good idea to check for a voltage selector switch, and where present it must obviously be set to the appropriate voltage before the supply is connected to the mains.

Fig.4.10 The mounting bracket has been transferred to the new suuply

Unlike the original power supply, the new one does not have a mains outlet for a monitor. Presumably this change has come about due to changes in the safety regulations, and modern PC supplies have an on/off switch in place of the mains outlet for a monitor. Either a new power lead for the monitor will be required, or the plug on the existing lead will have to be changed to a normal mains plug. Use a two or three amp fuse in the plug.

Before reconnecting everything to the PC and testing the new supply it is as well to check that no power connections have been omitted and that none of the other cables have come adrift during the swap. Make sure that the power supply is switched off (the "O" symbol of the on/off switch is pressed down) before reconnecting the mains lead. With everything connected up and ready to go, switch on the power supply and then switch on the PC itself. Everything should power up as normal, and the PC should be switched off at once if there are any obvious signs of a malfunction.

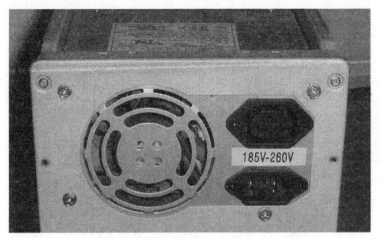

Fig.4.11 An AT supply is also held in place by four screws

The most likely problem is that there will be no response at all when the computer is switched on. This is usually caused by the power connector to the motherboard not being fully pushed down into place. This connector should lock, so it has not been connected properly if it can be pulled free without operating the locking lever. If the connection to the motherboard is correct, check any secondary motherboard connectors and the drive leads. The floppy drive's connector being out of alignment is the most likely cause of problems.

AT supply

Dealing with an AT power supply is not much different to dealing with an ATX type, but there are one or two differences of note. This type of supply is also held in place by four screws (Figure 4.11), and there could be a right-angle mounting bracket as well. However, any additional mounting is rarely used with AT power supplies. One of the main differences when dealing with AT supplies is that, as mentioned previously, there are two leads and connectors that carry power to the motherboard. Like all power connectors, they are polarised and can only be fitted to the board with the correct orientation. However, when reconnecting them it is important not to get the two connectors swapped over. The convention is for the black leads to be grouped together in the middle of the cluster, as shown in Figure 4.12. It is a good idea to check

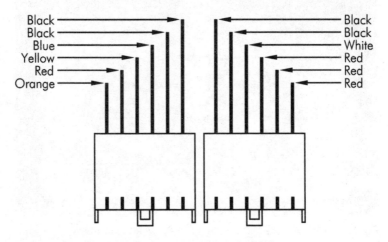

Black
Black
Blue
Yellow
Red
Orange

Black
Black
White
Red
Red
Red

Fig.4.12 The black leads are grouped in the middle

that your motherboard adheres to this convention before disconnecting
the supply from the motherboard.

Another significant difference between AT and ATX power supplies is
the on/off switching arrangement. An ATX power supply is normally left
switched on continuously, but it is in a sort of standby mode unless the
PC itself is actually operating. Operating the on/off switch activates the

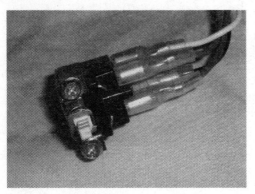

*Fig.4.13 An AT supply has an ordinary
on/off switch*

power supply and
switches on the PC.
The   normal
arrangement is for the
power supply to
be   automatically
returned   to   the
standby mode when
the operating system
has finished shutting
down. In effect, the
computer switches
itself off.

An AT power supply
does not support the
standby mode and

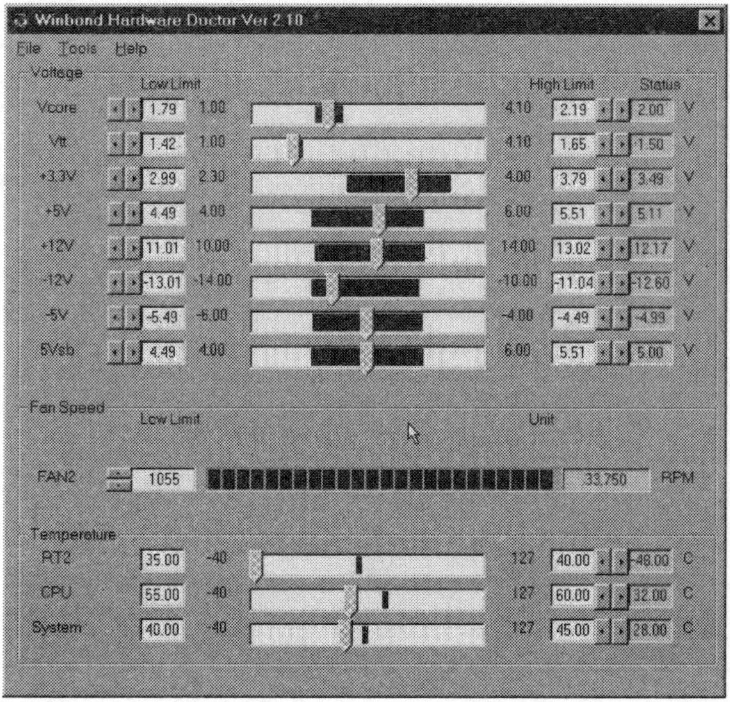

Fig.4.14 Many PCs are supplied with monitoring software

automatic switching. Instead, it has a conventional on/off switch (Figure 4.13). The new power supply is normally equipped with an on/off switch and lead, so the old switch must be removed and replaced as well. The on/off switch is bolted to the front of the case by two screws, but it might be necessary to do some dismantling at the front of the case to get at them. Double check that the power supply is not connected to the mains before attempting to remove the on/off switch. The connections to the switch should be fully insulated, but it is still inadvisable to try to remove a "live" switch. In fact it could reasonably be regarded as suicidal. Check the insulation on the switch of the new supply, and only fit it if the insulation is undamaged.

With the old supply removed it should not be difficult to fit the new on/off switch, bolt the supply itself in place, and reconnect the power leads. The computer is then ready for testing.

Monitoring

It is perhaps worth mentioning that many motherboards are now equipped with sensors that monitor various temperatures and voltages. With a PC that has this facility it is worthwhile using it to check the voltages from a power supply that seems to be giving problems. It could be that the supply is faulty or is being overloaded, and that a replacement or upgrade is needed. On the other hand, power supplies tend to be blamed for problems that have their origins elsewhere.

Figure 4.14 shows the HW Doctor program in action. Some of the monitored voltages might be produced by regulators on the motherboard rather than the power supply itself, so you need to read the documentation for the program to determine what is actually being monitored. An apparent fault in the power supply could actually be a problem with the motherboard. If a voltage drops well below its normal level when (say) a CD-ROM drive is used, and a malfunction then occurs, it is likely that the supply has an inadequate rating.

Points to remember

It is probably unnecessary to upgrade to a supply having a higher power rating if the present supply has insufficient power leads to accommodate extra drives. A supply splitter or adapter is probably all that is needed.

If the noise from your PC's power supply is excessive it is possible to replace it with a quiet type. Note that these are relatively expensive, and that any noise from other cooling fans and the hard drive will remain unaltered.

Before buying a new power supply, check to see if the existing unit has an extra connection to the motherboard. If it does, you require a "Pentium 4 ready" power supply unit. An ordinary ATX power supply has only one lead to carry power to the motherboard. Not all Pentium 4 motherboards require the additional lead and connector.

Always disconnect the power supply from the mains supply before starting to remove it. Do not open up the power supply and start delving around inside.

AT and ATX power supplies are mounted on the rear panel of the case by four screws. Occasionally there is additional support provided by a right-angle bracket. Where appropriate, this bracket must be transferred to the new power supply unit.

Replacing an AT power supply is complicated by the use of a conventional on/off switch. The new supply will come complete with a new on/off switch, so the existing switch must be replaced as well. You may have to partially dismantle the case in order to get at the on/off switch so that it can be swapped with the new one.

Many PCs are supplied complete with a monitor program that, amongst other things, shows the voltages present on the motherboard. These programs are useful if you think that the existing power supply is sometimes being overloaded and an upgrade is required.

4 Power supplies

Processor upgrading

Problems, problems

On the face of it, upgrading the microprocessor is the ideal way of giving a PC a new lease of life. A new faster processor would give the computer increased speed, enabling it to cope with the increasing demands of modern software. The cost of the upgrade would be quite low compared to the cost of a new PC, and would certainly justify the expense. Upgrading a processor is usually something less than straightforward though, if it is possible at all. Unfortunately, the older your PC the more it would benefit from a processor upgrade, but the lower the chances of it being feasible.

The problem with a processor upgrade is that as newer and better processors are developed, new and improved motherboards are also required. The most obvious problem is that of the processor requiring a faster clock speed than the motherboard can provide. Newly designed motherboards are often capable of going faster than the quickest of the processors available at the time. Although a motherboard is fitted with (say) a one gigahertz chip, it could be that it will actually work perfectly well with a 1.6 gigahertz type, even if that chip did not exist when the motherboard was made. On the other hand, the motherboard may have been struggling to accommodate the one gigahertz chip fitted when the PC was made, and there might be no upgrade path.

Even where an upgrade is possible, it will usually be necessary to upgrade the BIOS first, so that the motherboard recognises the new chip and can set the correct operating parameters for it. This process is covered later in this chapter. It is usually necessary to do some investigating at the web site of the relevant motherboard manufacturer in order to discover if there is an upgrade path available. Where there is, the updated BIOS is usually available as a free download from the manufacturer's web site.

In some cases there is no possibility of an upgrade because later processors used a different socket. Chapter one includes details of the various processor slots and sockets that have been used over the years, and a quick read through this material will quickly reveal the substantial number of changes that have occurred over the years. In some cases there are variations within each type of socket. There are two versions of Socket 370 for example.

A further complication is that AMD and Intel have gone their separate ways in recent years, and this means that different motherboards are required for each make of processor. If the existing processor in your PC is an Intel type, then there is no possibility of upgrading to anything other than another Intel chip. Similarly, if your PC currently uses an AMD chip, it is only possible to upgrade to another AMD chip, if an upgrade is actually possible.

The only exception to this is if you have a fairly old PC of the Socket 7 variety. As explained in chapter one, this type of socket was used for AMD, Cyrix, and Intel processors. Intel did not go beyond 233 megahertz Pentium MMX with this type of socket, but AMD used it for chips up to about 550MHz. With some Socket 7 motherboards it might therefore be possible to fit a faster processor, but there is a major practical problem. Suitable processors are now obsolete and are not sold for use in new PCs. This does not necessarily mean that they are unobtainable, but they might be. At best they are difficult to obtain, and are likely to be sold as spares at high spare part prices. It is worth looking out for sales of surplus stock though, as these sometimes feature old processors at giveaway prices. Also, old computer components are often available at computer fairs at quite low prices.

Overdrive

Various so-called "overdrive" processors have been available over the years, and these enable an old motherboard to be fitted with a relatively modern processor, even if the motherboard can not normally accommodate that processor. In most cases these processors are actually a bit more than just the processor, with built-in clock oscillators and possibly memory or other circuits as well. They are normally supplied as a full kit of parts, complete with heatsink, fan, and any other parts needed to complete the upgrade.

Where a suitable overdrive kit is available it does provide a relatively easy means of upgrading a PC, and in many cases it will represent the only upgrade path. These kits have something of a chequered reputation though. In tests some have proved to be quite effective, while others have produced little increase in performance. In fact some of the early overdrive units produced a slight reduction in performance when used with some PCs. Without actually testing one in your PC it is difficult to predict how well or otherwise it will perform. If you can get a suitable unit at a good price it is probably worth a try, but I would not recommend spending substantial amounts of money on this type of upgrade. Bear in mind that the processor will be new and relatively fast, but that the rest of the PC and the facilities it offers will remain unchanged.

There is another alternative in situations where a simple processor upgrade is not possible. Replace the motherboard and the memory as well as the processor. This is clearly much more expensive than a simple processor upgrade, but it usually produces huge benefits. There should be a huge increase in performance because it is possible to move on to a much more modern processor. Even the cheaper processors of today have far higher performance than those of several years ago. The processor should realise its full potential, since it will be backed up by plenty of modern memory and one of the latest chip sets on the motherboard. Some additional facilities will probably be obtained, such as USB 2.0 ports where the original PC only had USB 1.1 or no USB ports at all.

Changing the processor, memory, and motherboard is clearly a major undertaking, and it is not really the type of thing for someone new to computer upgrades. It is not that difficult though, and someone with a moderate amount of upgrading experience should be able to tackle the task. Having completed the upgrade, you have what is virtually a new computer. This form of processor upgrade is covered in the next chapter, which deals with "rescuing" an old PC that can no longer handle the latest software releases.

Options

The first task with a processor upgrade is to determine what processor is fitted at present. You will probably know this already if you are dealing with your own PC. When helping others with upgrades I have found that they usually have little knowledge of their PC's specification. The type of processor and its clock frequency are often displayed by the BIOS during the initial start-up period. The PC might be helpfully labelled something like "Pentium III 800MHz". Labels are not totally reliable because the PC could have already been upgraded, so if there is any doubt it is advisable

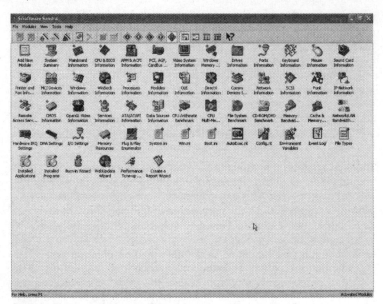

Fig.5.1 The initial screen of the Sandra system analyser

to use some system analysis software to check. This type of software can provide masses of useful facts for a "mystery" computer.

There are numerous analysis programs available, but this example will be based on the very popular Sisoftware Sandra Standard, which is available as a free download on the Internet. The Sisoftware Sandra web site is at:

www.sisoftware.co.uk/sandra

This program is available from several of the large shareware download sites such as www.download.com. Having downloaded, installed and run this program, a window like the one in Figure 5.1 is obtained. A number of program modules are available, with each one giving detailed information on a different part of the PC. In this case it is information on the processor that is required, and this is obtained by double-clicking the "CPU and BIOS Information" icon. Incidentally, CPU stands for central processing unit, and it is simply an alternative name for the processor.

The CPU and BIOS Information program produces a screen like the one in Figure 5.2, and the processor information is at the top. In this example

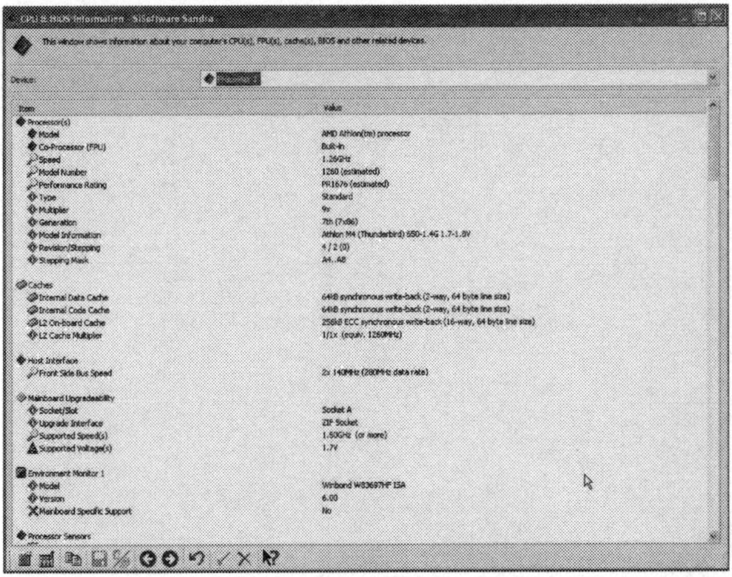

Fig.5.2 The program correctly identifies the processor

an AMD Athlon processor has been correctly identified. The processor is a 1.2 gigahertz type, but the program has correctly pointed out that it is actually running at 1.260 megahertz. This is because the motherboard's clock frequency has been set slightly too high, which has resulted in slight over-clocking of the entire system.

It is possible to get some basic information on a PC using the built-in facilities of Windows. From the Program menu select Accessories, System Tools, and then System Information. This produces a screen like the one of Figure 5.3. A great deal of useful information is available here, but it is usually too vague on the subjects that are of interest in the current context. The clock frequency of the processor and its manufacturer have been identified correctly, but there is no mention of it being an Athlon. The system manufacturer is given as VIA, which is the maker of the support chips. The motherboard is made by Jetway. For the present purposes it is better to use a program such as Sisoftware Sandra, which will give the more detailed information that is required in this case.

To obtain information on the motherboard using Sisoftware Sandra, close the CPU information window and then double-click the Mainboard

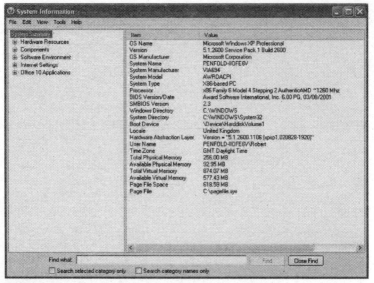

Fig.5.3 The Windows System Information Screen

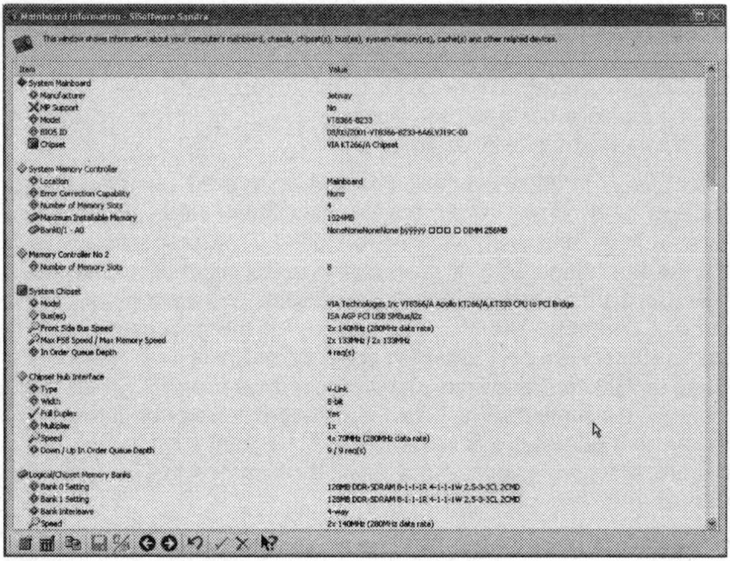

Fig.5.4 The Sandra Mainboard Information screen

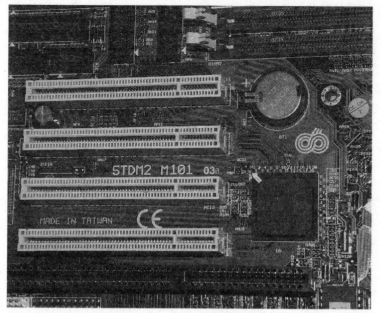

Fig.5.5 This motherboard is a Chaintech 5TDM2

Information icon in the main window. This launches a window like the one of Figure 5.4, and this shows a large amount of technical information about the motherboard. In particular, it provides the manufacturer and model number for the motherboard.

It has to be pointed out that the model number provided by the program can be different to the one used by the manufacturer when marketing the board. This complicates the next step, which is to go to the manufacturer's web site to look for information about the board and the availability of an updated BIOS. Where more than one type number is in use it is likely that the web site will give details for the board under both numbers. An Email to the manufacturer should soon get things sorted out if there is any doubt about the identity of a board. Do not try to update a BIOS unless you are certain that the new BIOS is suitable for your motherboard. Loading the wrong BIOS would almost certainly render the board unusable.

The type number of the motherboard plus the BIOS version and date are often shown near the top left-hand corner of the screen during the initial

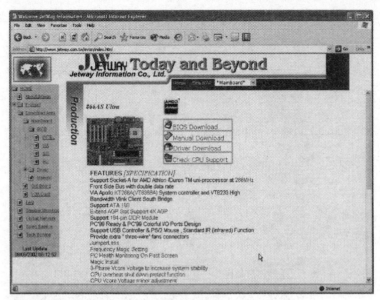

Fig.5.6 The page for the Jetway 866AS has useful links

start-up process. It can be difficult to make sense of all the material displayed during start-up, but it is worth noting it all down and looking for a correlation between the type numbers on the manufacturer's web site and the numbers you have noted.

If all else fails you can try looking on the motherboard itself for the board's name or type number. This might seem to be the obvious approach, but not all motherboards are actually marked with this information. Where it is present the situation will probably be confused by other markings. In the example of Figure 5.5 there is no manufacturer's name on the board, but the logo for Chaintech is present. The board is a 5TDM2, not an M101 or an O30.

A visual inspection of the board will probably reveal the name of the manufacturer and the model number for the board, but it might require a certain amount of sleuthing. It is worth looking through the documentation supplied with the PC. This might include a detailed specification including details of the motherboard. There could even be a copy of the instruction manual for the motherboard, which should tell you everything you need to know.

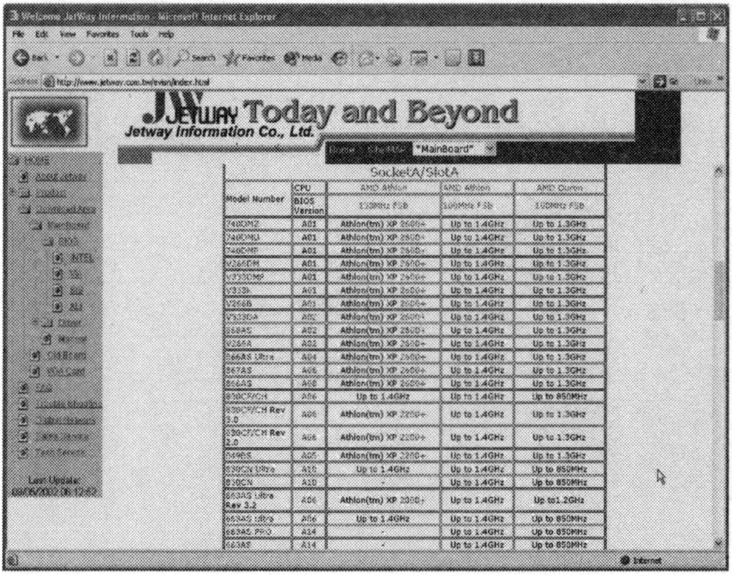

Fig.5.7   The CPU compatibility chart of Jetway motherboards

CPU compatibility

An Internet search engine should soon find the web site for the motherboard's manufacturer. Having found the site it is then a matter of looking for information about the CPU compatibility of the motherboard you are using. Most sites have charts that give information about the processor compatibility of each motherboard, and the various BIOS updates that are available. In this Jetway example I selected the Mainboards section of the site, followed by the VIA section, and then finally the page for the particular board fitted to the PC (a Jetway 866AS). This page of the site is shown in Figure 5.6, and it helpfully has links to a CPU compatibility page and one for BIOS updates.

Checking the CPU compatibility page is the next step. There is no point in upgrading the BIOS unless it is possible to fit a faster processor. Upgrading the BIOS is something that should not be done unless it is really necessary. Left-clicking the appropriate link produces the compatibility chart shown in Figure 5.7. With the original BIOS it is not possible to fit anything beyond a 1.4 gigahertz Athlon processor, which is not a great deal faster than the 1.2 gigahertz chip already fitted.

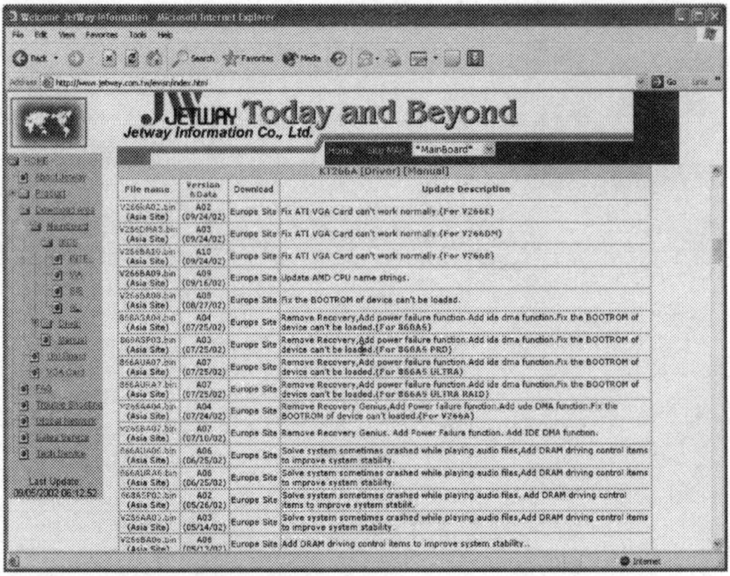

Fig.5.8 The list of BIOS updates. Make sure you download one intended for your motherboard

The aim is to fit an Athlon XP2000+ processor, which actually runs at about 1.633 gigahertz. The higher clock rate and improved circuitry of this processor means that it provides something like a 50 percent increase in performance over the existing processor. Surprisingly perhaps, the chart shows that this motherboard can accommodate Athlon processors up to the XP2600+ if it is equipped with the latest BIOS. Although a substantial upgrade, a Athlon XP2000+ is by no means stretching the motherboard to its limits.

The BIOS page (Figure 5.8) lists the available BIOS updates, and it is simply a matter of downloading it in the usual way. The BIOS file is usually just the data to be blown into the EEPROM chip on the motherboard. A program is needed in order to write this data to the chip. Your PC might have been supplied complete with this program, but if not it should be available from the manufacturer's web site.

Some modern PCs can do a BIOS update from within Windows, but this is not the normal way of doing things. Most motherboards require the PC to be booted into MS/DOS in order to update the BIOS. There should be some documentation available from the web site and (or) supplied with the PC that gives precise instructions for updating the BIOS. Read through this documentation a couple of times and follow the instructions "to the letter". Do not proceed until you are sure that you know exactly what you are doing.

Flash upgrade?

If you look through the specifications for motherboards you will often encounter something like "Flash upgradeable BIOS" or just "Flash BIOS". In days gone by the only way of upgrading the BIOS was to buy a new chip, or pair of chips as it was in those days. Some of the ROMs used to store the BIOS were actually re-programmable, but only by removing them from the PC and putting them into a programmer unit. This was not a practical proposition for most users. New BIOS chips were very difficult to obtain and you were usually stuck with the BIOS supplied with the motherboard.

The rate at which modern computing changes makes it beneficial to upgrade the BIOS from time to time in order to keep PCs up to date, and not just to accommodate a processor upgrade. The BIOS sometimes has to be updated to cure compatibility problems with certain items of hardware. There could even be one or two minor bugs in the original BIOS.

With a modern BIOS there is no need to replace the BIOS ROM chip or to remove it from the motherboard for reprogramming. The ROM for a modern BIOS can be electronically erased and reprogrammed while it is still on the motherboard. This is why it is possible to download a new BIOS and a "blower" program and upgrade the BIOS. Of course, an upgrade of this type is dependent on the motherboard having the BIOS in Flash memory. Unless you are using a very old PC there is little likelihood of it lacking support for the Flash method of upgrading the BIOS. If you are using an old PC and the manufacturer's web site does not give details of BIOS upgrades, it is reasonable to assume that the BIOS can not be upgraded.

Write protection

If you get an error message such as "Flash type unrecognised" during the upgrade, this does not mean that the BIOS is a non-reprogrammable type. It usually just means that the Flash memory is write-protected, making it impossible for the upgrade program to alter its contents. Write

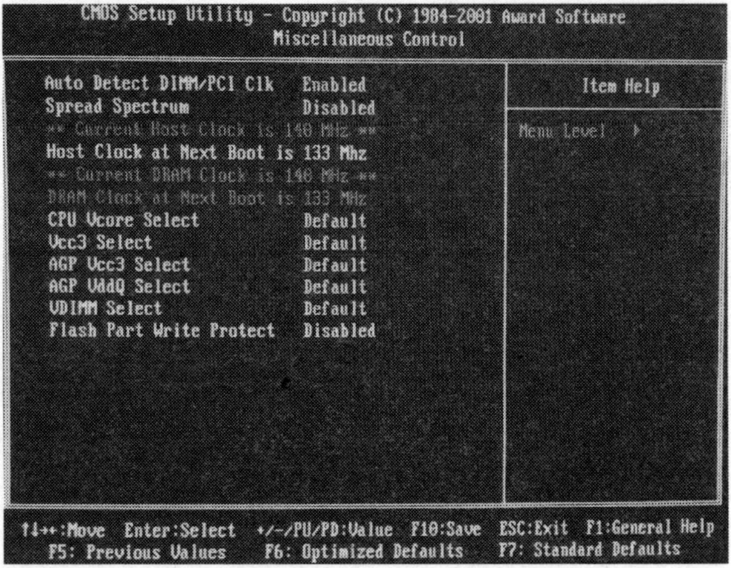

Fig.5.9 The BIOS can not be updated if it is write-protected

protection is used as a means of preventing viruses and other malicious programs from corrupting the BIOS and rendering the PC unusable. It would be prudent to check for write-protection before trying to upgrade the BIOS.

The manual for your PC or its motherboard should give instructions for disabling this facility. In some cases the write protection is provided via a switch or jumper on the motherboard. These days it is more usual for this facility to be controlled via a setting in the BIOS itself (Figure 5.9). There should be no difficulty in upgrading the BIOS once the write-protection has been switched off. Having completed the upgrade it is a good idea to enable this facility again, so that the BIOS is protected from attack.

Risk factor

It is only fair to point out that a BIOS upgrade is a bit risky. As explained previously, you need to be absolutely certain that the data file you are using is the correct one for your motherboard. Using the wrong BIOS data file could easily render the computer unusable, and if it will not

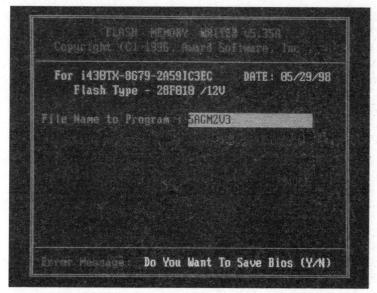

Fig.5.10 The BIOS upgrade program running from a floppy disc

boot-up correctly it is impossible to restore the original BIOS. Another slight worry is that a power failure during the upgrade could leave the PC with a BI (half a BIOS)! With an incomplete or corrupted BIOS it is unlikely that the PC could be rebooted to restore the original or complete the upgrade. It only takes a few seconds to carry out the upgrade, so you would be very unlucky indeed if a power failure interrupted the process, but it is a slight risk. A serious error when upgrading the BIOS could necessitate the fitting of a complete new motherboard.

The upgrade program usually has to be run from MS-DOS, and is very simple to operate (Figure 5.10). After you have supplied the name of the data file for the new BIOS (including any extension to the filename) the program should give the option of saving the existing BIOS onto disc. It is as well to do this so that you can revert to the original BIOS if the new version proves to be troublesome. After you have confirmed that you wish to continue with the upgrade the new data will be written to the BIOS ROM chip. Do not touch the computer during the flash upgrade, just stand back and let the upgrade program get on with it. The computer is then ready for rebooting and checking to see if the new BIOS has the desired effect.

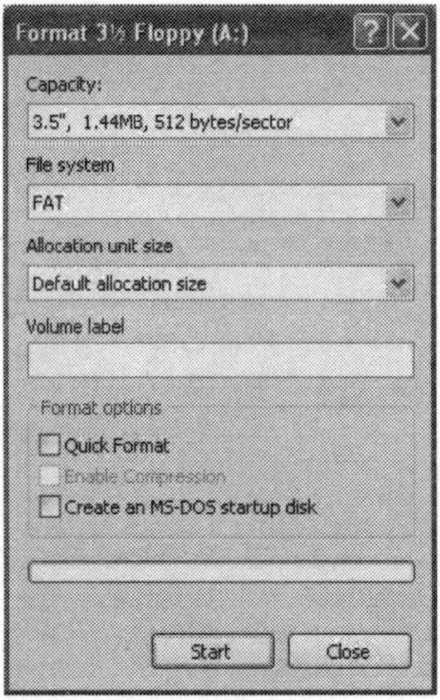

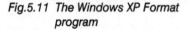

Boot disc

The boot disc used when upgrading has to be a very basic type that does not run some form of memory management software such as EMM386. Making a suitable boot disc from a system running Windows XP is very straightforward. Place a blank disc in the floppy drive, launch Windows Explorer, and then locate drive A in Windows Explorer. Right-click on the entry for drive A and select the Format option from the popup menu. This produces the window for the Format program, which looks like the one in Figure 5.11. Tick the Create an MS-DOS Startup Disc checkbox and then operate the Start button. A warning message will probably appear, pointing out

Fig.5.11 The Windows XP Format program

that any data on the disc will be lost. Operate the Yes button to continue and create the boot disc.

When the formatting has been completed, copy the BIOS data file and upgrade program to the floppy disc. Leave the disc in the floppy drive and restart the computer. With luck the floppy drive will be used as the boot drive and you will be ready to proceed with the upgrade once the boot process has been completed. It is possible that the computer will simply boot into Windows. This occurs because the floppy drive is not set as the first boot disc in the BIOS. The BIOS therefore looks for the hard drive first, finds it, and then boots into Windows as normal. Restart the PC, go into the BIOS and set the floppy as the first boot disc, then save the changes and exit the BIOS Setup program. The computer should then boot into MS/DOS using the floppy disc in drive A.

Unfortunately, the Windows ME Format program does not provide a boot disc option. It is possible to make a Startup disc via the Control Panel and the Add/Remove Programs facility. However, this option results in various utilities being placed on the disc, and some of these could interfere with the upgrade process. Make sure that the Minimal Boot option is selected from the boot options menu during the initial boot process, and the memory management programs, etc., will not be run. It should then be safe to go ahead with the BIOS upgrade.

Switches

Most BIOS upgrade programs accept certain switches to be added after the command name. For example, it is possible to specify the file containing the data for the new version of the BIOS. Another common option is one that clears the CMOS memory of all the BIOS settings. It is generally considered advisable to use this switch, since some of the original settings might be inappropriate to the new BIOS. Using this switch means that the BIOS will have no setting when the PC is restarted, and you must enter the Setup program so that the Load Setup Defaults option can be selected. If necessary, the defaults can then be "fine tuned" to suit your requirements. The date and time will have to be reset, but this can be done from the Windows Control Panel.

If the BIOS has been updated correctly a new BIOS version number and date should be displayed on the initial screen at start-up. It is also likely that Windows will detect that there has been a change and respond with various messages to the effect that new hardware has been detected. Actually, it is just detecting the same old hardware and reinstalling the drivers for it. Once this reinstallation has been completed the computer should perform much the same as it did before.

Out with the old

With the BIOS successfully updated it is time to move on to the hardware side of things. Switch off the PC and remove the outer casing so that you have access to the motherboard. There is likely to be a problem with access to the processor, which is often hidden away underneath the power supply. This is certainly a problem with the example PC, where the part of the processor's heatsink can just about be seen underneath the power supply (Figure 5.12).

It is impossible to change a processor without good access to the relevant section of the motherboard, so the power supply must be dismounted from the case. It should not be necessary to disconnect the supply from the motherboard or any of the drives. There should be good access to the processor if the power supply unit is placed on the drive cage. In this example, removing the power supply gave good all-round access to the processor (Figure 5.13).

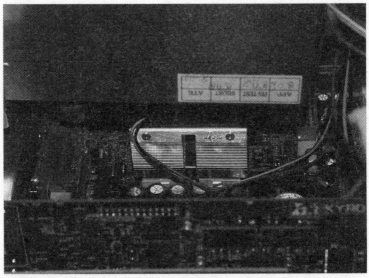

Fig.5.12 This processor is largely obscured by the power supply

Fig.5.13 Access is greatly improved by removing the power supply

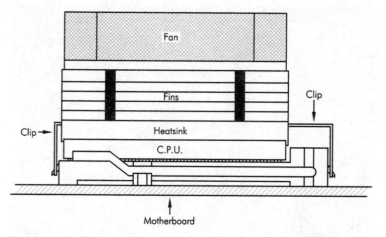

Fig.5.14 The heatsink and fan are clipped onto the processor's socket

Removing the old processor usually presents no problems, but the same is rarely true of its heatsink and fan. The heatsink normally clips onto the socket using the arrangement shown in Figure 5.14. The heatsink must be firmly clipped into place in order to ensure that it operates efficiently. The spring clip that holds it in place is therefore fairly strong. One side of the clip can be pressed down a relatively long way, but there is little movement on the other side. If you are lucky, pushing down on the side that has the greatest movement will result in it unhooking from the socket and the heatsink can then be pulled free.

In most cases it will not be quite as simple as this. Often it is necessary to use a screwdriver to gently lever the clip outwards as it is pushed downwards. This ensures that having been pushed down far enough it then moves out and free of the socket. Some heatsink clips can be very difficult to manoeuvre out of position because the clip is designed to press inwards quite firmly. Presumably it is done this way to make the heatsink easy to fit, with the clip tending to lock into place if it is pressed down far enough. Unfortunately, it makes things much more difficult when trying to remove the heatsink.

With some of them there is a notch in the clip that will take the blade of a medium size screwdriver. With the blade firmly fitted in place it is then quite easy to push downwards and then outwards to get the clip free of the socket. Take due care though. Slipping and gouging the motherboard with the blade of the screwdriver could seriously damage it.

Fig.5.15 The Athlon processor can be seen once the heatsink and fan have been removed

Do not get a case of "computer rage" if the heatsink is very reluctant to unclip. Trying to use brute force is a good way of damaging the motherboard and possibly injuring yourself in the process. In cases where the heatsink refuses to unclip there is little option other than removing the motherboard from the case so that you have totally unrestricted access to the heatsink. Try to get a good side-on view so that you can see what is preventing the clip from pulling free. What was previously an unsuccessful struggle can usually be solved in a few seconds once there is better access to the heatsink.

Some advocate removing the motherboard from the case whenever undertaking memory or processor upgrades. The reason for this is that both types of upgrade usually involve pressing down on the motherboard, causing it to flex slightly. This puts the motherboard at slight risk, but it is unlikely to be damaged unless you adopt a "hammer and tongs" approach. Some motherboards now have provision for extra stand-offs around the processor, which greatly reduces the risk of damage occurring. Removing the motherboard and reinstalling it is a time consuming business, and I suppose that it is not entirely risk-free. It is an approach that I only use where there is no other way of getting adequate access to the motherboard.

Fig.5.16 Older processors do not have the metal heat pad

With the heatsink removed you should be able to see the processor in the socket (Figure 5.15). The metal pad in the middle is the bit that conducts heat from the processor and into the heatsink. This is a feature of virtually all modern processors, but it is lacking on some older types (Figure 5.16). The four rubber pads are included on many processors, and they help to keep the underside of the heatsink parallel to the top of the processor. The heatsink would operate very inefficiently if it was allowed to keel over slightly. It is unlikely that any damage would occur, because most motherboards have protection circuits that shut down the system if the processor gets too hot. It is best not to put this type of thing to the "acid test" though.

Orientation

There should be a dot, arrow, or other marking near one corner of the processor. In the example of Figure 5.15 the top left-hand corner of the chip's case is missing. On the underside of the

Fig.5.17 A "missing" hole ensures that the processor can only be fitted correctly

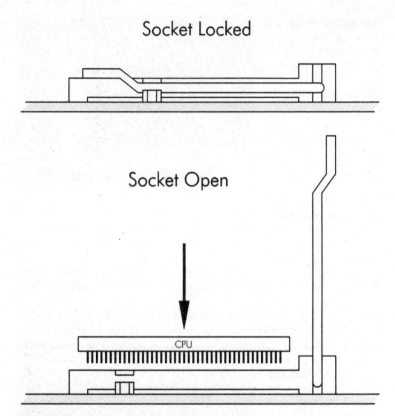

Socket Locked

Socket Open

CPU

Fig.5.18 The lever is raised to open the socket and lowered to lock it

processor there is one pin "missing" in this corner, which matches a missing hole in one corner of the socket. In Figure 5.17 the absent hole is in the top right-hand corner of the socket. The point of this is to ensure that the processor can only be inserted into the socket the right way around. Make a note of the processor's orientation so that it is quick and easy to fit the replacement.

The processors in modern PCs are fitted on the board via a form of ZIF (zero insertion force) socket. This simply means that the chip can be dropped into place without having to push it down into the socket. Similarly, the chip can be easily lifted from the socket with no need to prise it free or use any special tools. The socket has a locking mechanism that keeps the processor in place and electrically connected to the motherboard during use. In order to remove the processor it is merely necessary to raise the lever situated at one side of the socket to unlock it, and then lift the processor free. Figure 5.18 shows how this system of locking operates.

Next the new processor (Figure 5.19) is removed from its anti-static packaging and

Fig.5.19 The new Athlon XP processor in its anti-static packing

placed in the socket, being careful to get the orientation correct. Make sure that the standard anti-static handling precautions are rigidly observed

Fig.5.20 The Athlon XP processor installed on the motherboard

when dealing with the processors. Put the old processor in the anti-static packing so that it can be stored safely. The new processor should simply fall into place but it might take a certain amount of manoeuvring to get it into just the right position. Lower the locking lever back to its original position once the processor is in position. If the processor will not fall into place, check that its orientation is correct.

If it still fails to drop into place it is likely that one of the pins has become bent out of position. Look closely at all the pins and if necessary use the blade of a small screwdriver to carefully straighten any that are seriously bent out of place. Proceed very careful and gently, because the processor will be a write-off if one of the pins is broken off. Fortunately, the pins on modern processors are quite short and strong, so there should be no problems with bent pins unless the device has been seriously mistreated. Figure 5.20 shows the new AMD XP2000+ processor in place in the example PC.

New heatsink?

Next the heatsink and fan are fitted to the processor's socket. In general, heatsinks have become bigger over the years as more complex processors consume higher power levels and generate more heat. The latest processors actually consume less power than some of their predecessors even though they are more complex and operate at higher

clock frequencies. This is apparently due to the use of smaller transistors that give greater speed with reduced power consumption. Even so, it is a good idea not to simply fit the old heatsink and fan onto the new processor.

The safe option is to buy a new heatsink and fan assembly that is properly matched to the new chip. Most processors are offered in retail boxed

Fig.5.21 A fan fitted with a three-way lead and connector

and OEM (original equipment manufacturer) versions. The retail boxed version costs more, but it is usually complete with a heatsink and fan that are guaranteed to be up to the task. The heatsink and fan are not included with the OEM version. The retail boxed processor is the safer

option, and it is unlikely to cost much more than an OEM chip plus a heatsink and fan bought separately.

There is a potential problem with supplying power to the new fan since there is more than one way of powering PC cooling fans. The two most common methods are to power the fan from the motherboard via a three-way lead and connector (Figure

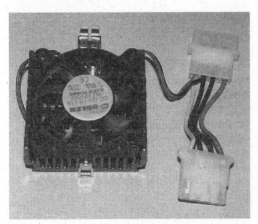

Fig.5.22 This fan taps off power from a 5.25-inch drive power lead

5.21), or to tap off power from the power lead for a drive (Figure 5.22). Most of the current fans have the three-way lead and connector for the motherboard. The third wire incidentally, enables the motherboard to monitor the speed of the fan and give a warning if it is too slow or stops.

If the original fan is a type that taps off power from a drive, and there are no fan power connectors on the motherboard, you must be careful to order a new fan that has drive power connectors. Alternatively, it will probably be possible to fit the fan from the old heatsink in place of the fan supplied with the new heatsink.

Heatsink compound

As supplied, the underside of the heatsink will probably look something like the one in Figure 5.23. The paper tear-off strip should be removed prior to fitting the heatsink. Removing it reveals a square of heatsink compound (Figure 5.24) that helps to produce a good thermal contact between the processor and the heatsink. This pad is not needed for older processors that lack the metal heat conductor on the top, and it

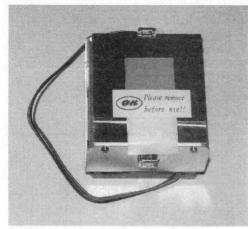

Fig.5.23 The heatsink compound has a
protective covering

will not be present on heatsinks intended for use with these processors.

If the heatsink from the original processor is being used for the new one, any existing pad of heatsink compound will be largely obliterated. The old pad must be carefully cleaned away and then some new heatsink compound must be added in its place. Most of the larger computer component retailers supply at least one grade of heatsink compound. One of the cheaper grades will suffice. The expensive types are intended for use in over-clocking and not for general use. Very little heatsink compound is needed, so one of the small sachets will be more than sufficient.

Fig.5.24 Here the heatsink compound has
been revealed

The heatsink is fitted in place by first clipping the less springy side of the clip under the lug on the socket. With the heatsink accurately in position on the socket it should then be reasonably easy to press the other side of the clip down and into place. Heatsinks are usually much easier to install than they are to remove. It is advisable to pull firmly on the heatsink to

Fig.5.25 The heatsink and fan in position on the processor

make sure that it is reliably secured to the socket. There could be dire consequences for the processor if the heatsink should come adrift. Figure 5.25 shows the heatsink securely fitted in place in the example PC.

Pentium 4

The method of mounting the heatsink described previously is the one used for most processors, including those that fit Socket 7, Socket 370, and Socket A boards. There are some processors that use a different type of heatsink. The Slot processors fall into this category, but it is unlikely that a suitable processor to upgrade one of these boards will be obtainable. Pentium 4 processors are another exception, and these are much more likely upgrade candidates.

The socket for a Pentium 4 processor looks quite conventional (Figure 5.26), and there is the usual lever that is used to lock or release the processor. Figure 5.27 shows the processor fitted into its socket. The processor itself also looks fairly conventional, but it is smaller than

Fig.5.26 A Pentium 4 requires a different heatsink and fan

Fig.5.27 The Pentium 4 processor installed in its socket

Fig.5.28 The heatsink and fan for the 2.4 gigahertz Pentium 4

previous Pentiums, Athlons, etc. Around the processor there is a black plastic mounting bracket that is used to clip the heatsink in place. This can be seen in Figure 5.26 and 5.27. The heatsink itself (Figure 5.28) is relatively large, and it has two locking levers, one at each end.

Fitting the heatsink onto the motherboard is very easy, and it simply presses down into place on the black plastic mounting bracket. If it is reluctant to fit into place you probably have one or both of the levers in the locked position, and correcting this should enable it to be pressed down into place. The levers are set to the locked position once the heatsink has properly clipped into place. The levers operate a cam mechanism that forces the heatsink down onto the processor. Figure 5.29 shows the heatsink locked into place, and one of the cams can be seen in the side-on view of Figure 5.30.

Fig.5.29 The heatsink and fan locked in position

Fig.5.30 One of the locking cams can be seen in front of the fan

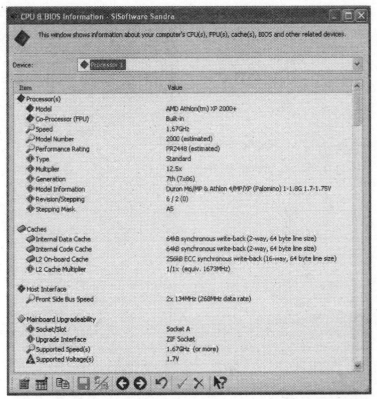

Fig.5.31 The Sandra analyser program shows that the new processor is present and correct

Jumperless

With the heatsink and fan in place it is time to do any reassembly such as refitting the power supply, check that no cables have come adrift, and then try out the new processor. It is assumed here that the motherboard is a so-called "jumperless" type that does not require things such as voltages and clock frequencies to be set via jumpers or switches on the motherboard. With an older motherboard it might be necessary to adjust some settings to produce the right operating conditions for the new processor. Some modern motherboards have a few settings set via switches or jumpers, and the front side bus frequency is often set in this way. The motherboard manufacturer's web site should have details of

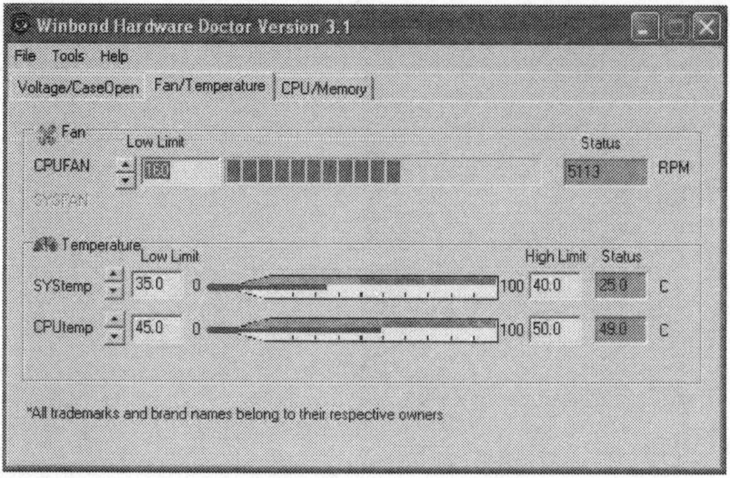

Fig.5.32 The motherboard's monitor program in action

the correct settings for each processor that the board will accept. Motherboards settings are covered in the next chapter, so refer to this if necessary.

With the example PC the new processor was detected and the BIOS automatically configured itself to suit. The onscreen messages during the start-up procedure suggested that the new chip was installed and functioning well. This was confirmed using the CPU reporting section of Sisoftware Sandra. As can be seen from the results (Figure 5.31) the processor is operating at the correct speed of 1.67 megahertz and it has been correctly identified as an AMD Athlon XP2000+. The system proved to be very stable with the new settings.

If the motherboard has a built-in temperature monitor for the processor it is advisable to use this after the PC has been running for a few minutes. The BIOS often displays the CPU temperature during the initial start-up sequence, or POST (power on self test) as it is often called. This enables the temperature to be checked by restarting Windows and watching the screen carefully during the POST sequence. The CPU temperature can usually be checked by going to the relevant section of the BIOS Setup program.

Many PCs are supplied with a monitoring utility for the motherboard, and this provides the most convenient means of checking the processor's temperature, fans speeds, etc. Figure 5.32 shows the monitor program for the example PC, and with the processor at only 49 degree Celsius it is operating quite coolly by current standards, and the upgrade has been completely successful.

It is only fair to point out that each processor upgrade tends to be a bit different to any other processor upgrade. With so many different processors and motherboards being manufactured in the last few years there are numerous permutations, with each one being slightly different in points of detail. Consequently, it is often necessary to use some common sense in order to get everything sorted out correctly. If your PC was not supplied with a manual for the motherboard it is definitely worthwhile searching the manufacturer's web site for a downloadable version. Even the skimpier manuals should tell you any important facts that you need to know when dealing with the processor.

Points to remember

The processor upgrade options available, if any, are determined by the motherboard fitted to your PC. Each motherboard only takes a limited range of processors, and modern boards are only designed to handle processors from one manufacturer (either AMD or Intel).

It is often possible to extend the range of processors that a board can accommodate by upgrading the BIOS. Most modern boards have the BIOS in Flash memory, and it can be upgraded using the appropriate program and a new BIOS downloaded from the Internet.

Overdrive and similar processors permit upgrades to processors that are otherwise beyond the capability of a motherboard. This type of upgrade is sometimes very successful, but it can produce disappointing results.

Check the available options before deciding on an upgrade. Find the model name or number of the motherboard and its maker. Some delving on the Internet should then produce a choice of available upgrade options. If the motherboard was "a bit long in the tooth" when the PC was built it is possible that there will be no upgrade options.

If a BIOS upgrade is needed, follow the manufacturer's upgrade instructions "to the letter". Make absolutely certain that you are using the correct BIOS data file. A mistake when upgrading the BIOS could leave the motherboard unusable, so only upgrade when it is really necessary.

Some motherboards are supplied with utilities that permit the BIOS to be upgraded from within Windows. In most cases though, it is necessary to make a boot disc and boot from drive A. The disc should provide a very basic MS/DOS system with no memory management software or anything else that could cause the BIOS upgrade program to malfunction.

Do not use the "armstrong" method if the old heatsink is difficult to remove. Using brute force is more likely to damage the motherboard than to release the heatsink. If necessary, remove the motherboard from the case in order to gain better access to the heatsink.

The heatsink for the old processor is unlikely to be suitable for the new one. The safest option is to buy a retail boxed version of the processor that includes a matching heatsink and fan.

If the motherboard does not have a three-terminal power connector for the fan, you must use one that takes its power from one of the drive power connectors via a simple adapter. This will presumably be the same system that is used to supply power to the existing fan.

With many motherboards it is unnecessary to change any settings in order to get the motherboard to function correctly. The BIOS will detect the new processor and make any adjustments that are required. In some cases it will be necessary to make one or two changes, such as increasing the bus speed of the motherboard. Sometimes this is done via switches or jumpers on the motherboard, but in most cases it is just a matter of changing one or two BIOS settings.

Adding
drives

Floppy drives

For a stand-alone PC at least one disc drive is an essential feature, because the operating system is loaded from a disc drive and is not built-in. While in theory a single floppy drive will suffice, these days the single floppy approach is only used for troubleshooting. For normal use the minimum requirement is a fairly large hard disc, one floppy drive, and a CD-ROM drive. Most software will actually run quite happily without a CD-ROM drive, but software is mainly distributed on CD-ROMs, and without a suitable drive there is no way of installing it onto the hard disc drive.

Those dealing with large amounts of data will almost certainly require some form of interchangeable disc drive having a high capacity, such as a CD-RW type. However, most users still require a humble floppy disc drive even if their PC has a CD-RW drive, Zip drive, or whatever. It is essential in order to install or reinstall some versions of Windows. Windows NT4, 2000, and XP can be installed by booting from the installation CD-ROM, but this approach is not possible with Windows 95, 98, or ME. The computer has to be booted from a floppy disc and then installed from the CD-ROM, making the floppy disc drive non-optional.

There are five types of floppy disc drive used with PCs, and these are listed below. All five types use both sides of the disc incidentally.

3.5-inch, 80 track, 720k capacity

3.5-inch, 80 track, 1.44M capacity

3.5-inch 2.88M capacity

5.25-inch, 40 track, 360k capacity

5.25-inch, 80 track, 1.2M capacity

The data on a floppy disc drive is stored magnetically on the metal oxide coating. This is much the same as the way in which an audio signal is recorded onto the tape in an ordinary compact cassette. In the case of a floppy disc though, the data is recorded onto a number of concentric tracks, or "cylinders" as they are sometimes termed. Each track is divided into a number of sectors, and there are nine sectors per track for a 5.25-inch 360k disc for example.

Originally the 5.25-inch 360k drives were used on PCs, PC XTs, and compatibles, while the 5.25-inch 1.2M type were used on ATs and compatibles. 3.5-inch drives have been adopted as the industry standard, and 3.5-inch 1.44M drives have gradually take over from the 5.25-inch variety. Even the 3.5-inch 720k type is now obsolete. 1.2M 5.25-inch drives are still available, but they are increasingly difficult to track down. It is unlikely that they are still in production, so those that are available must be either old stock or second-hand.

At one time it was common for PCs to have a 1.44M 3.5-inch drive and a 5.25-inch 1.2M drive. The former is used to read and write new data discs, with the latter providing compatibility with the numerous 5.25-inch discs that many users (particularly business users) still possessed. Of course, 5.25-inch discs can have their contents copied onto 3.5-inch discs, but this is time consuming and expensive if you have large numbers of old discs. Hence many users simply opted for the two-disc system. With 5.25-inch drives now well and truly obsolete it is a good idea to copy any 5.25-inch discs onto 3.5-inch discs or CD-ROMs while it is still possible.

The 2.88M disc drives were designed to replace the 1.44M drives as the standard for new PCs. With PCs tending to produce ever-larger files there is a definite advantage in the higher capacity of a 2.88M drive. Despite this, 2.88M drives have remained something of a rarity, and the vast majority of new computers are still fitted with 1.44 megabyte drives. The high initial price and a reputation for poor reliability certainly hindered the progress of the 2.88M drives. Consumer resistance to yet another change in the standard floppy disc format probably played its part as well. Another factor is that 2.88 megabytes is not much data by current standards.

Extra floppy

Most PCs are supplied with a single 3.5-inch 1.44M floppy as standard, and for most purposes this is all that is required. However, if you will need to do a lot of disc copying it will be somewhat easier with the aid of

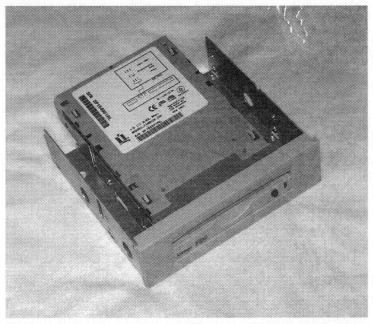

Fig.6.1 A 3.5-inch format (Zip) drive fitted in a 5.25-inch bay adapter

a second floppy disc. The first point to bear in mind when adding a disc drive to a PC is that it must be of a type that is supported by the BIOS. Also, it must be a type that the computer's floppy disc controller can handle. There should be no difficulty when adding any standard size drive to a modern PC, since the BIOS and built-in floppy controller will almost certainly support all five types. If you need to add a 5.25-inch drive so that old discs can be copied, then this should be possible. As always though, it is best to check and not jump to conclusions. The manual for the computer or its motherboard might have the information you require, but it is easy to go into the BIOS and cycle through the floppy disc options.

Of course, before fitting a floppy drive you must ensure that the computer's case can accommodate it. You need a free drive bay of the correct size, and with a floppy drive it must be an open type that gives access to the front of the drive. Unfortunately, many modern PC cases have only one free 3.5-inch drive bay that meets this requirement. There is a potential solution if an open 5.25-inch bay is available. It is possible

Fig.6.2 The metal plate and plastic cover removed from a drive bay

to obtain an adapter that permits a 3.5-inch drive to be used in a 5.25-inch bay (Figure 6.1). An adapter of this type should be usable with any 3.5-inch drive and not just with floppy drives. It is actually a Zip drive that is fitted in the adapter shown in Figure 6.1.

There are two basic tasks to complete when fitting a floppy disc drive. The first is to get it physically fixed in place, and the second is to get it connected to the controller correctly. There are plastic covers over the external drive bays, and these must be removed at the positions where drives are to be fitted. These are easily pushed out from the rear, but there will probably be a slight snag here in the form of a metal plate behind each plastic cover. These plates are partially cut from the case, and must be removed from any bays where externally accessible drives will be fitted. They can usually be left in place where other drives, such as the hard drive or drives, will be fitted.

These plates are removed in the same way as other blanking plates in the case. Unclip the plastic cover first. There are usually a couple of holes in the metal plate so that you can push out the plastic cover from the rear by poking a screwdriver through one of these holes. With a bit of pushing and shoving it should be possible to turn the plate through about 30 degrees or so, although it can take a while to get the blanking plate completely free. You can then get hold of one edge, and with a bit of waggling the plate should soon break away from the case. With a few cases the plates are held in place by screws, so check this point before you try the flexing method. With the plate and plastic cover removed (Figure 6.2) the bay is ready for the drive to be fitted.

With modern PCs the disc drives normally fit directly into the drive bays, and are then fixed in place using two screws each side. Figure 6.3 shows the drive bay and fixing screws for a 5.25-inch drive, but the same method is used for both types. The screws fit into the threaded holes in the side panels of the drives. If you are lucky, your computer will have been supplied with some additional drive fixing screws and one or two other odds and ends of hardware.

Fig.6.3 Drives are mormally held in place by two screws each side

Alternatively, disc drives are sometimes supplied complete with a set of four fixing screws, but this is not usually the case with floppy drives.

If not, it could be difficult to locate a source of suitable screws, but your local computer store might be able to help. It is important that these screws are quite short. There is otherwise a risk of them penetrating too far into the drive and causing damage. This will not be a problem if you use screws specifically intended for mounting drives, but could be if you have to improvise with whatever you can obtain. Screws longer than 10 millimetres should certainly not be used. Provided you have the correct fixing screws, fixing a drive into this type of computer is unlikely to give any real difficulties.

Early PCs used a somewhat different method of drive fixing. Two plastic guide-rails were required, and these were bolted one per side onto the drive. This assembly was then slid into place in one of the drive bays, and the rails were bolted to the drive bay. This method is now long obsolete, but some recent PC cases use an updated version of the guide-rail idea. The general scheme of things is to have a guide-rail fitted to

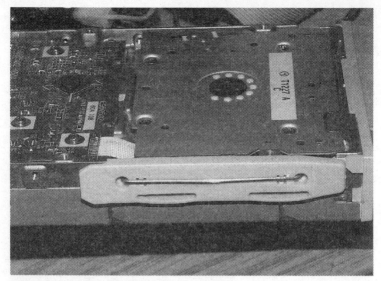

Fig.6.4 A drive fitted with a clip-on guide-rail

one side of the drive (Figure 6.4), and it is usually held in place via a wire clip. This side of the drive is not bolted into place and is only supported by the guide-rail. The other side is held in place by two screws in the normal fashion.

As viewed from the front of the PC, it is the right-hand side of the drive that is fitted with the guide-rail. I assume that the idea is to avoid using fixing screws on the right-hand side of the drive, which is usually less accessible than the left-hand side. In fact I have encountered PCs where it is only possible to access these screws by removing the motherboard. Some spare guide-rails should have been supplied with your PC if it uses this method of fixing, and it will not be possible to fit an additional drive properly without one. The guide-rails are normally used for the 3.5-inch bays with the 5.25-inch types having mounting screws both sides, but there could be some exceptions.

Connections

You must also connect the power supply to the disc drive. Modern PC power supplies have about five or six leads and connectors for disc drives.

Simply connect the plug on any spare lead to the power socket on the disc drive. This is a properly polarised plug, and it is impossible to connect it to the drive the wrong way round. With old PCs there may not be a spare disc drive power cable. You will then need to obtain an adapter which takes one of the drive power leads and splits it to permit connection to two drives.

Note that there are two sizes of power connector. The larger type is used for 5.25-inch floppy drives, CD-ROM drives, and most hard disc drives. A miniature version of this power connector is used for 3.5-inch floppy drives. However, if a 3.5-inch drive is fitted in a chassis to permit it to fit into a 5.25-inch bay, this might include an adapter that enables the drive to be connected to a standard (full size) disc drive connector. If there is a spare power cable but it is the wrong size, obtain an adapter lead to convert it to the correct type of connector, or use one of the splitter cables mentioned previously.

The 5.25-inch power connectors tend to be rather stiff but are otherwise reasonably foolproof. The 3.5-inch variety fit into place much more easily and are supposedly polarised. In practice the connectors on the drives are sometimes very basic and permit the power leads to be connected incorrectly. The slightly concave side of the connector faces towards the connector on the drive. Another potential problem is that the lead can sometimes be connected one set of pins along from the correct position, so check carefully to ensure that the two connectors are properly aligned. With the lead

Fig.6.5 A 3.5-inch power connector fitted correctly

connected properly you should have something like Figure 6.5, with no power pins visible on either side of the connector. Getting the power lead connected incorrectly can "blow" the drive, so check that this connector is fitted correctly.

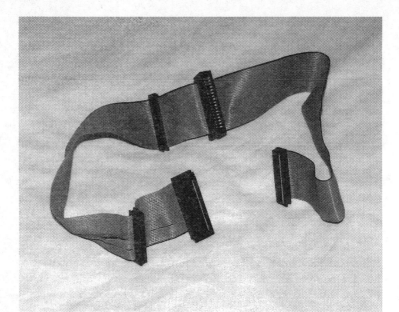

Fig.6.6 A floppy drive cable having two sets of drive connectors

Floppy cables

The standard PC floppy disc drive cable consists of a length of 34-way ribbon cable, which is fitted with 34-way edge connectors and IDC connectors at the floppy drive end. 3.5-inch floppy drives require the IDC connectors, and 5.25-inch types connect to the edge connectors. The connector at the controller end is not totally standardised, but anything other than an "antique" PC will require a 34-way IDC connector. Most cables are for twin drives, and therefore have two sets of drive connectors. This makes like easier when adding a second drive, because you can normally use the existing cable. Figure 6.6 shows a standard floppy drive data cable, complete with two pairs of drive connectors. Note that modern floppy cables often lack the edge connectors and are only suitable for use with 3.5-inch drives. A full floppy cable will be needed if you wish to add a 5.25-inch floppy drive.

In a standard floppy drive set-up, the two connectors would be wired in exactly the same way. Pin 1 at the controller would connect to pin 1 of both drives, pin 2 would connect to both of the pin 2s, and so on. The two drives do not operate in unison, and both try to operate as drive A, because there are jumper leads on the drives which are set to make one operate as drive A, and the other as drive B. Provided one drive is set as drive A and the other is set as drive B there will be no conflicts. The jumper blocks are normally a set of four pairs of terminals marked something like "DS0", "DS1", "DS2", and "DS3" (or possibly something like "DS1" to "DS4"). The instruction manual for the disc drive (in the unlikely event of you being able to obtain it) will make it clear which of the many jumper blocks are the ones for drive selection. Drive A has the jumper lead on "DS0", while drive B has it on "DS1".

Things could actually be set up in this fashion in a PC, but it is not the standard way of doing things. Instead, both drives are set as drive B by having the jumper lead placed on "DS1". The so-called "twist" in the cable between the two drive connectors then reverses some of the connections to one drive, making it operate as drive B. This may seem to be an unusual way of doing things, but there is apparently a good reason for it. If you obtain a PC disc drive, whether for use as a replacement for a worn out drive A, or as a newly added drive B, the same drive configured in exactly the same way will do the job. This avoids the need for dealers to stock two different types of drive, which in reality is exactly the same type of drive with a slightly different configuration.

For the DIY PC upgrader it makes life easier in that any drive sold for use in a PC should work perfectly without the need to alter any of the configuration jumpers. In fact many 3.5-inch drives are manufactured specifically for use in PCs, and do not actually have any configuration jumpers. Of course, if you buy a drive that is not specifically for use in a PC, it might not be set up correctly for operation in a PC. The elusive instruction booklet for the disc drive is then more than a little useful. Since a new 3.5-inch floppy drive for a PC only costs a few pounds there is little point buying one that is not intended for use in a PC.

The computer will still work if you get the connections to two floppy drives swapped over, but the one you required as drive A: will be drive B:, and vice versa. The connector at the end of the cable couples to drive A, while the other one connects to drive B. Figure 6.7 shows this general scheme of things. When adding a drive to an older PC you might find that the cable only has edge connectors for the drives, but that the new drive requires an IDC connector. A suitable edge connector to IDC adapter could be impossible to obtain these days, and there will probably be no alternative to buying a new floppy drive cable. Unless you are upgrading a really old PC you are unlikely to encounter this problem.

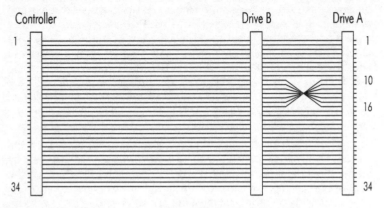

Fig.6.7 The arrangement used for a PC floppy drive cable

Getting the floppy drive cable connected to the new drive should be straightforward, because the two connectors should be polarised, so that they can not be fitted the wrong way round. The necessary "key" is just a small metal rod on the edge connector, which fits into a slot in the connector on the drive. A lump and a slot on IDC connectors serve the same function. Unfortunately, the polarising "keys" are sometimes missing. Another unhelpful variation is the floppy drive that has the polarising on both the top and bottom edges of the connector.

You should find that the connector numbers, or some of them, are marked onto the connector on the disc drive and on the motherboard. Incidentally, on modern computers the floppy drive controller is invariably part of the motherboard. The numbers might also be marked on the drive lead connectors, and a coloured lead (as opposed to the grey of all the others) on the cable itself should denote the pin 1 end of the lead/connector. Of course, pin 1 of the floppy drive controller couples to pin 1 of the drive's connector.

Termination resistors

In the past every disc drive had a set of eight termination resistors. These connected to certain inputs of the drive, and tied them to the +5 volt supply rail. They are termed "pull-up" resistors. However many disc drives are used, only one set of termination resistors should be present. It is only the drive at the end of the cable that should have these resistors. Therefore, if you fit a second drive to a PC, as it will fit mid-cable, it will not require its termination resistors. These resistors are normally in the form of a single component, rather than eight individual resistors. They will be mounted in a socket of some kind, and this will often be of the standard 16-pin d.i.l. integrated circuit type. A socket of this type has two rows of eight terminals 0.3 inches apart. The resistor pack itself will probably be in the form of a black plastic component having two rows of eight pins. The resistors have a value of 220 ohms, and so the component will be marked something like "220R", plus some other characters in most cases.

Some drives have a s.i.l. (single in-line) resistor pack. These have nine pins in a single row, usually with 0.1-inch pin spacing. Like the d.i.l. resistor packs, they are mounted in a socket so that they can be easily removed. In fact the s.i.l. variety are generally more easily removed than the d.i.l. type. With any d.i.l. component it is a good idea to use a screwdriver to carefully prise it free from the socket. Keep the termination resistor pack safe somewhere in case it should be needed at some later time. In fact you should always keep anything removed from the computer when performing upgrades. You never know when these odds and ends will be needed again.

It is only fair to point out that many modern floppy drives do not have removable termination resistors. If you install a 5.25-inch drive it will probably have them, but I have not encountered termination resistors on 3.5-inch drives for quite some time. With drives that lack these resistors you simply connect them up to the motherboard and hope they work (which they invariably seem to).

Having installed an additional floppy drive it is likely that the PC will simply ignore it when the computer is booted into Windows. This happens because the existing BIOS setting will be for no drive B. Consequently the BIOS ignores the new drive, as does the operating system. The new drive will only work straight away if the BIOS detects the new drive and alters the relevant setting itself. Assuming this does not happen; you must go into the BIOS Setup program and make the change yourself. The floppy drive settings are usually in the Standard CMOS section of the program. It is just a matter of working through the options for drive B until the appropriate drive type is found.

Hard discs

A hard disc is very much like an ordinary floppy type, but in a highly refined form. In fact modern hard disc drives are so highly refined that they manage to cram incredible amounts of data onto a small disc. The disc itself is a permanent part of the drive, and is not interchangeable like floppy discs (hence the alternative name of "fixed" disc). The disc is made of metal and is rigid (hence the "hard" disc name). The disc spins at a much higher rate that is about ten or more times faster than the rotation speed of a floppy disc. Furthermore, it rotates continuously, not just when data must be accessed.

This is an important factor, since one of the main advantages of a hard disc is the speed with which data can be accessed. Having to wait for the disc to build up speed and settle down at the right speed would slow down disc accesses by an unacceptable degree. In fact the high rotation speed would result in accesses to a hard disc actually being slower than those to a floppy disc. A slight drawback of this continuous rotation is that computers equipped with hard discs are notoriously noisy! The high rotation speed of the disc aids rapid data transfers. Data can typically be read from disc in less than a tenth of the time that a floppy disc would take to handle the same amount of data. In fact modern hard drives are probably several hundred times faster than floppy drives.

Although the disc of a hard disc drive is not changeable, it has a very high capacity so that it can accommodate large amounts of data and several large applications programs if necessary. This is achieved by having what are typically many hundreds of cylinders (tracks) with numerous sectors per cylinder. Early hard discs had capacities of about 10 to 20 megabytes, but the lowest capacity currently offered by most suppliers is 10 or 20 gigabytes (1000 megabytes). Hard discs having capacities in excess of 100 gigabytes are quite commonplace. In most cases the "disc" is actually two, three, or four discs mounted one above the other on a common spindle. This enables around three to eight record/playback heads and sides of the disc to be used, giving higher capacities than could be handled using a single disc.

An important point that has to be made right from the start is that hard discs are highly intricate and quite delicate pieces of equipment. Modern hard drives are somewhat tougher than the early units, most of which had warning notices stating that the mildest of jolts could damage the drive. Even so, they must be treated with due respect, and protected from excessive jolts and vibration if they are to provide long and trouble-free service. You are unlikely to damage a modern hard disc drive simply by picking up the computer in which it is fitted, and carrying it across to the other side of the room. On the other hand, dropping a hard drive or the computer in which it is fitted could well result in serious damage to the hard disc drive.

Hard disc units are hermetically sealed so that dust can not enter. This is crucial, due to the high rotation speed of the disc. Apparently, the heads are aerodynamic types, which glide just above the surface of the disc, never actually coming into contact with it. If the two should come into contact, even via an intervening speck of dust, the result could easily be severe damage to the surface of the disc, and possibly to the head as well. Never open up a hard disc drive if you ever intend to use it again!

Interfaces

Adding a hard disc drive to a PC breaks down into four basic tasks. First the configuration jumpers must be checked and altered if they are not appropriate for your set-up. Then the drive must be bolted in place inside the computer. Next it is connected to the power supply and a suitable hard disc controller. Finally, it must be formatted and made ready for use with the operating system.

Usually the operating system will be installed on the hard disc so that the computer boots-up from the hard disc at switch-on. Of course, this is not necessary when adding an extra hard disc rather than swapping the existing disc for a higher capacity type. Assuming the original disc has one partition (drive C), the new one will become drive D and any others such as CD-RW drives will move up by one letter. As we shall see shortly, formatting and making a hard disc ready for use is a slightly more complex business than formatting a floppy disc.

If a second hard disc is installed it will usually be the slave device on the primary IDE channel, with the original (boot) hard drive as the master device on this channel. The new disc drive will be the master on the primary IDE channel if the original drive is being replaced with a higher capacity type. The various configuration options are covered later in this chapter, but whether it is a master or slave device, the drive should be correctly configured before it is mounted in the case. The configuration jumpers are usually inaccessible once the drive has been installed. These days there is almost invariably a configuration chart on the drive itself, so determining the correct jumper settings should be straightforward.

Physically installing a hard disc is much the same as installing a floppy disc. All PC floppy disc drives, with the possible exceptions of some very early types, are of the half height variety. The same is true for PC hard disc drives. A PC drive bay should therefore be more than ample for modern hard disc units. As there is no disc swapping with a hard disc drive, it does not need to be mounted in a drive bay that has an open front. In fact the convention is for hard disc drives to be mounted out of sight in an internal drive bay.

A variety of hard disc controllers have been used in the past, but there is now only one type in common use. This is the IDE type, which has developed into a range of "turbo" interfaces starting with the UDMA33 type. This method of hard disc interfacing is basically just interfacing the drive direct onto the ISA expansion bus, or in the case of the UDMA33 interface, onto the faster PCI expansion bus. The hard disc controller is contained within the drive. The UDMA33 interface was replaced by the UDMA66 type, followed by the UDMA100 and UDMA133 types.

There is full compatibility between the oldest version of the IDE interface and the modern varieties. Even the oldest of IDE hard disc drives should work perfectly well if it is connected to a modern IDE interface such as a UDMA133 type. Similarly, a modern UDMA133 disc drive should work perfectly well if it is used as a replacement or upgrade drive in a computer that has an old IDE or EIDE hard disc interface. Of course, in order to gain the faster transfer rates of (say) a UDMA100 drive it must be used in a PC that has a UDMA100 or later interface. Using an old drive on a UDMA133 interface will not give an increase in performance either, but the drive will still work as a standard IDE type. In order to get a UDMA133 drive to operate at full speed the PC must have a UDMA133 interface, suitable BIOS support, and an operating system equipped with a suitable hard disc driver. The speed at which the hard drive operates is determined by the oldest and slowest part of the hard disc subsystem.

Connections

With any reasonably recent PC there will be at least two IDE ports on the motherboard. Connections from the controller to the hard disc drive are made via a 40-way ribbon cable, and most IDE cables have provision for two IDE devices. Note that drives having UDMA66 or later versions of the IDE interface require a special cable having 80 leads in order to exploit the higher data transfer rates supported by these interfaces. Using a 40-way cable effectively downgrades these drives to UDMA33 operation.

With two drives per IDE port and two ports on the motherboard, up to four IDE devices can be accommodated. Most PCs only have a single hard disc drive, but the IDE ports can also be used for CD-ROM drives, CD writers, and high capacity drives that have removable media such as Zip drives. It is therefore conceivable that all four IDE channels could be used, but two or three are usually sufficient. Unlike PC floppy drives, a twist in the cable is not used to determine which drive is the master IDE device and which is the slave type. Instead, configuration jumpers on the drives are used to set each IDE device as a master or a slave. There might only be the master and slave options, but there is often a third option that is called something like "cable select". This seems to be non-essential in a PC context and should be ignored.

With some IDE devices, but mainly hard disc drives, there are two master options. One of these is used where the drive is the only device connected to that IDE interface, and the other is used where there is a slave device as well. The convention is for the boot drive to be the master device on the first IDE interface, although it will probably be possible to boot from the hard drive if it is used on one of other IDE channels. If you do not wish to boot from a hard drive it can certainly be used on any available IDE channel, as can CD-ROM drives and CD writers.

However, it is important to bear in mind that an IDE interface can not operate as (say) a UDMA133 type when it is accessing a hard disc drive and a UDMA33 type when it is controlling the data flow to a CD-ROM drive. The interface will operate at a speed that suits the slowest device it is controlling. It is therefore best to keep the hard disc drive or drives on one IDE interface and connect CD-ROM drives, etc., to the other. This lets the hard disc operate at maximum speed, or as close to maximum speed as the interface can manage. Of course, with an old motherboard the IDE interfaces might not support any "turbo" modes anyway, and this gives greater choice over the channelling of the drives.

Connectors

The IDC connectors used for IDE data cables are polarised, and in theory can not be connected the wrong way round. In practice the connectors on the motherboard are simplified versions which allow the cable to be connected either way round. Also, the connectors on the cable sometimes lack the polarising "key" which ensures that they can not be connected the wrong way round. You then have to look carefully at the circuit boards, drives, and instruction manuals to find pin one on the IDE port and the drives. You then just follow the convention of making sure that the red lead of the cable connects to pin one of both the IDE port and drive connectors.

The only other common form of hard disc interface is the SCSI (small computer systems interface) type. This is actually a general-purpose interface that can be used wherever high-speed data transfers are required. It is not just used for internal devices such as hard discs and CD-ROM drives, and is often used with scanners and other external peripherals. Up to eight devices can be connected in chain fashion to a SCSI interface. SCSI hard disc drives have never been very popular amongst PC users, and have mainly been used in network servers rather than stand-alone PCs. The speed advantage of SCSI hard discs has been largely eroded by the faster IDE interfaces, and the substantial additional cost does not seem to be justified for most stand-alone PCs.

Formatting

Once you have configured the jumpers on the hard drive, mounted it in the case, and connected it to the controller and the power supply, it is time to switch on and try it out. However, there is still a fair amount of work to do before the computer will boot from the hard drive. The first step is to go into the BIOS Setup program and enter the appropriate parameters for the particular drive you are using. The BIOS Setup program is covered in detail in chapter 2, so refer to this chapter if you are unsure about configuring the BIOS to operate with a new hard disc. The settings for the hard disc are normally in the Standard CMOS section of the BIOS.

When using a high capacity drive in an old PC there can be problems due to the BIOS not supporting disc capacities of more than 528 megabytes. This does not mean that a hard disc having a capacity of more than 528 megabytes is unusable with a computer of this type, but it does mean that it can only use the first 528 megabytes of its capacity. If you set drive parameters that give a higher capacity the BIOS will not accept them. There are actually ways around the 528-megabyte limit, and some hard drives are provided with utility software that can handle this problem. However, there is no guarantee that this type of quick fix will not produce problems in use.

Fitting a more modern BIOS or (where possible) upgrading the program in the existing BIOS ROMs is a better solution, but is often impractical. Finding a more modern BIOS that is compatible with the motherboard is likely to be problematic, and could also be quite costly. It would probably be more cost effective to undertake a major upgrade, including the replacement of the motherboard with a modern type having a BIOS that properly supports modern high capacity drives. Fortunately, there can be few PCs still in use that have this BIOS limitation, so it is unlikely that you will encounter it.

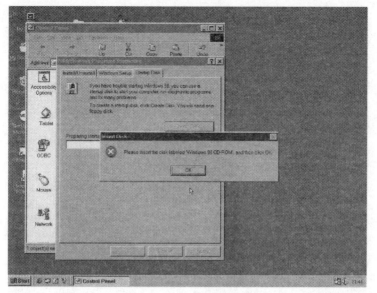

Fig.6.8 A Startup disc can be made using Windows 95, 98 or ME

FDISK

Once the BIOS has been dealt with it should be possible to boot from an MS-DOS or Windows 95/98/ME system disc in floppy drive A. If the computer is otherwise working but will not boot from drive A, it is probably because it has not been configured to attempt to boot from drive A. This can be corrected by going back into the BIOS Setup program and setting a suitable boot-up sequence, which means any sequence that includes drive A. In the BIOS Setup program you might find a section that can undertake a low-level format of the hard disc drive. Unlike a floppy drive, a hard disc must be low-level formatted before it can accept high-level formatting from the operating system. However, IDE hard drives are supplied with the low-level formatting already done, and a low-level formatting program must not be used to process them.

With the computer booted-up and running MS-DOS or the Windows 95/98/ME equivalent of MS-DOS, the hard drive will not be accessible. It must be high-level formatted using the MS-DOS "FORMAT" program, but first you must first prepare the disc using the "FDISK" command. The system disc in drive A should contain copies of both programs.

They are included on Windows 95/98/ME Startup discs. A Startup disc is normally created when the operating system is initially installed, but one can be created by going to the Windows Control Panel and double-clicking the Add/Remove Programs icon. Operate the Startup Disk tab followed by the Create Disk button, and then follow the onscreen prompts (Figure 6.8).

Large drives

FDISK is used to create one or more DOS partitions, and with discs of 2.1 gigabytes or less you may wish to have the whole of the disc as a single partition. The hard disc drive then becomes drive C. By creating further partitions it can also operate as drive D, drive E, etc. The primary partition is the boot disc, and this is where the operating system must be installed. The MS/DOS and Windows 95 file systems set the 2.1-gigabyte partition limit. There is also an 8.4-gigabyte limit on the physical size of the drive. With Windows 98 and any reasonably modern BIOS these limits do not apply, but you must use the FAT32 file system. To do this simply answer yes when FDISK is first run, and you are asked if you require support for large hard disc drives. Even if you do not wish to have a large disc organised as one large partition, it is still best to opt for large hard disc support. FAT32 utilizes the available disc space more efficiently and reduces wastage. Note that if you only require a single partition you must still use the FDISK program to set up this single partition, and that the FORMAT program will not work on the hard drive until FDISK has created a DOS partition.

Some hard discs are supplied complete with partitioning software that will also format the disc and add the system files, which will be copied from the boot disc. Where a utility program of this type is available it is probably better to use it instead of the FDISK and FORMAT programs. These MS-DOS programs are fairly straightforward in use, but using the software supplied with the drive will almost certainly be even easier. These programs are usually very quick in operation. If you use the FDISK and FORMAT programs, make sure that you are using modern versions of them. Versions of MS/DOS earlier than version 3.3 are not able to provide two partitions, and are not really suitable for use with a modern PC.

Using FDISK

Once you are in FDISK there is a menu offering these four choices (see also Figure 6.9):

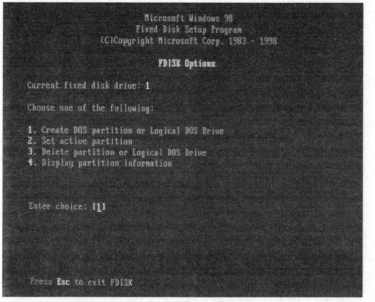

Fig.6.9 The main FDISK menu has four options

1. Create DOS partition or logical DOS drive

2. Set the active partition

3. Delete partition or logical DOS drive

4. Display partition information

The first thing we need to do is create a DOS partition, so select option one, which will be the default. This takes you into a further menu offering these three options (Figure 6.10):

1. Create primary DOS partition

2. Create extended DOS partition

3. Create logical DOS drive(s) in the extended DOS partition

It is a primary DOS partition that is required, so select option one, which should again be the default. You will then be asked if you wish to use the maximum space for the partition and make it the active partition. If you answer yes, the whole disc, or as much of it as FDISK can handle, will be used for the partition. It will also be made active, which simply means

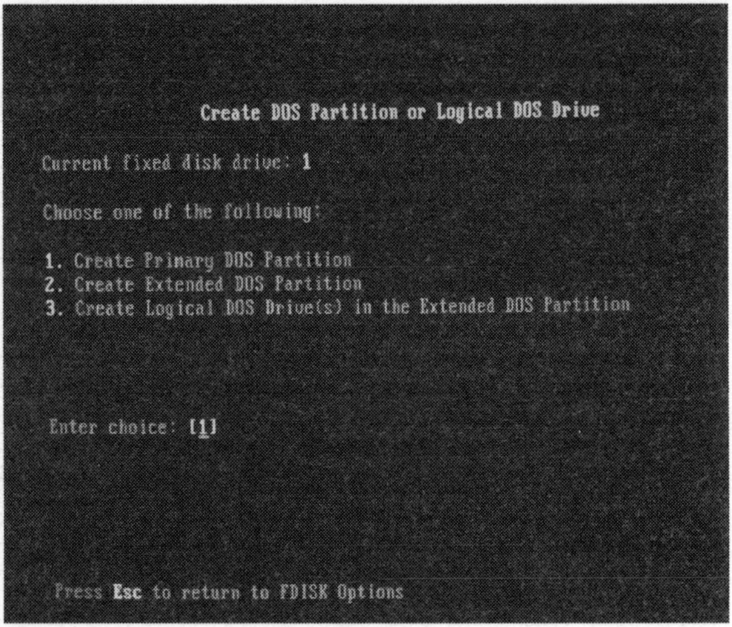

Fig.6.10 The FDISK partition creation menu

that this is the partition that the computer will try to boot from. This is the partition to which the operating system should be installed. If you answer no, you will then have to specify the size of the primary partition in megabytes. This creates the partition, but does not make it active. Having created the partition you then press the Escape key to return to the original menu. It is a good idea to select option four to check that the partition has been created successfully (Figure 6.11).

If you did not use the maximum space for the partition it will not have been made active. To do this select option two from the main menu and then enter the number of the partition you wish to make active. As there is only one partition this will obviously be partition number one. Press Return to implement this command, and then press the Escape key to return to the main menu again. It is then a good idea to use option four once again to ensure that everything has gone smoothly. In the Status column there should be an "A" to indicate that partition one is active (as in Figure 6.11).

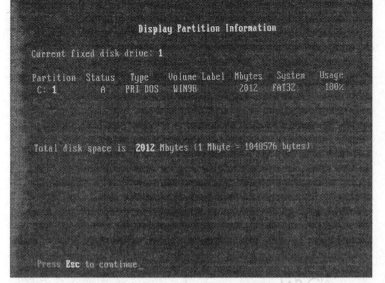

Fig.6.11 Using FDISK to check the partition information

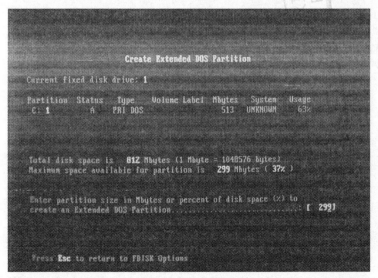

Fig.6.12 Creating an extended DOS partition

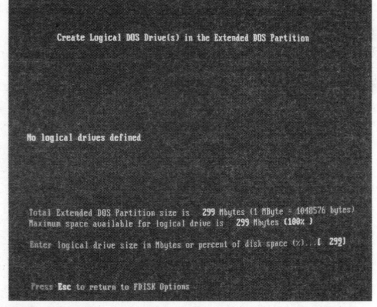

Create Logical DOS Drive(s) in the Extended DOS Partition

No logical drives defined

Total Extended DOS Partition size is   299 Mbytes (1 Mbyte = 1048576 bytes)
Maximum space available for logical drive is   299 Mbytes (100%)

Enter logical drive size in Mbytes or percent of disk space (%)...[299]

Press **Esc** to return to FDISK Options

Fig.6.13 Creating an extra partition does not create a logical drive

If a further partition is required select option one, and then option two, which is "Create extended DOS partition" (Figure 6.12). Enter the size of the partition you require and press the Return key to create the partition. Then press the Escape key, which will bring up a message saying "No logical drives defined" (Figure 6.13). In other words, you have created a partition, but as yet it does not have a drive letter. Assuming you require all the space in the partition to be one logical drive, simply press the Return key. This will make the partition drive D, and a screen giving this information will appear (Figure 6.14). Press the Escape key to return to the main menu, and use option four to check that the partition has been created successfully.

Formatting

Having created the partitions you require, the "FORMAT" command can then be run. First you will have to press the Escape key twice to exit FDISK, and then the computer must be rebooted so that the new partition information takes effect. If the original disc drive has been replaced with

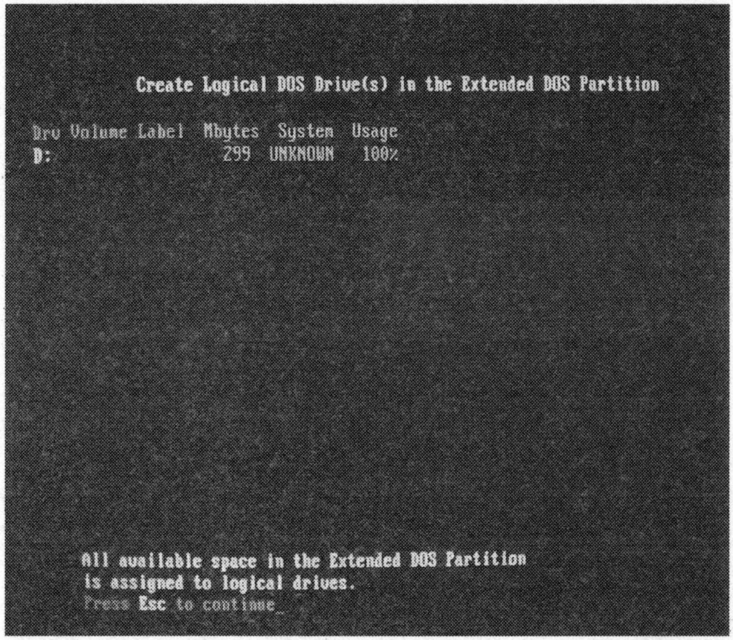

Fig.6.14 This screen confirms that logical drive D: has been created

a larger one, the new drive will be drive C. Use this command to format drive C:

format C:

This will bring up a warning to the effect that all data in drive C will be lost if you proceed with the format. As yet there is no data to lose, so answer yes to proceed with the formatting. It might take several minutes to complete the task, since there are a large number of tracks to be processed and checked. If the hard disc has more than one partition and is operating as drive C, drive D, etc., each partition must formatted using a separate "FORMAT" command. This command will format drive D:

format D:

If the new drive is in addition to the boot drive rather than replacing it, the original drive will be drive C and the new one will be drive D. Where the original disc has more than one partition, the new disc will be one letter up from the last drive letter used by the original disc. For example, the new one will be drive F if the original drive has three partitions (C, D, and E). Of course, CD-ROM drives, etc., will be moved up one drive letter when the new hard disc is added, or by two or more letters if it has more than one partition.

Easy copying

An additional drive does not require the operating system to be installed, since the PC will still boot in the normal way from the original drive. The same is not true if the original drive is replaced by the new unit. First the operating system must be installed, then all the applications programs must be installed, and finally the data on the old drive must be transferred to the new one. It is a good idea to backup any data on the old drive before starting the upgrade, but the easiest way of transferring the data is to have the old drive as the slave device on the primary IDE channel. Data can then be dragged from one drive and dropped in the other using Windows Explorer.

Starting the installation from scratch with the new drive has its advantages, and the main one is that it provides a "clean" installation that is free from all the rubbish that tends to accumulate on a hard disc drive during normal use. The drawback is that it can be very time consuming. Getting everything installed and running properly on the new drive could literally take all day, or even a couple of days if things do not go smoothly. Buying a program such as Power Quest's Drive Copy is definitely worth considering if a quicker method is needed. The amount of time that can be saved using a program such as this is amazing.

The basic idea is to have the new drive installed as drive C and the old one as drive D. Using a program such as Drive Copy it is possible to clone the old drive onto the new one. The image taken from the old drive is placed onto the new one in such a way that the operating system will boot from the new drive. In fact everything should work exactly as before, including any customisation of the operating system and applications programs. Note that passwords or other information stored in concealed files are unlikely to be copied and will have to be entered again when the relevant programs are run. The time taken to make the copy varies considerably from one system to another, but is often less than an hour.

Having completed the cloning process the old drive can either be removed, or it can be left in place and reformatted to clear its contents.

Assuming the old drive has a reasonably high capacity, it makes sense to leave it in place and use that capacity rather than simply discarding it. Another option is to leave its contents intact. It then acts as a backup drive. If the installation on drive C becomes so badly damaged that it can not be repaired, any important data is first backed up and then the old disc is once again cloned onto the new one.

Incidentally, it is a requirement of most cloning programs that the new disc is equal to or larger than the original one. In an upgrading context this should not be an issue, since you would not upgrade to a smaller hard disc.

The hard way

If the clone system is not used, the next step is to install the operating system onto the new disc. In the unlikely event that you have the floppy disc version of Windows 95/98 there should be no difficulty in loading it onto the hard disc once the hard disc is bootable. It is more likely that Windows will be installed from CD-ROM, and this should also be perfectly straightforward provided you opt for CD-ROM support when the menu appears during the boot process. Simply type Setup and press the Return key to run the Setup program on the Windows 95/98/ME installation disc. It is then just a matter of following the on-screen prompts to complete the Windows installation.

Note that you can install the upgrade version of Windows 95, 98 or ME onto a "clean" hard disc, and that it is not essential to load your old version of Windows first so that you have something to upgrade. However, during the installation process you will probably be asked to prove that you have a qualifying upgrade product by putting the Setup disc into the floppy drive or CD-ROM drive, as appropriate. Do not throw away or recycle your old Windows discs, as this could leave you unable to reinstall the Windows upgrade.

Windows XP

Windows XP is easier to install than Windows 95/98/ME, and there is no need to format the hard disc drive when installing Windows XP. This can be done during the installation process. In fact the partitioning of the disc can also be handled by the installation program, so FDISK is not needed either. The Windows XP installation CD-ROM is a bootable type, so it is possible to boot from the CD-ROM straight into the Setup program. No floppy boot disc is required.

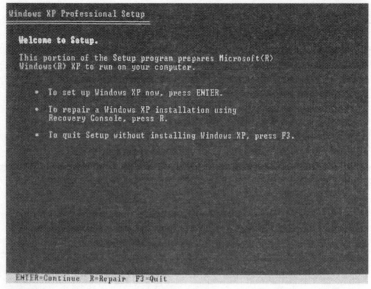

Fig.6.15 The opening screen of the Windows XP Setup program

The first step is to boot from the installation CD-ROM, and this might require changes to the BIOS settings. The BIOS must be set to boot from the CD-ROM drive before it tries to boot from the hard disc. It is unlikely that the computer will attempt to boot from the CD-ROM drive if the priorities are the other way around, and it will certainly not do so unless the CD-ROM is set as one of the boot devices. If all is well, a message will appear on the screen indicating that any key must be operated in order to boot from the CD-ROM drive. This message appears quite briefly, so be ready to press one of the keys. The computer will try to boot from the hard disc if you "miss the boat". It will then be necessary to restart the computer and try again.

After various files have been loaded from the CD-ROM, things should come to a halt with the screen of Figure 6.15. The Setup program is needed to install Windows XP, so press the Enter (Return) key. The Next screen (Figure 6.16) is the usual licence agreement, and the F8 key is pressed in order to agree with the licensing terms. Note that Windows XP can not be installed unless you do agree to the licensing conditions. Things should now move on to a screen like the one of Figure 6.17 where there is sometimes the option of repairing any existing installation or

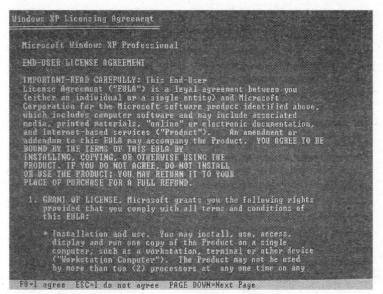

Fig.6.16 *You must agree to the conditions in order to proceed*

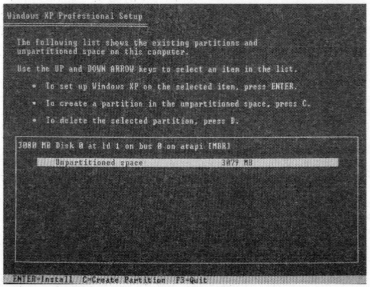

Fig.6.17 *There are a few options for the "raw" disc space*

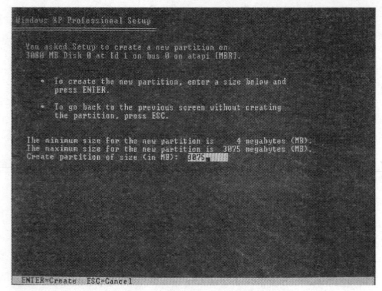

Fig.6.18 The first task is to produce a new partition

installing Windows XP from scratch. In this case there is no existing installation, so you are presented with various options for the "raw" hard disc space.

The first task is to produce a new partition by operating the C key, which produces the screen of Figure 6.18. By default the Setup program will use the whole disc as a single partition, but you can enter a smaller size if desired. The remaining space can then be partitioned using the same method used to produce the first partition. Here we will keep things simple and settle for a single partition equal to the full capacity of the disc. This is achieved by pressing the Return (Enter) key, which brings up the screen of Figure 6.19. Operate the Return key again, which will produce the new partition and install Windows XP onto it.

This moves things on to the screen of Figure 6.20 where the desired file system is selected. Unless there is a good reason to use the FAT or FAT32 file systems, such as compatibility with another file system, choose the NTFS option. This file system makes the best use of Windows XP's capabilities. Having selected the required file system, press the Return

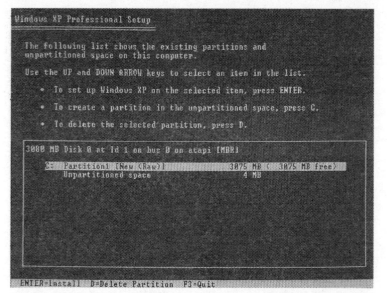

Fig.6.19 Press Return to create the partition and install Windows on it

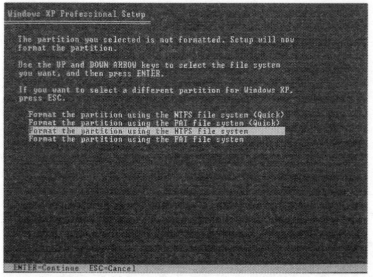

Fig.6.20 NTFS is the file system normally used with Windows XP

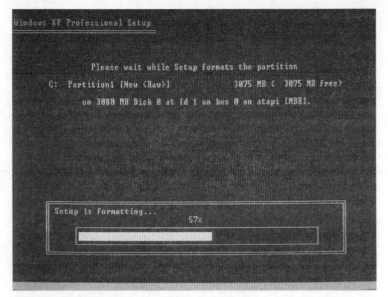

Fig.6.21 The bargraph shows how the formatting is progressing

key to go ahead and format the partition. This brings up the screen of Figure 6.21, complete with the usual bargraph to show how far the formatting has progressed.

Once the partition has been created and formatted, the Setup program will start copying files to the hard disc (Figure 6.22). Once this stage has been completed you are prompted to restart the computer (Figure 6.23), but this will happen in a few seconds if you do not respond. Having rebooted, the computer will go into the initial screen of the Setup program (Figure 6.24), and installation then carries on in normal Windows fashion.

XP second drive

Windows XP has been designed as an MS/DOS-free zone, and it is not necessary to use the MS/DOS FDISK and FORMAT programs when a second hard disc is added to a Windows XP system. I suppose that these programs could be used, but it would definitely be doing things the hard way. There is a built-in program that greatly simplifies the partitioning and formatting of hard drives. This program can be run by

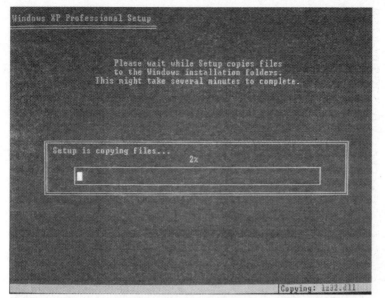

Fig.6.22 With the formatting completed, files are copied to the disc

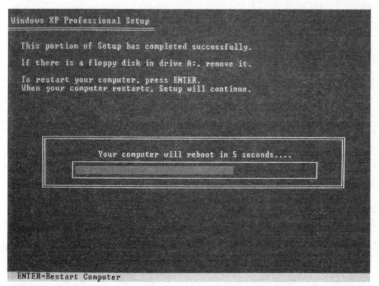

Fig.6.23 Restart the computer once the copying has been completed

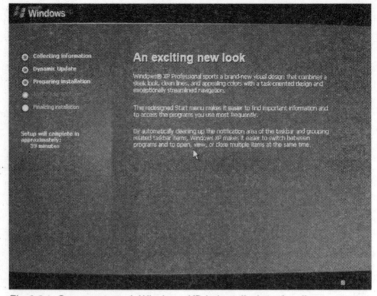

Fig.6.24 Once restarted, Windows XP is installed on the disc

going to the Windows Control Panel and double clicking the Administrative Tools icon. This produces a window like the one of Figure 6.25, and double clicking the Computer Management icon produces the new window of Figure 6.26. Several utilities are available from the Computer Management window, but the one required in this case is Disk Management. Left clicking this entry in the left-hand panel changes the window to look something like Figure 6.27.

Details of the boot drive are given at the top of the right-hand panel. The bottom section gives details of both drives, and the new drive is Disk 1. This is described as "Unallocated", which means that it is not partitioned or formatted at this stage. The black line to the right of the Disk 1 label and icon also indicates that it is not partitioned. To partition the disc, right-click on the black line and then select the New Partition option from the popup menu. This launches the New Partition Wizard (Figure 6.28). Windows XP can use two types of disc, which are the basic and dynamic varieties. The New Partition Wizard only handles basic discs, and these use conventional partitions that are essentially the same as those used by MS-DOS and earlier versions of Windows. For most purposes a basic disc is perfectly adequate.

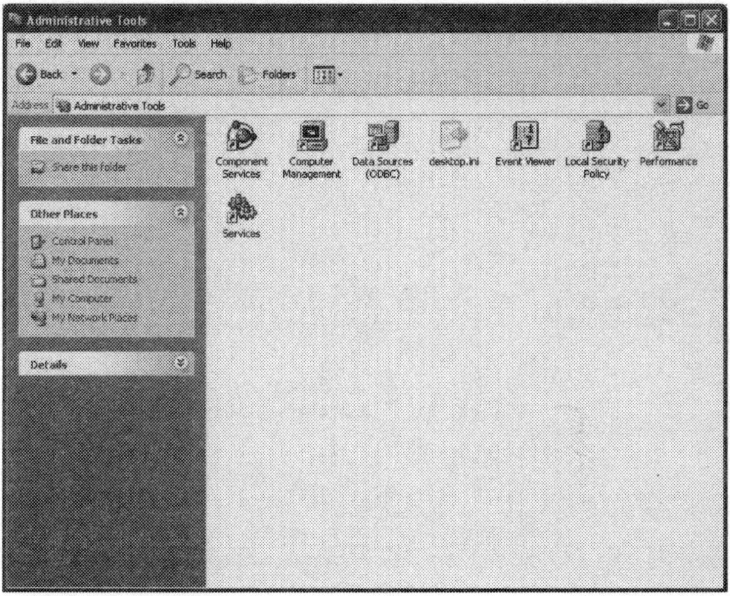

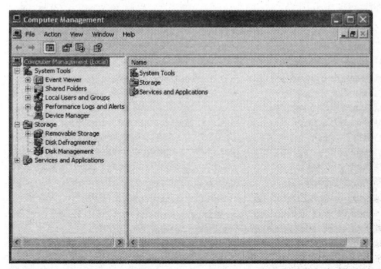

Fig.6.25 The Administrative Tools window

Fig.6.26 The Computer Management screen offers a range of options

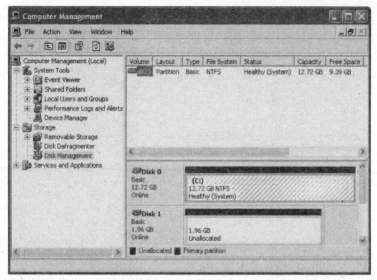

Fig.6.27 The window with the Disk Management facility selected

Operate the Next button to move on with the partitioning, and a window like the one in Figure 6.29 should appear. Either an extended or a primary partition can be selected using the radio buttons, and in this case it is a primary partition that is needed. The size of the partition is selected at the next window (Figure 6.30), and the maximum and minimum usable sizes are indicated. All the available disc space will be used by default, but a different size can be used by typing a value (in megabytes) into the textbox. Operating the Next

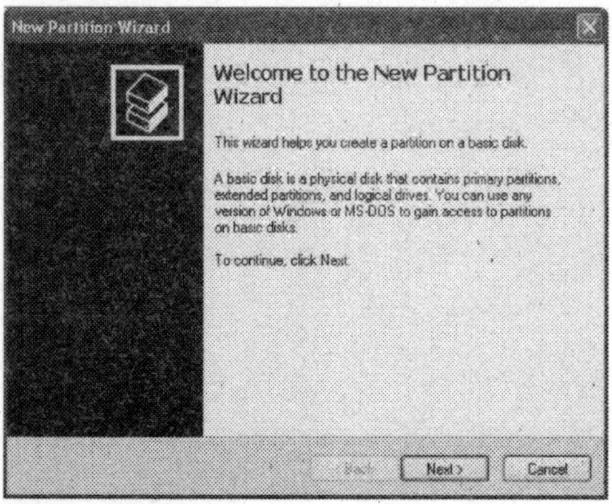

Fig.6.28 The opening screen of the New Partition Wizard

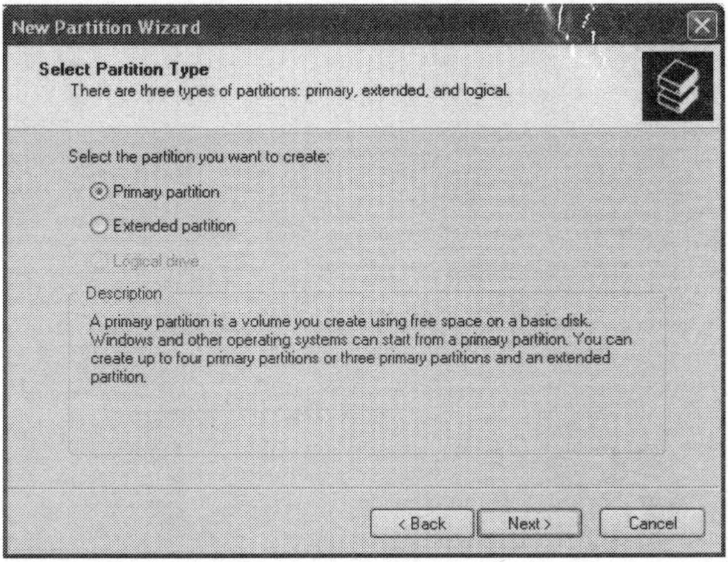

Fig.6.29 Use this window to select the partition type

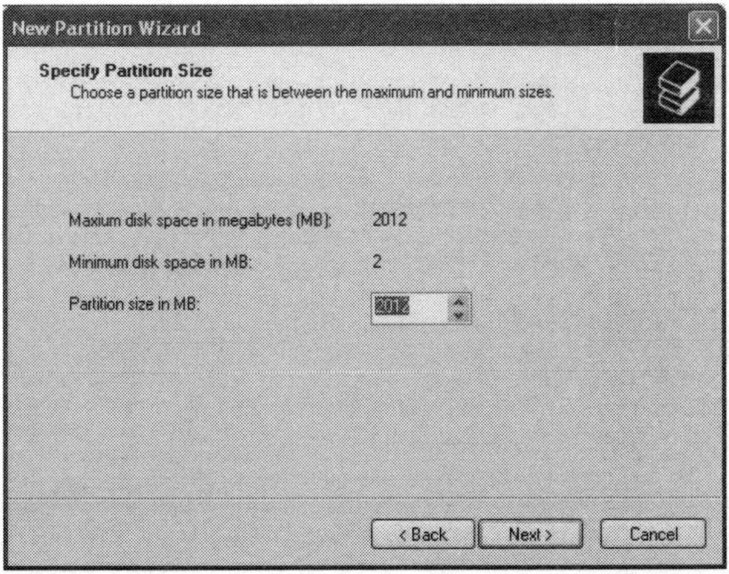

Fig.6.30 This window is used to set the partition size (in megabytes)

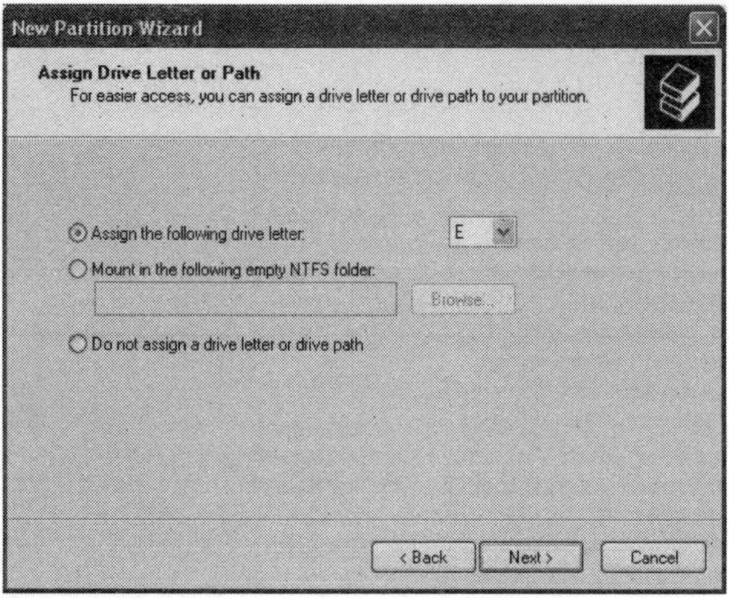

Fig.6.31 Here a drive letter is assigned to the new partition

button brings up the window of Figure 6.31 where a drive letter is assigned to the new partition. Unless there is a good reason to do otherwise, simply accept the default drive letter.

At the next window (Figure 6.32) you have the choice of formatting the new partition or leaving it unformatted. Since the partition will not be usable until it is formatted, accept the formatting option. One of the menus offers a choice of FAT, FAT32, or NTFS formatting. Settle for the default option of NTFS formatting unless you need compatibility with another Windows operating system. Also settle for the default allocation unit size, which will be one that is appropriate for the partition size. A different name for the drive, such as "Backup", can be entered into the textbox if desired. Tick the appropriate checkbox if you wish to enable file and folder compression.

Left-click the Next button when you are satisfied with the settings. The next window (Figure 6.33) lists all the parameters that have been selected, and provides an opportunity to change your mind or correct mistakes. If necessary, use the Back button to return to earlier windows and change

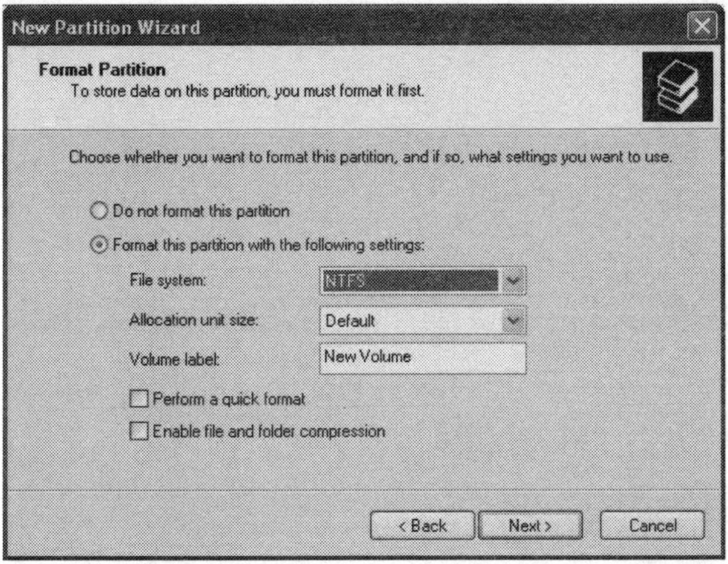

Fig.6.32 The partition can be formatted as an NTFS, FAT, or FAT32 type

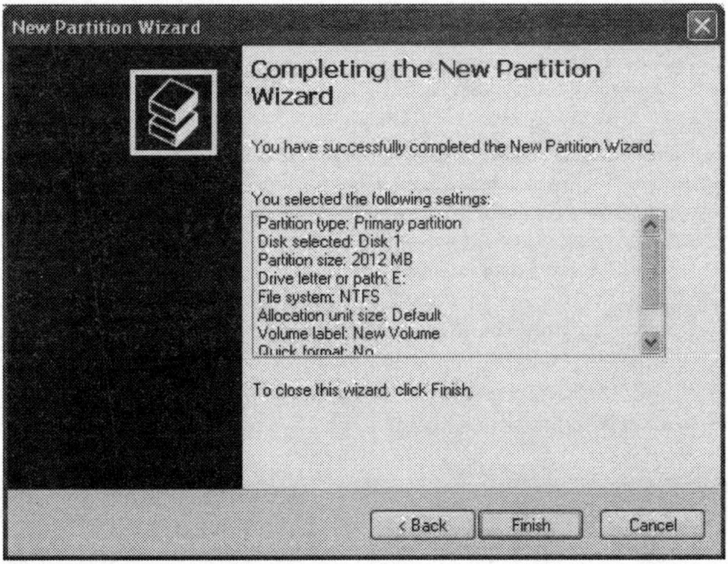

Fig.6.33 This window lists the parameters that have been selected

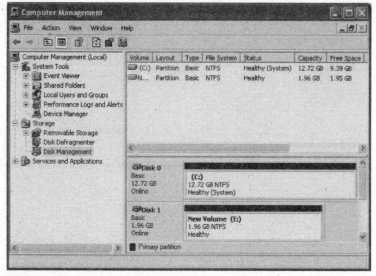

Fig.6.34 The Disk Management window shows the new partition

some of the settings. Operate the Finish button if all the settings are correct. The partition will then be created, and it will appear as a blue line in the Disk Management window. It will then be formatted, and this may take half an hour or more for a large partition. The area below the blue line indicates how far the formatting process has progressed. Eventually the formatting will be completed, and the Disk Management window will show the new disc as containing a primary partition using the appropriate file system (Figure 6.34). Once the formatting has been completed, files on the main drive can be copied to the new partition using the Cut and Paste facilities of Windows Explorer.

If space has been left for a further partition on the disc, right-click on the black section of the line that represents the vacant disc space. Then select the New Partition option from the popup menu, and go through the whole partitioning and formatting process again. A maximum of four primary partitions can be used on each physical disc.

The rest

There are now numerous other types of internal drive for PCs, including CD-ROMs, CD-ROM writers, DVD drives, and various types of removable hard disc drive. Installing one of these is very much like installing a hard disc drive, and the new drive will normally interface to one of the IDE ports. There are a few exceptions, such as drives which use a SCSI interface card, or their own dedicated interface card.

With IDE drives it is a matter of going into the BIOS Setup program to see if there is specific support for the type of drive you are fitting. There are often options for CD-ROM, Zip, and LS120 drives, but you are unlikely to find specific settings for any other drives. Note though, that DVD drives, CD-RW types, etc., are all plain CD-ROM drives as far as the BIOS is concerned. It is the operating system and supporting software that takes them beyond basic CD-ROM operation. The drive's instruction manual should give advice on the BIOS settings for any non-standard drives, but in most cases it is just a matter of setting the appropriate IDE channel as occupied, but with all the parameters set to zero. The drive should be supplied with drivers for the popular operating systems, together with full installation instructions.

When buying removable hard disc drives, CD ROM writers, etc., you need to make sure you know exactly what you are buying, and that it is suitable for use in your system. IDE versions of some drives are only usable if they are supported by the BIOS in your PC. If not, either an external parallel port, USB, or SCSI version of the drive will have to be used. This is unlikely to be a problem unless you PC is several years old, but it is as well to check this point before buying a drive for an old PC.

If the drive requires a SCSI or other form of controller card is it supplied as standard or is it an optional extra? A suitable controller card can be quite expensive, and in some cases it costs nearly as much as the bare drive it controls. With a CD-ROM writer or CD-RW drive, is it supplied with full supporting software? These drives can be used in Windows 95/98/ME much like any other drive, albeit with some restrictions. However, they can only do so with the aid of suitable software, such as Adaptec's Easy CD Creator or Nero. Again, this type of software can significantly add to the cost of a drive if has to be bought as an extra. Windows XP has some built-in support for CD-RW drives, but additional software is still needed in order to fully exploit this type of drive.

Audio cable

The configuration jumpers on CD-ROM drives, Zip drives, etc., normally have only the three basic settings (master, slave, and cable select). Make sure that you configure the drive before mounting it in the case, because

Fig.6.35 There is usually an analogue audio output on CD-ROM drives

the jumper block is likely to be inaccessible once the drive is in position. With any form of CD-ROM or DVD drive there is invariably an audio output socket on the rear of the unit, usually between the configuration jumper block and the power input socket (Figure 6.35). This enables audio CDs to be played on the drive to be heard through the computer's sound system.

This coupling is not really necessary if you will not play audio tracks on the CD-ROM drive, or if audio tracks will be monitored via the headphone socket on the CD-ROM drive. It is not essential if the new drive is in addition to an existing CD-ROM or DVD drive, and the original unit is coupled to the audio system. CDs can simply be played through the original drive. However, it makes sense to connect the socket just in case you need to play audio tracks on the new drive via the soundcard.

There are a couple of potential snags, one of which is simply that more than one type of connector has been used at both the CD-ROM and the soundcard ends of these cables. An audio cable is usually supplied

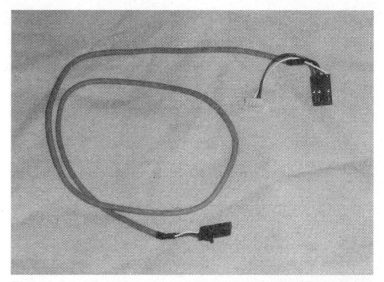

Fig.6.36 An audio lead that has two types of connector at the end which connects to the motherboard or soundcard

with any form of CD-ROM or DVD drive provided you buy the retail boxed version and not an OEM unit. This usually has a relatively large and flat connector at each end, which is the only type used in current equipment. Where an old PC is being upgraded it is possible that the soundcard or motherboard will use a different type of connector. The audio cable supplied with the drive might have two connectors at one end (Figure 6.36). One or other of the connectors at this end should suit the connector on the soundcard or motherboard. It will otherwise be necessary to buy a suitable cable.

The other potential problem is that there might not be a spare audio input on the soundcard or motherboard. Soundcards are more accommodating in this respect, and any reasonably modern type should have at least two audio input ports. The integrated audio circuits on motherboards are often fairly basic, but some motherboards do have two or three audio inputs. There is no easy solution if the audio system lacks a suitable input, and the audio connection will then have to be omitted.

Points to remember

A PC can have two floppy disc drives and it is worth adding a second drive if you will need to do a lot of disc copying. The vast majority of PCs are equipped with a twin floppy cable and have a spare power lead on the power supply unit. All you need is the drive itself and a few fixing screws.

Having installed a new drive, floppy or otherwise, do not forget to go to the BIOS Setup program and make the necessary changes in the Standard CMOS section. Unless the drive is set up correctly in the BIOS it will not be recognised by the operating system.

A modern high-speed hard disc drive such as a UDMA133 type will only work at its full rated speed if the correct (80-way) cable is used and the motherboard has the appropriate interface. However, the high-speed drives are compatible with earlier IDE interfaces and 40-way IDE cables, and will work with them at reduced speed.

A hard disc drive must be partitioned and formatted before it can be used. It must still be partitioned even if its full capacity will be used as one huge partition. With Windows 95/98/ME the formatting and portioning are carried out with the aid of a Windows Startup disc, and the FDISK and FORMAT commands on this disc.

With Windows XP it is possible to boot from the installation CD-ROM. The Windows Setup program can then be used to partition and format the new drive prior to installing the operating system. If the new drive is in addition to the boot drive, boot into Windows XP and then use its facilities to partition and format the new drive.

When adding a second drive it must be partitioned and formatted, but there is no need to install the operating system on it. In fact adding the operating system onto a second hard drive would waste some of its capacity and could confuse the original copy of the operating system.

There are programs available that will make a clone of the original drive using the new and bigger drive. This represents the quickest and easiest way of getting the PC "up and running" again when upgrading to a larger drive.

Cloning the original drive is a quick and easy way of handling a hard disc upgrade, but reinstalling everything from scratch can have a big advantage. There is little point in cloning an installation that has become clogged up with thousands of unused files and is running slowly or with poor reliability. In this situation it is worth taking the time to produce a new and "clean" installation.

CD-ROM and similar types or drive normally have an audio output socket. This can be connected to an audio input on the soundcard or motherboard so that audio CDs can be played through the computer's sound system. This facility can not be implemented if there is only one audio input connector and it is already in use by another drive.

Memory upgrades

Chip memory

With so many modern programs requiring large amounts of memory in order to work at their best (or to work at all in some cases), it is not surprising that adding memory is the most popular form of hardware upgrade. Memory upgrading is a potentially confusing subject, since there are now several types of memory in common use, and numerous types have been used over the years. PCs prior to the 80386 processor had their memory in the form of integrated circuits that plugged into rows of holders on the motherboard. In some cases there were about three dozen of these sockets.

Upgrading on-board RAM was a fiddly and time consuming process. If you ran out of sockets it was possible to increase the RAM further using expansion cards, but this gave rather poor performance due to the relatively low operating speed of the ISA expansion bus. Memory expansion cards are now totally obsolete, but you can probably still obtain the chips for on-board memory upgrades. This type of memory is well and truly obsolete though, and it will not be considered further here.

Memory map

Memory that comes within the normal 640k MS/DOS allocation is usually termed "base memory". With a modern PC there will be no need to expand the base memory, as the computer will have been supplied with the full 640k of RAM as standard. RAM, incidentally, stands for "random access memory", and is the form of memory used for storing application programs and data. The contents of the RAM in a PC are lost when the computer is switched off, and it is, for all practical purposes, lost if the

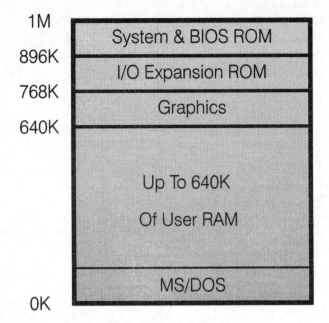

Fig.7.1 The memory map for a PC's base memory

computer is reset (whether a hardware or software reset is used). ROM (read only memory) is used for programs that must not be lost when the computer is switched off, which in the case of a PC means its BIOS program. The 8088 series of microprocessors can address 1 megabyte (1024 kilobytes or 1024k) of memory, but in a PC only 640k of this is allocated to RAM for program and data storage. The rest is set aside for purposes such as the ROM BIOS and the video RAM. Figure 7.1 shows the original memory map for PC.

Modern PC processors can operate in modes that permit large amounts of RAM to be accessed. Even on the most modern of PCs the maximum RAM limit is usually imposed by the motherboard design and not the processor, with an upper limit that is usually around 256 to 1024 megabytes or even more. This is much greater than is needed for most modern applications, the majority of which will run under Windows ME with about 32 megabytes of RAM. This is not to say that these programs will not run better with more RAM. Probably the most frequently asked of frequently asked PC questions is "how much RAM do I need." This is very much a "how long is a piece of string" style question, and it is entirely dependent on the applications software that you will be running.

The software manuals should give details of the minimum requirements, but the minimum is the bare minimum needed to run the software at all. Most programs can run in a relatively small amount of RAM by using the hard disc for temporary storage space. This usually works quite well, but gives noticeably slower results than when using RAM as the temporary data store. With complex graphics oriented programs the operating speed can be painfully slow unless the PC is equipped with large amounts of RAM. There will probably be a recommended minimum system to run the software, a typical system, or something of this type. I tend to regard the amount of RAM recommended for a typical system as the minimum that will really be usable in practice.

For most software at present, 32 megabytes of RAM is sufficient provided the operating system is Windows 95, 98, or ME. This is the absolute minimum though, and upwards of 64 megabytes is preferable. The story is very different with Windows XP, where 128 megabytes represents a realistic minimum. At least 256 megabytes of memory is preferable. Some applications require much larger amounts of memory, and programs that handle photographic images or other large bitmaps are particularly demanding in this respect. Programs that handle video also require large amounts of memory, and probably hard disc space as well.

As an example, when handling large bitmap images in PhotoShop it is recommended that the amount of RAM in the PC should be at least double the size of the bitmap. In order to handle scanned bitmaps of around 25 to 30 megabytes at least 60 megabytes of RAM would therefore be required. Fitting the PC with 64 megabytes of RAM should therefore give workable results, but 96 or 128 megabytes would probably give noticeably quicker and smoother running. With Windows XP you would probably have to add at least 96 megabytes to these figures.

Bear in mind that large amounts of RAM can be needed in order to run several programs at once. In theory you do not need (say) 48 megabytes of RAM to multitask with two programs that require 16 and 32 megabytes of RAM. Somewhat less than 48 megabytes should suffice, because you are only running one copy of the operating system, and the two programs will share some resources. Practical experience would suggest that 48 megabytes would actually represent a realistic minimum in this situation.

Although memory has been very expensive in the past, it is currently quite cheap and putting large amounts of RAM into a PC is likely to be well worth the modest cost involved. Memory is like you know what and hard disc space: you can never have too much of it. You do not hear people claiming that they have wasted money putting too much memory in their computers, but you do hear people expressing regret for not having specified more RAM when buying their PC.

SIMMs

Memory in the form of individual chips was replaced by SIMMs (single in-line memory modules). A memory module of this type is a small printed circuit board, which is fitted with miniature DRAM chips of the surface-mount variety. A 30-pin SIMM is shown in Figure 7.2 where it is the smaller of the two memory modules.. This board plugs into a socket on the motherboard, and this set-up is like a sort of miniature version of the standard expansion slot system.

80386 and 80486 based PCs mostly use 30-pin SIMMs. These modules are available with normal eight-bit wide memory, and nine-bit wide memory. It is the nine-bit variety that is needed for most 80386 and 80486 PCs. The additional bit, incidentally, is used for a method of error checking known as parity checking. These modules come in 256k, 1 megabyte, and 4 megabyte varieties, reflecting the type of DRAM chip they use.

These modules are also available in a variety of speed ratings, again reflecting the type of DRAM chip they utilize. From the early days of memory chips to the latest memory modules there has always been RAM of the same general type but with various speed ratings. Consequently, when buying RAM you have to make sure that you obtain the right type and memory of adequate speed rating. With 80386 based PCs the modules normally have to be used in pairs or even in sets of four, but some 80486s can use odd numbers of these modules. There may also be restrictions on using SIMMs of different sizes. In general, later PCs are more accommodating, but it is still advisable to check for memory restrictions before buying any memory modules.

Bigger and better

30-pin SIMMs are now long obsolete, and have not been used in new computers for many years. They were been superseded by 72-pin SIMMs, which provide capacities of more than 4 megabytes per module. 72-pin SIMMs are available in 4, 8, 16, 32, and 64 megabyte versions.

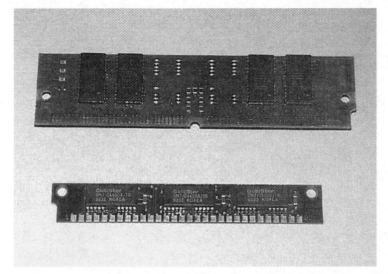

Fig.7.2 A 72-pin SIMM (top) and a 30-pin type (bottom)

Like the 30-pin variety they are available with or without the parity bit. The larger memory module in Figure 7.2 is a 72-pin SIMM. Unlike the 30-pin SIMMs, it is the modules that lack the parity bit that are normally used in PCs. Some motherboards can actually accommodate either type, but in practice the non-parity type are used because they are significantly cheaper.

Two types of memory are available in 72-pin SIMM form. The original modules of this type were fitted with fast page memory (FPM), and this type of memory is based on ordinary DRAM chips. Later 72-pin modules use an alternative form of memory called extended data output (EDO) RAM. This usually gives somewhat faster performance than fast page memory, although the improvement obtained is unlikely to be more than about 10 percent or so. 72-pin memory modules are now obsolete, but you may need to use them if you upgrade the memory of an old PC. Obviously care has to be taken to obtain the right type.

If in doubt, it is a matter of checking the manual for the computer or the motherboard to determine which type or types of memory module are supported. The BIOS usually displays details of the installed memory during the start-up procedure, and programs such as Sisoft's Sandra will supply this information.

Fig.7.3 A 168-pin DIMM (dual in-line memory module)

SIMMs were superseded by DIMMs (dual in-line memory modules). These look like outsize SIMMs (Figure 7.3), and have 168 terminals. SIMMs operate from a 5 volt supply, but the DIMMs used in PCs operate from 3.3 volts (like the input/output terminals of a Pentium processor of the same period). However, 5 volt DIMMs are produced. Fast page and EDO DIMMs are available, but it is SDRAM (synchronous dynamic random access memory) DIMMs that are normally used in PCs. Many PC motherboards will actually operate with fast page and EDO DIMMs, but as these are more difficult to obtain, slower, and usually more expensive than SDRAM, there would seem to be no point in using them. Buffered and unbuffered SDRAM DIMMs are available, but it is the unbuffered variety that is normally required for use in PCs.

SDRAM DIMMs are available with capacities of 16, 32, 64, and 128 megabytes, but many of the early Pentium motherboards that accept this type of memory are incompatible with the larger sizes. In fact some of the first boards to accept DIMMs will only take the 16-megabyte type.

SDRAM is available in various speeds. For ordinary Socket 7 and Pentium II computers the 12ns variety is sufficient, but the faster 10ns DIMMs are also suitable. PCs that use faster motherboards which operate at 100MHz, such as 350MHz and faster Pentium II systems, require 10ns SDRAM.

The modules that use this memory are usually referred to as "PC100" DIMMs in advertisements. Although this type of memory has not been used in new PCs for some time, it is quite likely that this is the type that will be needed if an old PC is upgraded.

Many older motherboards only have sockets for DIMMs, but there are plenty of boards that can take DIMMs or SIMMs. A typical Socket 7 motherboard of this type has sockets for two DIMMs and four 72-pin SIMMs. Some PC upgraders get into difficulty because they assume that it is possible to utilize all six sockets. Using a mixture of DIMMs and SIMMs is not a good idea, and is strictly prohibited with many motherboards. Even where the manufacturer of the motherboard does not ban this practice, I would certainly advise against it. The problem in using a mixture of the two memory types seems to stem from the fact that they operate at different supply voltages rather than any differences in their timing.

Whatever the cause, I have never managed to get satisfactory results when using a mixture of these two types of memory module. If you read the "fine print" in the motherboard's manual you will almost certainly discover that one bank of SIMM sockets is connected to use the same address space as the DIMM sockets. Regardless of any other considerations, it is not possible to use both of these sets of sockets, as there would be a hardware conflict.

Modern memory

As processor speeds have increased it has been necessary for new types of memory to be produced in an attempt to keep pace. 168-pin DIMMs have been used in new PCs until quite recently, but in a faster version. These are known as PC133 DIMMs, and they look much the same as the slower versions. This type of memory is not quite obsolete, but it is now little used in new PCs. The most popular form of memory for recent PCs is the DDR (double data rate) variety.

The "double" part of the name refers to the fact that the memory operates at twice the clock frequency of the motherboard. Clock frequencies of 200 megahertz and 266 megahertz are used with the original versions of DDR memory, and these respectively use motherboard bus frequencies of 100 and 133 megahertz. I think it is fair to say that DDR memory did not give the sort of speed increase that many had hoped for, but it did give a significant improvement. When the price of DDR memory became comparable to the PC100 and PC133 varieties it was inevitable that it would gradually take over.

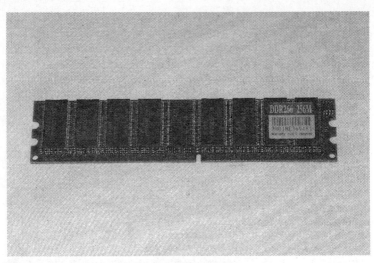

Fig.7.4 This is a 184-pin PC2100 DDR DIMM

DDR memory is sold in the form of 184-pin DIMMs (Figure 7.4). From the physical point of view a DDR DIMM is essentially just a slightly scaled-up version of the 168-pin components. The 200 and 233 megahertz DDR modules are sometimes sold as such, but they are more usually called PC1600 and PC2100 modules respectively. The number in each case refers to the bandwidth in megabits per second. The PC1600 modules seem to be relatively difficult to obtain these days, but the faster PC2100 type can be used instead. Things move on, and faster (PC2700 and PC3200) DDR modules are now starting to appear. The PC2700 modules are for use at 333 megahertz and the PC3200 modules are for operation at 400 megahertz. Of course, these are the operating frequencies for the memory modules, and in standard DDR fashion the motherboards operate at half these frequencies.

With DDR memory, and possibly with other types, you may encounter a rating such as "CL3" or "CL2.5". This refers to a memory timing parameter in the BIOS Setup program, where it is usually called something like CAS Latency. A low figure here gives higher performance, but there is no guarantee that "bog standard" memory modules will work reliably with so-called "aggressive" memory timing. If you wish to push the system to its limits it is essential to obtain modules that are guaranteed to operate with a low CAS Latency setting.

RIMMs

There is an alternative form of high-speed memory in the form of RIMMs (Figure 7.5), which are memory modules from Rambus Inc. Each Rambus DRAM (RDRAM) can operate at up to 800 megahertz over a 16-bit wide channel. RIMMs are often called PC800 modules, with the 800 being derived from the maximum operating frequency. Note that a PC1600 DDR module is not twice as fast as a PC800 RIMM. The 1600 refers to the bit rate, whereas the figure of 800 is the frequency for a 16-bit bus. The PC800 modules should be something like eight times faster than the PC1600 variety, but the difference in overall performance is, of course, very much less than this. The latest RIMMs (PC1066) operate at up to 1066 megahertz.

Fig.7.5 A Rambus memory module (RIMM)

RDRAM memory is certainly very fast, and it was used with many early Pentium 4 based systems. Its drawback was the very high price tag which added substantially to the cost of the complete computer system. Although RIMM prices have come down over the years, this type of memory remains relatively expensive. This has led to the widespread use of PC133 and DDR memory with Pentium 4 systems. A memory upgrade will be relatively expensive if you have a PC that uses RIMMs.

The types of memory detailed previously are the ones that have been in common use over the past few years. It is only fair to point out that there are variations such as 200-pin SODIMS and that some PC manufacturers have gone their own way with so-called proprietary memory. The memory chips on these modules are much the same as those on equivalent types of standard memory, but the modules are physically different to the standard types. Of course, a memory module will only work in your PC if it has the right kind of memory chip and it is physically compatible with the memory sockets.

The right memory

When purchasing memory for a modern PC it is clearly imperative to proceed carefully, as it would be very easy to buy the wrong type. I think it is fair to say that determining the type of memory needed is usually more difficult than actually fitting the new memory. There is really no alternative to reading the relevant section of the computer's manual, or the manual for the motherboard if that is what was supplied with the PC, to discover what type or types of memory module are usable.

Do not use more than one type of memory. If the PC already has two fast page SIMMs, use two more fast page SIMMs to increase its memory and not a couple of EDO SIMMs. If a motherboard has sockets for (say) four PC133 and two PC2100 memory modules, it is highly unlikely that a mixture of the two types can be used. With very few exceptions, SIMMs must be used in pairs in Pentium PCs, but DIMMs can be used in multiples of one.

It will sometimes be necessary to remove one or more of the existing memory modules in order to increase the memory capacity of the computer. With only a few memory sockets on the motherboard, you can not go on increasing the amount of memory fitted by simply adding more and more memory modules. It therefore pays to think ahead and fit large memory modules, rather than working your way up to high capacity modules, wasting a lot of smaller ones along the way.

Do not jump to conclusions about the maximum memory capability of your PC. Recently I was asked for help by someone with a PC that had 512 megabytes of DDR memory in the form of a single memory module. This left one free memory socket, and the owner of the PC wished to add an extra 256 megabytes via this socket. Although this seemed to be entirely reasonable, a quick inspection of the manual for the motherboard revealed that the maximum memory limit of 512 megabytes had already been reached. Although the PC had a free memory module it was of no practical value. The maximum memory capacity of many older PCs is quite low when compared to the amounts of memory often fitted into modern PCs. A limit of 256 megabytes or less is quite common.

In a similar vein, do not assume that a motherboard is compatible with any memory module that is physically compatible with its memory sockets. As explained previously, the same sockets have been used with different memory types and (or) speeds. Also, the higher capacity modules are sometimes incompatible with certain motherboards. This is usually because the higher capacity modules simply did not exist when these motherboards were designed. The sockets used for memory modules have minor variations that prevent most unsuitable modules from being fitted, but there are some exceptions. Before buying extra memory it is essential that it fully compatible with your PC, and that the PC can actually take additional memory.

If you are not sure of the way in which the memory of you PC is made up, one solution is to simply look inside to see which memory sockets are occupied. This may not be necessary, because the BIOS start-up routine usually produces a screen that gives this sort of information about the system hardware. The BIOS will probably report the amount of memory in each bank of sockets, and the exact type of RAM fitted.

Unfortunately, system testing and analysing programs are not usually very forthcoming with precise information about the memory. The amount of physical memory present will be reported, but it is unlikely that any further information will be given. The BIOS is usually the best source of information. Also look through the information provided with the PC when you bought it. This should include a detailed specification that gives full details of the memory.

It is not possible to work out the best way of expanding the computer's memory unless you know what memory is already fitted. You really need to look at all the possible upgrade options, and cost them. Older types of memory tend to be more expensive than newer types, presumably because the older types of memory module no longer sell in large quantities. If your PC will take a more up-to-date form of memory than the type currently fitted, it might actually be cheaper to dump the original memory and start "from scratch". Apart from being cheaper, changing to a more modern form of memory will probably provide a modest increase in performance. Where appropriate, it is certainly worth considering this option.

Fitting memories

Fitting numerous RAM chips into their sockets is a tedious task, and it is easy to accidentally buckle one of the pins or fit a chip around the wrong way. Memory modules were produced in an attempt to make fitting and removing memory much easier, and something that practically anyone could undertake. Fitting DIMMs is certainly very easy, and it is impossible to fit them the wrong way round because the circuit board has a polarising "key". This is just an off-centre notch cut in the circuit board that matches a bar in the DIMM socket (see Figure 7.6). In fact there are two of these

Fig.7.6 A DIMM has a polarising key that matches a bar in the socket

keys (Figure 7.7), and they are apparently in slightly different positions depending on the supply voltage of the module and the type of RAM fitted. This should make it impossible to fit a DIMM of the wrong type.

Fig.7.7 There are actually two polarising keys in each DIMM

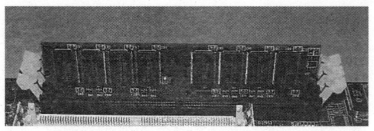

Fig.7.8 A DIMM fitted into its socket but not yet locked into place

When fitting a DIMM always look for the notch that is well off centre. This, plus the bar in the socket, makes it clear which way round the module must be fitted. The module simply drops into place vertically and as it is pressed down into position the plastic lever at each end of the socket should start to close up. Pressing both levers into the vertical position should securely lock the module in place. Of course, the two levers must be set fully downwards and outwards before you start to insert the module.

Do not try to fit these modules by simply pressing hard until they click into place. They will probably fit into place correctly using this method, but it risks damaging the motherboard. Operating the levers enables modules to be fully inserted into their sockets without having to exert much force on the modules and motherboard. Figures 7.8 and 7.9 respectively show a DIMM before and after it has been locked into place. To remove a DIMM, simply press the two levers outwards as far as they will go. This should unlock the memory module so that it can be lifted free of the socket.

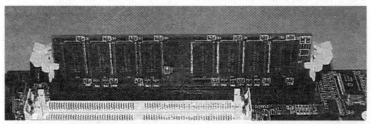

Fig.7.9 Here the DIMM has been fully pushed down into the socket and locked into place. The locking levers have gone right into the cutouts in the module

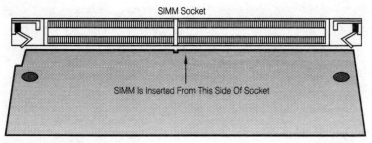

Fig.7.10 A SIMM is fitted in the socket at an angle and then raised to a vertical position

Fitting SIMMs

In my opinion at any rate, SIMMs are slightly more awkward to fit. Although in theory it is impossible to fit a 72-pin SIMM the wrong way round, in practice it does happen occasionally. This seems to be due to the rather flimsy and slightly too basic SIMM holders used on some motherboards. There is the usual polarising notch in the module and matching bar in the socket, but they are small and only very slightly off-centre. Also, there is one corner of the circuit board missing. The old 30 pin SIMMs seem to be somewhat easier to deal with. They have the missing corner, but not the notch incidentally. These days it is only the 72-pin type that you are likely to encounter.

The method of fitting both types is exactly the same. When fitting SIMMs, orient the motherboard so that the sides of the sockets having the metal clips are facing towards you, and the plain sides are facing away from you (Figure 7.10). Take the first SIMM and fit it into the first socket, which is the one that is furthest away from you, but it must be leaning toward you at about 45 degrees and not fully vertical. Once it is right down into the socket it should lock into place properly if it is raised to the vertical position.

If it refuses to fit into position properly it is almost certainly the wrong way round. If you turn it through 180 degrees and try again it should fit into place correctly. You can then move on to the next socket, and fit the next SIMM in the same way. Figures 7.11 and 7.12 respectively show a SIMM before and after it is locked into position.

Because SIMMs have to be inserted into their sockets at an angle, and the sockets are tightly grouped on the motherboard, you normally have to fit them in the right order. Otherwise you put in one SIMM which then

Fig.7.11 A SIMM before it has been locked in place

blocks access to the socket for one of the others. You therefore have to work your way along the sockets in a methodical fashion. To remove a SIMM, pull the metal clips at each end of the socket outwards. The SIMM should then slump forwards at about 45 degrees, after which it is easily lifted clear of the holder. SIMMs have to be removed in the opposite order to the one in which they were fitted.

Fig.7.12 Here the SIMM has been raised to a vertical position and it has locked into place successfully

*Fig.7.13 Memory modules should be supplied in some form of
anti-static packing*

Dummy RIMMs

When dealing with RIMMs you might find that one memory socket is
fitted with the genuine article while the other is fitted with a sort of dummy
RIMM. Apparently the dummy memory module has voltage regulators
that are needed to ensure that the real module is supplied with the correct
voltages. The dummy module is not needed if a second (genuine) RIMM
is added, and the new memory module is fitted in place of the dummy.
The manual for the PC or the motherboard should explain when the
dummy module is and is not required. If a dummy module does have to
be removed, store it safely in case it is required at some time in the
future.

Static

Remember that memory modules are vulnerable to damage by static
charges, and can be "zapped" by charges that are too small to produce
any noticeable sparks and "cracking" sounds. Apart from processors,

memory modules are probably the components that are most vulnerable to static damage. They are normally supplied in some form of anti-static packing, which is most usually in the form of a bag made from conductive plastic (Figure 7.13). Always leave memory modules or any other static-sensitive components in the protective packing until it is time to fit them into the computer. Observe all the usual anti-static precautions when dealing with memory modules. Some memory modules are quite expensive, so be especially careful with any that fall into this category.

Points to remember

Memory is no longer added to PCs in the form of individual memory chips. Instead, all current PC memory is in the form of modules that are much quicker and easier to fit.

The hardest part of a memory upgrade is determining the correct type of memory to use. Start by ascertaining the amount and type of memory already fitted to the PC and the number of free memory sockets. Then check the maximum amount of memory that can be used and the maximum size per module. You are then in a position to work out the upgrade possibilities.

Do not use memory modules that have an inadequate speed rating. If you fit memory modules that are too slow it is unlikely that the PC will even start the POST (power on self test), and they will certainly not work reliably at the higher speed.

Bear in mind that SIMMs normally operate in pairs, so adding one SIMM is not usually an option. DIMMs are more accommodating and using odd numbers of them is usually permissible.

With few exceptions, it is not possible to mix the type of memory used in a PC. It is normally acceptable to use a fast memory module if a slower module is unobtainable or relatively expensive, provided both modules are otherwise of the same basic type. Any memory mixing that goes beyond this is almost certainly doomed to fail.

Not all PCs use standard memory modules. There will be a relatively few sources of supply if your PC uses proprietary memory modules. In the case of an old PC it might not be possible to obtain suitable modules at all.

A DIMM is fitted by pressing it down into the holder and then raising the two locking levers. A SIMM is placed into a socket at an angle and then raised to a vertical position. In both cases the module must be fitted into the socket the right way round.

Memory modules are vulnerable to static charges, so observe the standard anti-static handling precautions when dealing with them.

Major
upgrades

Major upgrade?

One reason for the success of PCs is undoubtedly their modular construction, which makes it easy to add new features such as CD writers, or to upgrade existing facilities. If your video card is not up to the latest 3-D games, you can simply remove it and fit the latest high-speed 3-D video card instead. If the hard disc drive no longer has sufficient capacity for the latest mega-powerful software suites, it can be replaced with a higher capacity drive that will provide you with all the storage space you could possibly want.

In theory, you can go on upgrading a PC for ever, keeping it fully up-to-date with all the latest "bells and whistles". In practice there is a limit to the length of time that you can continue with this form of gradual upgrading. Eventually the basic PC becomes so out of date that it can no longer accommodate the latest PC peripherals, etc. This obsolescence occurs due to the changes in the PC interfaces, and there can also be problems with the BIOS when trying to use the latest gadgets in an old PC.

Does this mean that a PC can not go on indefinitely? Not really, it just means that after a number of years a major upgrade will be required in order to keep the computer up to date. As explained previously, upgrading the processor often involves upgrading the motherboard and memory as well, so it is not only "golden oldie" PCs that are candidates for a major upgrade. When considering any substantial upgrade you first need to ask yourself whether or not it is worth upgrading the computer at all. If the answer is yes, you then have to work out exactly what you are going to replace, and what you are going to replace it with.

Deciding whether or not a computer is worth upgrading is to some extent a subjective matter. There is relatively little to be gained in the case of a recent computer that needs a new motherboard to accommodate a more modern processor. Unless you genuinely need more speed it would be a pointless and costly exercise. On the other hand, a major upgrade is more cost effective than buying a new PC in situations where more speed is essential.

If you have a computer based on an early to middle period Pentium grade processor that has been kept up to date with multimedia add-ons, a high-capacity hard disc drive, etc., you probably have an ideal candidate for a major upgrade. The PC has plenty of modern components that will work well in a "new" computer. By replacing the motherboard, processor, and memory you are getting rid of the oldest and slowest components in the PC, and the gain in performance should be substantial.

At the other extreme, a PC of similar vintage that is still in its original form is unlikely to be worth upgrading. It would actually be possible to bring a computer of this type up to a modern specification, but so much would have to be changed and added that very little of the original PC would remain in the upgraded computer.

In all probability, at best only the floppy drive, case and power supply unit would be carried through to the "new" computer. In a worst case scenario only the floppy drive would be of use, with the AT case and power supply having to be upgraded to modern ATX types. It might also be possible to use the keyboard, mouse, and monitor with the upgraded machine, but the input devices are likely to be well worn, and the monitor might not do justice to a modern PC.

People sometimes ask me for advice about upgrading 80486 PCs, or even earlier computers. With computers of this vintage it is probably not worthwhile attempting to give them a major upgrade. My advice is to continue using computers such as these with their original software rather than trying to get them to run modern programs. Adding more memory and other easy fixes will not enable a ten year old PC to run modern software. The only viable alternative is to build a new PC "from scratch" using any modern components that can be salvaged from the old PC. Unfortunately, in most cases there will be little or nothing that can be usefully moved on into the new computer.

Ringing the changes

If you have a PC that is worthy of a major upgrade, just what has to be changed in order to bring it up to a modern specification? In an ideal world you would simply compare the current specification of the PC with the specification of the PC that you would like. You would then replace anything in the current machine that fell short of your requirements. In the real world this could well cost very much more than you are prepared to spend on the project. If financial restrictions dictate the implementation of a minimal upgrade, it will still be necessary to replace much of the existing PC.

The obvious way of providing a PC with an increase in speed is to upgrade the processor. As explained previously, it is not possible to simply remove an early Pentium processor and replace it with the latest multi gigahertz wonder chip. Older processors are physically and electrically incompatible with modern Pentium devices. It is often possible to produce a worthwhile improvement by upgrading the processor to one of a moderately higher specification, but anything beyond that is impractical. Unfortunately, with an old PC the upgrade processor is likely to be well and truly obsolete and it might not be possible to obtain one.

Being realistic about matters, upgrading from an early or middle period Pentium processor to a modern type will involve much more than simply swapping the processor and re-configuring the motherboard. There are two main problems when attempting a Pentium-to-Pentium upgrade. One of these is simply the physical and electrical difference between early and modern Pentium processors. The 60 and 66MHz Pentium processors require motherboards fitted with a socket known as "Socket 4", and these were followed by Pentiums requiring Socket 7-equipped motherboards. Next there were Pentium II processors with their slot technology and the Slot 1 connector. These were followed by two versions of Socket 370 and then the sockets that are in use today.

Processor compatibility

The other potential problem is that the motherboard of your computer may not support faster Pentium processors even if it has the right type of socket. If these faster processors were not available at the time the computer was built, it would be unreasonable to expect the motherboard to support them. The manual for the motherboard should provide details of the processors that are supported, together with details of how to reconfigure the board for each of these chips.

As explained previously, the motherboard might be able to accommodate faster processors with the aid of a BIOS upgrade. Where this is possible it certainly represents the best approach, but in general it only applies to PCs that are no more than about two years old. Even with a PC that is one or two years old there is no guarantee of an easy processor upgrade path.

Upgrading to a more modern motherboard often brings a small but worthwhile improvement in speed, together with other advantages such as a more modern BIOS and the ability to take more and faster memory. A change in motherboard can also provide more modern interfaces such as the USB (universal serial bus) and the AGP (advanced graphics port) varieties. In the case of a recent computer the upgrade might provide USB 2.0 ports in place of USB 1.1 types, together with a faster version of the AGP interface. Additional time and effort put into a motherboard upgrade is likely to be well rewarded.

Case problems

If the current motherboard can not accommodate modern processors, the obvious solution is to replace the motherboard as well. A low-cost motherboard plus a budget processor need not cost very much, and is likely to give far higher performance than something like an old 233 or 300 megahertz Pentium II. Apart from the increased speed of the new processor, the support chips on the motherboard are likely to be far superior to those on the old board.

Also, the new motherboard will probably have useful features such as USB 2.0 ports, and perhaps a LAN (local area network) adapter or RAID controller as well. However, before proceeding it is essential to ascertain how much of the existing PC is compatible with the proposed new motherboard. In most cases it will be necessary to change more than just the processor and motherboard.

The case and power supply are a likely cause of problems. While the vast majority of recent PCs and probably all new ones use ATX cases and power supplies, in the past the AT case and power supply was very popular. Consequently, there is a good chance that the PC you wish to upgrade will have an AT case and power supply. There is no problem if you can find an AT motherboard that matches your requirements, but few if any AT motherboards are currently produced.

You may be able to find one that offers a reasonable upgrade from your PC's current specification, but your options (if any) will be very limited. Although many AT motherboards can be used with ATX cases and power supplies, there is no compatibility in the opposite direction. If you switch to an ATX motherboard, the case and power supply must also be changed.

It is tempting to say that it is not worthwhile trying a large-scale upgrade of an AT style PC, but some ATX cases and power supplies are now available at surprisingly low prices. Where the existing PC has a number of good modern components it might be worth rebuilding it into a new case. However, this is really building a new PC using some components from the old computer and it goes beyond what would normally be regarded as an upgrade. Consult BP534 (Easy PC Construction) for details of building your own PC.

If you are not sure which type of case and power supply is fitted to your PC it is not difficult to find out. The most reliable way to tell is to open up the case and look at the power supply. With luck this will be labelled "AT" or "ATX". If not, look at the power connectors on the motherboard. An ATX power supply has only one motherboard power connector whereas an AT type has two (refer back to Figures 4.2 and 4.3). Note that the ATX boards used in many Pentium 4 computers have two additional power connectors (refer back to Figure 4.4). The power supply is an ATX type if these are present, even if they are not needed by the motherboard.

Lost memory

Changing the motherboard is likely to enforce the fitting of new memory. Early PCs had their memory in the form of memory chips fitted directly on the motherboard. 80386 and 80486 PCs mostly had their memory in the form of 30-pin SIMMs (single in-line memory modules). Early Pentium motherboards used 72-pin SIMMs and these were replaced with 168-pin DIMMs (dual in-line memory modules) in later Pentium PCs. These were later replaced by 184-pin DIMMs. There is a chapter of this book that covers memory, so it is not something that will be considered in detail here.

With the current low price of memory it would probably be advisable to scrap the existing memory and upgrade to more modern memory modules that will enable the computer to reach its full potential. It is unlikely that the existing memory will be compatible with the new motherboard anyway. It is even more unlikely that the existing memory would enable the new board to reach its full potential.

I would certainly take the opportunity to increase the amount of memory. The upgraded computer would then have no difficulty in running modern operating systems and applications software. Bear in mind that a lack of memory can seriously slow down many applications programs. There is little point in spending money on a large upgrade if the final product will be held back by a lack of memory.

Video card

The video adapter is another possible problem area when undertaking a major upgrade. If the existing video card is a PCI type there should be no difficulty in using it in one of the PCI expansion slots of the new motherboard. Similarly, there should be no difficulty in using an AGP video card on a new motherboard, even if it is an early and relatively slow example of an AGP card. If the existing video card requires some other form of expansion slot such as a VESA or ISA type there is no chance of using it with a modern motherboard. It might be still be possible to find a motherboard that has an ISA expansion slot, and the video card might work in this slot. It would severely limit the speed of the PC though, and could certainly not be recommended.

The best video cards of a few years ago are quite slow when compared to most of the cheaper boards that are available today. Discarding the old video adapter and replacing it with an inexpensive modern type is likely to give a large increase in performance. If you are heavily into any form of graphics application it would almost certainly be worthwhile upgrading to one of the modern high-speed video cards. These can greatly increase the operating speed of many heavyweight graphics applications.

Bear in mind that many modern motherboards have built-in graphics adapters. It would be unrealistic to expect one of these to give the same level of 3-D performance as an expensive AGP graphics card, but they are more than adequate for 2-D applications. They have at least some 3-D capability, and are adequate unless you are heavily into 3-D gaming. Note that some of the graphics adapters use part of the system memory. Therefore, with (say) 32 megabytes of video memory there is 32 megabytes less for the operating system and applications programs to use. With the current low cost of memory this is not a major drawback, and fitting 256 megabytes of memory would not "break the bank".

Hard choices

The hard disc drive tends to be one of the weakest points of older PCs. Although the speed of data transfers tends to be quite slow by current standards, the level of performance obtained is usually just about adequate for modern software. It is the amount of storage capacity available that is the main problem. Older PCs generally have hard disc capacities of around two gigabytes, whereas modern PCs usually have hard discs with about 10 to 60 times this capacity. For most purposes there is probably considerable "overkill" in the largest of today's hard drives, but an old drive having a capacity few gigabytes is rather limiting.

If you are upgrading a PC that still has its original hard disc drive, and you will need to run a modern operating system such as Windows ME or XP on the upgraded machine, a new hard drive may well be essential. Apart from its slow speed and limited capacity, there has to be a question mark over the reliability of any hard disc drive that is more than about five years old. Unless you are very unlucky, a new hard disc drive should operate reliably and keep your data safe for many years to come.

Of course, because hard disc drives tend to fill up; this is an aspect of a PC that is often upgraded after a few years. The hard disc often has a more modern version of the IDE interface than the motherboard, and upgrading the motherboard will enable the hard disc to reach its full potential. It is a PC that has received a hard disc upgrade, plus perhaps other drives such as a DVD and (or) CDR/W type, that is the best candidate for a major upgrade. Replace the processor, motherboard, and memory with new units, buying a motherboard with integrated sound and graphics if necessary, and you will have a PC with a modern specification for a relatively modest outlay. You are virtually building a new PC if you have to buy disc drives as well, and starting from scratch is probably the better option.

Heatsink

Last, but by no means least, bear in mind that all modern Pentium class processors require a heatsink and fan in order to ensure that there is no danger of the processor overheating. Even if the existing processor is equipped with a heatsink and (or) cooling fan, this is unlikely to be of any use with the new processor. Some Pentium class processors require larger heatsinks and more efficient fans than others, and when ordering the processor it is important to ensure that you obtain an adequate cooling system for it.

It is advisable to buy the heatsink and fan at the same time as you buy the processor. Any reputable PC component supplier should know exactly what is and is not suitable for each processor that they sell, and should be able to supply you with a suitable heatsink and fan. As pointed out in a previous chapter, most processors are available complete with a heatsink and fan in the retail boxed versions. Buying one of these ensures that the processor will be equipped with an adequate cooling system, and this is certainly the method I recommend.

It is perhaps worth mentioning that modern motherboards almost invariably lack ISA expansion slots. While it might be just possible to track down a board that has one or two ISA slots, it is more likely that nothing suitable will be found. This means that any ISA expansion cards can not be used in the upgraded PC. The situation is the same if you opt for a completely new PC, and it is just a fact of PC life that ISA expansion cards are getting past their "use by dates". Unfortunately, it can be expensive to replace specialist ISA cards with modern PCI equivalents. An ISA audio card is less of a problem, since most motherboards now have the audio circuits built in, and you will probably not wish to use the old audio card anyway.

It has to be admitted that changing the processor, motherboard, and memory of a PC means replacing a high percentage of the computer. While this is certainly not going to be cheap, when you look at the advantages gained it could be regarded as "cheap at the price." In days gone by people often used to spend quite large sums of money in order to obtain an increase in speed of about 30 to 50 percent. By upgrading an old Pentium PC using one of the current budget processors you are likely to gain something like a five or even tenfold increase in speed. A computer that could previously not operate satisfactorily with modern software, if it could run it at all, will be transformed into one that will work well with practically any current software title.

Risks

Many PC users are understandably rather reluctant to attempt an upgrade that involves changing the motherboard. In truth, it is not really that difficult, but things can go wrong. If you buy a new computer or pay someone to perform a major upgrade for you, presumably you will be covered by some form of guarantee, and the risk will be minimal. When performing an upgrade yourself you are covered to some extent by the guarantees for the new components that are being added. On the other hand, if you make a mess of things and damage one or more of the components, these guarantees will be of no help and you have to take responsibility for this type of thing yourself.

Looking at things realistically, the chances of damaging one of the components are quite small provided you take the necessary anti-static handling precautions and do not go at things like the proverbial " bull in a china shop". PC components are not ultra-delicate, but if you start forcing things into place you may well seriously damage one or more of the parts. The cost of repairing PC components tends to be greater than they are worth, so if something should become damaged it will probably be a write-off. However, provided you proceed carefully and patiently it is highly unlikely that any of the components will come to grief.

It is only fair to point out that even if you get everything just right there is still an outside chance that the finished computer will fail to work absolutely perfectly. PCs are notorious for obscure incompatibility problems, and although it is fair to say that problems of this type are quite rare, they remain a very real possibility. Most hardware incompatibility problems are actually caused by problems with the driver software rather than any real problems with the hardware. The majority of problems are minor niggles and not major failures. In due course the hardware manufacturers usually make improved drivers available on their web sites.

ATX standard?

Before starting a major upgrade it is as well to check that the PC is built from standard components. In particular, some of the larger PC manufacturers do not always use standard ATX power supplies and motherboards. If your PC is a non-standard type it could be impossible to upgrade it unless the case and power supply are also replaced. Some

Fig.8.1 Mini tower cases are neat but may not take all motherboards

Fig.8.2 This ATX motherboard is very small and will fit almost any case

manufacturers have their own forms of memory module, but this will not be of importance if the memory is being replaced.

Only proceed with an upgrade if you are sure that your PC is one of the standard types or you are prepared to replace the case and power supply with standard ATX types. As pointed out previously, ATX motherboards are incompatible with AT cases and power supplies, so the situation is the same if the PC is an AT type. You need to choose the motherboard carefully if the case is one of the very small ATX towers (Figure 8.1), or any other very compact case. Many of these will only take the so-called "micro" format ATX boards (Figure 8.2), which are much more compact than the standard variety.

Even if the case has sufficient space for a full-size motherboard, in practice it might not be usable in the case. Once the board is in place the drives might obscure the memory modules, or there could be insufficient space for the processor's heatsink and fan due to the power supply unit getting in the way. With small ATX cases it is safer to opt for one of the smaller motherboards.

Decisions, decisions

Once you have definitely decided to upgrade an old PC and have chosen the parts to be replaced, the next step is to select the new processor. A big advantage of replacing the motherboard is that it removes any restrictions on the choice of processor. Apart from any restrictions imposed by your budget, any current processor can be used. It is probably not a good idea to opt for the latest high-speed wonder chip as these tend to cost many times more than budget processors. This increased cost is not usually reflected in a similarly large increase in performance.

Power consumption is also an issue if the power supply is not being upgraded as well. There is a risk of some of the faster processors requiring more power than the existing supply can provide. Actually, some of the slower processors also have quite high current consumptions, but in general they are safer options.

Another point to bear in mind is that some Pentium 4 motherboards require two additional power connectors, and these will probably not be present on the existing power supply. It is not difficult or expensive to upgrade the power supply to a modern 300 watt unit, and it might be better to do this rather than have restrictions on the choice of processor. Choose a processor and motherboard that have simple power requirements if you wish to avoid changing the power supply.

Before buying a new motherboard, make quite sure that it is suitable for the processor you have chosen. The same processor is sometimes available in two versions. The difference is that one is designed for a motherboard that operates at a higher bus speed, effectively making that version slightly faster. Most motherboards can accommodate both bus frequencies, but it is best not to assume that a board can handle both versions of the processor.

Be especially careful with motherboards that are being offered quite cheap. These "special offer" boards usually represent very good value for money, but are unlikely to have an up to the minute specification. Check the manufacturer's web site, which should give concise details about the compatibility of each motherboard. In general, it is better to use the version of the processor that runs at the higher bus frequency, even if this means using slightly more expensive memory. Opt for the slower versions if the budget is limited. The upgraded PC will still "fly" compared to the original.

It is often possible to download the instruction manuals for the motherboards in standard PDF format. Most motherboard manufacturers seem to have this facility. These files can be displayed using the free Acrobat Reader program which is available from www.adobe.com. In addition to specifying the compatible processors, the manual should list the accessories supplied with the board and explain how to install and set up the board. This enables you to check that it precisely meets your requirements, and that there is no aspect of installation that will prove awkward. I never buy a motherboard unless I have seen the manual first. It can avoid some nasty surprises and wasted money.

Memory type

Having obtained the new processor, a matching heatsink and fan, and a suitable motherboard, you can then move on to any other components that need to be upgraded. As pointed out previously, it will almost certainly be necessary to obtain new memory modules. It is a good idea to obtain the motherboard before deciding on the type of memory to use, or download the manual. The manual for the motherboard should make it clear which type or types of memory are supported. There is a chapter of this book that deals specifically with memory matters, and this material will not be repeated here. Consult the relevant chapter if you are unsure about the differences between the various types of memory that are available.

Nuts and bolts

Once all the parts for the upgrade have been obtained it is time to open up the PC and remove the old motherboard. Ideally you should find a reasonably large and uncluttered table to work on. PCs tend to have more than their fair share of sharp corners and bits of metal that protrude slightly, so protect the top of the table with plenty of newspaper or cloths. The manual for your computer should give details of how to remove the outer casing, but this usually just involves removing three or four screws at the rear of the case. With ATX tower cases the top and sides are separate pieces, and it will probably be necessary to remove both of them in order to remove the motherboard. With a desktop case it is the top and bottom panels that have to be removed.

The panels usually pull backwards and away once the screws at the rear of the case have been removed. With some older PCs the front fascia is also part of the removable outer casing, and with these the outer casing is removed by pulling it forwards and away from the main unit. Cases of this type sometimes have the retaining screws on the underside of the case rather than at the rear. As always with the cases of electronic equipment, it can require some careful investigation in order to find the way in.

Before the motherboard can be removed it must be disconnected from the power supply, loudspeaker, on/off LED, etc. The expansion cards must also be removed, and it might be necessary to remove the power supply as well. The old motherboard can sometimes be removed with the power supply in place, and it might also be possible to slide the new board into place. However, if it is going to be a tight squeeze it is better to remove the power supply. Flexing the new board and trying to slide it past small obstructions gives a good chance of damaging it. Remember that the expansion cards are static-sensitive. Where no suitable anti-static packing is available they can be temporarily stored on a piece of earthed metal foil.

Depending on the type of case involved and the number of drives fitted, it might be necessary to remove one or more of the disc drives in order to permit removal of the motherboard. If you are upgrading the hard disc drive you may wish to remove the old unit. However, if the case can accommodate both hard drives it may be as well to leave the old unit in place, and operate the computer with two hard drives. In the long term you will probably wish to phase out the old drive, but initially it can be useful to include it in the computer.

Having the two drives operating side-by-side makes it easy to copy files from the old drive to the new one. Where possible, leave the data cables connected to the drives. If the cables are found to seriously impede work on the computer they must be completely disconnected and removed. It is then advisable to make some simple sketches or notes so that there is no difficulty in reconnecting them correctly.

Stand-offs

You may find that removing the old motherboard simply requires five or six screws to be undone, and that the board will then lift clear of the chassis. With most boards though, there will only be one or two screws to remove. The board will still be held in place by a number of plastic stand-offs, but in most cases it can be slid sideways and then clear of the chassis. The plastic stand-offs will still be attached to the

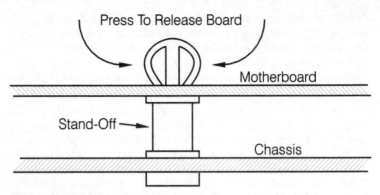

Fig.8.3 Some plastic stand-offs have to be squeezed to release the motherboard

motherboard, and must be removed so that they can be used with the new board. This requires the tops of the stand-offs to be squeezed inwards using a pair of pliers and then pulled free of the board (Figure 8.3). If the motherboard can not be slid free from the chassis, you may find that the stand-offs can be released on the underside of the case. They may fit into the chassis in much the same way that they fit into the motherboard, or they may be held in place with fixing screws.

The construction of some PC cases is such that it may not be possible to free the stand-offs from the case. You then have the task of removing the motherboard with the stand-offs still fixed to the case. This tends to be rather awkward because the motherboard is likely to be somewhat inaccessible, and there is also a tendency for one stand-off to slip back into place while you are freeing the next one. You may need a helper to hold the board and prevent it from slipping back into place while you unclip the stand-offs. Alternatively, you could try improvising some simple wedges to prevent the board from dropping back into place.

Pre-fabrication

It is advisable to do as much work as possible on the new motherboard before it is mounted in the case, because it is far more accessible when it is on the worktop. The amount of setting up required varies greatly from one board to another, and with some boards there is no need to bother with any configuration switches or jumpers. The correct clock frequency and processor supply voltages are set using the BIOS Setup program when the computer is run for the first time. In most cases the

BIOS will automatically detect the processor type and configure the board accordingly. You only need to intervene if the BIOS makes a mistake or you wish to use over-clocking techniques in an attempt to improve performance.

If the motherboard has hardware rather than software configuration, it will be necessary to set up either a DIP switch or a number of jumpers to produce the correct operating conditions for the processor. A DIP switch is simply a bank of small switches mounted on the motherboard, and there will normally be either eight or 10 switches. Jumpers are simply small pieces of metal that are normally encased in plastic, and they are used to bridge pins on the motherboard. The pins may be grouped together in a single bank, but they are usually scattered around the board in small groups. The motherboard's manual should give details of how to set up the DIP switches or jumpers to suit each of the supported processors. Refer back to chapter two if you need more information about DIP switches and jumpers.

It is not essential to understand what you are doing when you configure the motherboard, but it can often be helpful. It is necessary to set a suitable clock frequency for the processor, but this is not as straightforward as you might think. Although the processor will probably be operating at around one gigahertz or more, the motherboard and memory will be operating at a much lower frequency or frequencies.

The original Pentium motherboards operated with a maximum system frequency of just 66MHz, and (say) a 233MHz Pentium is accommodated by running the processor at 3.5 times the board's clock frequency. Modern motherboards run at bus frequencies of 100 megahertz or more, giving a huge discrepancy between the motherboard and processor frequencies. This discrepancy between the two frequencies is clearly undesirable as it reduces the increase in speed provided by a super-fast processor. The processor tends to spend much of its time waiting for everything else to catch up. This is the only way that the current technology can handle things though.

Clock speeds

Matters are further complicated by the fact that the quoted clock speed of some processors is slightly different to the frequency actually used, which is nothing new. The old Cyrix/IBM processors used these equivalent ratings, where the specified speed was that of an equivalent Pentium processor. The actual processor clock frequency was significantly lower. AMD uses the same system with their XP processors, where the figure in the type number indicates the chip's equivalent speed in terms of Pentium 4 clock rates. The XP2100+ for example, is slightly faster than a Pentium 4 running at 2100 megahertz (2.1 gigahertz). The actual clock frequency is much lower at 1.75 gigahertz.

Modern processors almost invariably have the multiplier locked. In other words, the motherboard detects the type of processor fitted and sets the appropriate clock multiplier. On the face of it you can not accidentally set the wrong clock rate, but it is not quite as simple as that. The multiplier is usually locked, but the operating frequency of the motherboard is not. If you set (say) a 100 megahertz bus frequency for a chip designed for operation with a 133 megahertz motherboard, the processor's clock frequency will be too low. It will probably work, but the whole computer will be operating much slower than it should.

A mistake in the other direction would set the processor's clock frequency much too high. This is unlikely to result in any damage, but it does give a slight risk of the processor overheating. There is little chance of the PC operating reliably, and it is very unlikely that it would even make it through the POST.

Processors do not all operate at the same supply potential, but these days the motherboard usually detects which processor is fitted and sets a suitable supply voltage. There might be jumpers or BIOS settings that permit the processor voltage or voltages to be altered, but these are usually included for those that wish to try over-clocking. The ability to alter the processor's multiplier or "fine tune" the motherboard's bus frequency is included for the same reason. Do not alter any of these settings unless you know exactly what you are doing. Also bear in mind that overclocking a processor invalidates its warranty.

The instruction manual for the motherboard should give details of any switches or jumpers. Where appropriate, give them the correct settings before fitting the motherboard in the case. It can be very difficult to alter jumper settings once the motherboard is installed, so make quite sure that any jumpers are set prior to installation. It is advisable to fit the microprocessor and memory modules before fitting the motherboard into the case. Fitting memory modules is dealt with in the chapter that covers memory matters, and this aspect of things will not be considered further here. Fitting the processor and heatsink was also covered earlier, and it will not be described again here.

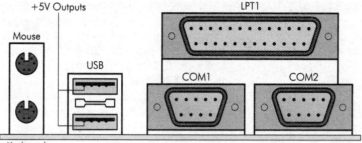

Fig.8.4 The basic port cluster for an ATX motherboard

Rebuilding

Once the board has been configured, and the processor and memory modules have been fitted, the motherboard can be mounted on the chassis. There should be no difficulty in using the old fixings with the new board, and fitting the new motherboard is generally easier than removing the old one. There is one potential problem in the form of the various connectors at the rear of the board. These are the connectors for the various ports (mouse, keyboard, USB, etc.), plus those for additional features such as the game port, and audio inputs and outputs. The main ports are well standardised, and there are conventions for the placement of additional connectors such as audio and video types.

The most common arrangement is the one shown in Figure 8.4 and in the photograph of Figure 8.5. These days many motherboards have integated audio, and use the same basic layout with the game and audio ports added to the right of the parallel ports. Some motherboards have LAN ports or additional USB ports, and these are usually added above the standard pair of USB connectors. Motherboards that have integrated video adapters often use a totally different layout.

There should be no problem when using a new motherboard that has nothing beyond the standard ports, or no more ports that those present on the original motherboard. The situation is different when the new motherboard has more ports than the old one. There will be no access holes for these additional ports in the case. The holes might be present but covered with blanking plates. It is then just a matter of unscrewing or pressing out the blanking plates, as appropriate.

Fig.8.5 This PC only has the basic ATX ports. Most have more ports

One or two alternative plates for the ports (Figure 8.6) are sometimes included in the bits and pieces supplied with PCs, or a suitable one might be included with the motherboard. It is then just a matter of fitting the new plate before installing the motherboard. If all else fails it should be possible to remove the existing plate and not replace it with anything.

Fig.8.6 An alternative plate to suit some non-standard ATX boards

This is not a particularly neat solution, but it will give excellent access to the ports. It will permit dust to get into the PC, but modern cases are riddled with ventilation holes so the dust will get in anyway.

Power leads

With the motherboard installed, any drives that were removed to enable the change of motherboard should be reinstalled in the case, and any new drives should also be fitted at this stage. If the power supply was removed it must also be fitted back into place at this stage. It is advisable to connect the power lead for the motherboard before fitting the power supply back in place. An ATX power connector can only be fitted the right way around, but make sure that it is fully pushed down into place. Any secondary power connector for the motherboard should also be fitted at this stage.

The drives will either fit direct into the drive bays, or they will have to be fitted with guide-rails first. The original type of guide-rail is now long obsolete, but a few cases use an updated version. This has the drive clipped into place on one side using a metal or plastic rail while the other side is bolted into place in the normal fashion. This avoids having to get access to both sides of the drive in order to fit or remove one. An extra guide-rail will be needed if you are adding a drive, and one or two "spares" should have been supplied with your PC. Hard disc drives and CD-ROM drives are often supplied with a set of four fixing screws, but if not there will probably be some spares in the odds and ends supplied with the computer.

The next task is to fit the expansion cards, assuming that they are needed in the new PC. It is likely that one or more of the expansion cards used in the original PC will not be needed for the upgraded version. Modern motherboards have all the normal interfaces included on the board, including such things as the serial and parallel ports, the hard and floppy disc interfaces, USB ports, and possibly even LAN or Firewire adapters. Expansion cards that only duplicate functions provided by the motherboard are not needed in the upgraded PC, and fitting them could prevent the PC from operating properly.

If it is very difficult or impossible to fit the expansion cards in place, the motherboard is probably slightly out of position. Slightly loosen the motherboard's mounting screws, fit one of the cards in place, shifting the motherboard fractionally if necessary, and then tighten the screws again. The manual for the motherboard will include a diagram that

Fig.8.7 An AGP card uses a two-tier system to get in all the terminals

identifies the ISA, PCI, and AGP expansion slots, but there is no risk of fitting a card in the wrong type of slot because they use connectors of different sizes.

Note that modern AGP slots have a locking lever at the front of the slot, which avoids the common problem of the card skewing slightly when the mounting bracket is bolted to the case. There are a lot of terminals crammed into a small space on an AGP connector (Figure 8.7), so even

a slight skewing of the card could cause problems. The locking mechanism in the AGP slot latches into a cut-out in the front of the video card's connector (Figure 8.8).

This is rather like the locking mechanism used at each end of a DIMM, and the locking lever on the slot certainly looks very similar (Figure

Fig.8.8 The cut-out for the locking lever at the front of an AGP card

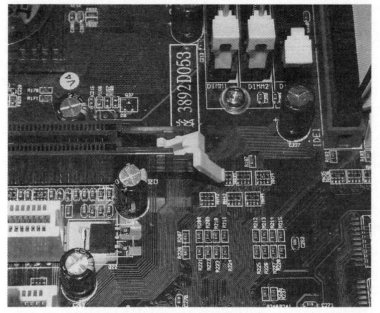

Fig.8.9 The locking lever of an AGP expansion slot

8.9). However, only one locking mechanism is used for an AGP card. Make sure that the lever is in the open (down) position before attempting to fit the video card. The lever will probably move into the locking position automatically when the video card is inserted into the AGP slot, but if necessary it can be given a little help. Figure 8.10 shows an AGP card locked into its expansion slot, with the lever in the locked (up) position.

Seeing red

There are quite a few connecting cables in the average PC, and getting everything connected correctly deters many would-be PC upgraders. Getting everything connected properly is actually much easier than you might expect. If you look at the connectors on the motherboard for the parallel ports, disc interfaces, etc., you will probably find that each connector has a pin that is marked as pin "1". This marking is also present on the data connectors of most drives, including the CD-ROM and floppy varieties. The manuals for you computer components should also have diagrams that show the pin numbering for each connector. If

Fig.8.10 Here the video card has been locked in the AGP slot

you look at the cables supplied with the motherboard, and those of the original PC, you will notice that they are made from grey "ribbon" cable. This type of cable always has a red line running down one side of the cable, and the convention is for this to carry the pin one connection.

In order to get all the ribbon cables connected correctly you merely have to ensure that the red leads always connect to the pin one end of the connectors on the drives and motherboard. In theory, the connectors are all polarised anyway, giving no possibility of connecting them the wrong way round. In practice the connectors are often somewhat cut-down and simplified versions of the "real thing", and reverse connection is possible.

Fortunately, modern motherboards and drives are generally better in this respect than those from some years ago. Anyway, always check carefully that both ends of every cable conforms to the "red to pin one" convention. If you made sketches and notes before dismantling the PC, which is a good idea for anyone new to this type of thing, these should prove helpful when refitting the data cables.

The chapter that covers floppy disc drives explains the reason for the "twisted" floppy drive cable and you should consult this if you are unsure about the right method of connection. The IDE interfaces on modern motherboards seem to cause a certain amount of confusion, and it is important to bear in mind that each IDE interface can support two drives. The two interfaces are sometimes just referred to as IDE1 and IDE2, in other places you will find them respectively called the primary and secondary IDE interfaces.

The two drives connected to each interface are the master and slave devices. Of course, you do not need to have two devices connected to each one, or indeed any IDE devices connected at all. However, a modern PC normally has at least two IDE drives, which are the hard disc and some form of CD-ROM or DVD drive. The hard disc drive will normally be the primary device on the primary IDE interface (IDE1).

UDMA66, etc.

A set of IDE cables is normally supplied with the motherboard, and you will also have the set supplied in the PC. The easiest way of handling things is to leave the original cables connected to the drives, and then reconnect them to the motherboard once the new one has been fitted. It might be worthwhile switching the data cable for the hard disc drive for the one supplied with the new motherboard. If the hard disc is an upgrade it is likely that it will support one of the high-speed IDE interfaces (UDMA66, UDMA100, etc.).

It is odds on that the old motherboard only supports UDMA33, and it will therefore use an old-style IDE data cable. The new motherboard should certainly support at least UDMA100, and should give better results with the hard drive. However, a special cable having twice as many leads is needed for anything beyond UDMA33. At least one of the cables supplied with the motherboard should be a UDMA66 type, and this should be used if the hard disc supports UDMA66 or higher.

IDE cables usually have provision for two drives, and the CD-ROM drive could be wired up to the second connector on the hard drive's cable. It then becomes the primary slave device. In practice it is usually better to have the CD-ROM drive on the secondary IDE interface. This is particularly important if the hard drive supports one of the high-speed data modes, because having a CD-ROM or similar drive on the same IDE interface could restrict the hard disc to UDMA33 operation.

This method requires a second IDE data cable, but as pointed out previously, you should have plenty of these. An old style (40-way) IDE cable is perfectly adequate for CD-ROM drives, DVD drives, etc., since they only have a UDMA33 interface. If there is a third IDE drive such as another CD-ROM or a Zip type, this should be used as the slave device on the secondary IDE interface.

Master/slave

Unlike PC floppy drives, the IDE drives are set as the master or slave devices via jumpers on the drivers, and not by way of a "twisted" cable. CD-ROM drives normally have jumper settings for master and slave operation, plus a third called something like cable select. In a PC context it is only the master and slave options that are of interest. Hard disc drives sometimes have the same options, but there are often two master settings. One setting is used if the drive is the only device on that IDE interface, and the other is used if there is also a slave device on that IDE channel. When dealing with hard disc drives it is best to read the manuals carefully and then set the jumpers accordingly, rather than jumping to conclusions and possibly getting things wrong. The web sites of the hard disc manufacturers usually have jumper settings for any drives that they have produced in the last five years or more. Most modern hard disc drives are marked with a chart showing the jumper settings for each option.

More wiring

There is still plenty to do once the drives and external interface connectors have been wired up. If it was not connected earlier, the power supply unit must be connected to the motherboard. Remember to connect the two additional power leads in the case of Pentium 4 motherboards that use this feature. Also make sure that all the disc drives are wired to the power supply unit. There will be various "flying" leads coming from LEDs, switches, and the loudspeaker mounted on the case (Figure 8.11). There will also be

Fig.8.11 The connector block on the motherboard

various connectors on the motherboard to accommodate this sort of thing (Figure 8.12). The chances of the facilities offered by the motherboard matching up with those provided by the case are pretty remote. This potential mismatch is not of any great practical importance though.

Fig.8.12 The leads and connectors for the switches, speaker, etc.

With these minor functions it is really just a matter of implementing any that are common to both the motherboard and the case, and leaving any others unconnected. This usually means connecting the power on/ off indicator and IDE activity LEDs, the loudspeaker, and the reset switch, and ignoring anything else. The LEDs will only work if they are connected with the right polarity. There may be "+" markings on the leads and the motherboard to indicate the polarity, but these are often missing. Often vague markings or colour coding are used, and neither are likely to be of any real help. Where necessary you can adopt the "suck it and see" method. The LEDs will not light up if they are connected with the wrong polarity, but they will not be damaged either.

The audio output socket of the CD-ROM drive is usually connected to the audio input connector of the sound card, or the motherboard in the case of integrated audio circuits. Audio CDs played in the drive can then be heard through the PC's sound system. There should be at least one audio input connector on the motherboard if it has an integrated audio facility, and most sound cards now have several audio inputs. The existing cable can be used if the original soundcard has been retained.

It is possible that a new cable will be required if a switch is made to integrated audio on the motherboard. Two or three audio connectors have been used in the past, and the existing cable might use one that is now defunct. A suitable cable can be bought from a large computer store or at a computer fair for no more than a few pounds. Of course, if you will only play audio CDs into headphones connected to the CD-ROM drive's headphone socket, or do not intend to use the drive for audio CDs at all, this cable is not required.

Depending on the facilities of the PC, there could be one or two additional cables to connect. Some modems can have additional cables, as can DVD decoders and video capture cards. This is just a matter of copying the method of connection used in the original PC. Where the original PC has any unusual features and cabling it is definitely a good idea to make some sketches and notes prior to dismantling it. Rebuilding the PC should then be straightforward. Where appropriate, make sure that you obtain a new motherboard that supports these special features.

Blast-off

With everything installed in the case and the cabling completed, it is time to give everything a final check before reconnecting the monitor, mouse and keyboard, and switching on. At switch-on the computer should go through the usual BIOS start-up routine, but this routine will probably be slightly different to the one performed by the original computer. This is due to the change of BIOS that accompanied the change to a new motherboard.

It is advisable to break into the start-up routine and run the BIOS Setup program before the computer tries to boot-up. A modern BIOS is very good at detecting the hardware present in the computer and adjusting itself accordingly. The user still has to set a few things manually in order to ensure correct operation of the computer. Refer to chapter two for an in-depth look at BIOS settings. This aspect of things will not be considered in detail here.

You will need to go into the part of the Setup program that deals with the standard BIOS settings, and here you must set the correct IDE and floppy drive types. If you do not know the correct parameters for the hard disc drive this will probably not matter. The "Auto" option will get the BIOS to read the correct settings from the drive and configure itself correctly. It will probably be possible to set the time and date from the operating system once the computer is fully operational, but while you are in the standard BIOS part of the Setup program you might as well take the opportunity to set these.

Once the standard CMOS settings have been dealt with it is likely that the computer should work quite well. You can alter the defaults for things like the printer port's operating mode, and whether Num Lock is on or off at switch-on, but in most cases the standard CMOS settings are the only ones that you must set up correctly before the computer will work

Auto detection

If you have not changed the hard disc drive, once you have saved and exited from the Setup program the computer will try to boot into Windows. The computer will probably start to boot-up in the usual fashion, but the Plug N Play feature will soon start to detect the hardware changes and load the appropriate drivers. In some cases it may have suitable drivers available already, but you will usually have to put the appropriate drivers disc into the floppy or CD-ROM drive when prompted by the on-screen Windows messages. The new motherboard should have been supplied with a disc containing any drivers needed for its hardware. It may be necessary to use the Windows installation CD-ROM at some stage in the proceedings, so have this disc handy just in case.

Read the installation instructions provided with the various items of hardware that you have bought for the upgraded PC. Most hardware does things in standard Windows fashion, and apart from providing the drivers disc when prompted, you have to do nothing more than sit back and watch while Windows gets on with it. Some hardware requires additional installation though, and there may also be some useful utility software on the discs that has to be installed separately.

On the face of it, there is little hardware that will need new drivers. A change in the video or sound circuits will necessitate new drivers, but one might reasonably expect everything else to work normally. It can therefore be rather puzzling when Windows starts reporting all manner of new hardware, and announces that it is finding and loading new software to support this hardware. In some cases it is simply rediscovering old hardware, and loading drivers that are already there. Windows 95 seems to be especially prone to this problem, but later versions of Windows are not much better.

Unfortunately, you often seem to end up with a PC that has two sets of drivers, neither of which are working properly. Again, Windows 95 is more prone to this than the later versions of Windows. Normally the only solution to this problem is to go into the control panel, select System and then Device Manager, and then delete both versions of the offending driver. Next exit Windows and re-boot the computer. When the operating system starts to load it should detect the "new" hardware and load the drivers for it. You may not have to provide it with the drivers disc, as it may well find that it already has the necessary files on the hard disc and reinstall them from there.

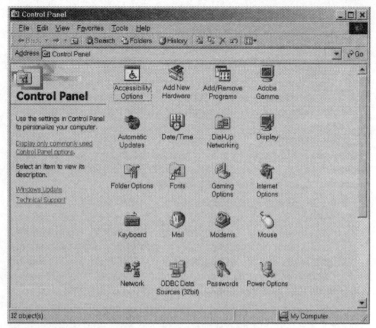

Fig.8.13 The Windows XP version of the Control Panel

Port drivers

In addition to drivers for any new expansion cards, Windows will load drivers for new hardware on the motherboard. These drivers accommodate such things as improved hard disc and parallel ports, and the USB ports. The computer will probably re-boot two or three times as part of the installation process, but with luck you should eventually end up with the Windows desktop displayed on the screen, and the computer ready to run your applications.

It is worth going into the Device Manager and checking that none of the hardware entries are marked with the dreaded exclamation marks, which indicate that all is not well. If there is a problem with one or more of the drivers, I usually find that deleting the offending driver or drivers and re-booting the computer clears the problem. During the re-boot the drivers are reinstalled, and they normally reinstall correctly. With an awkward

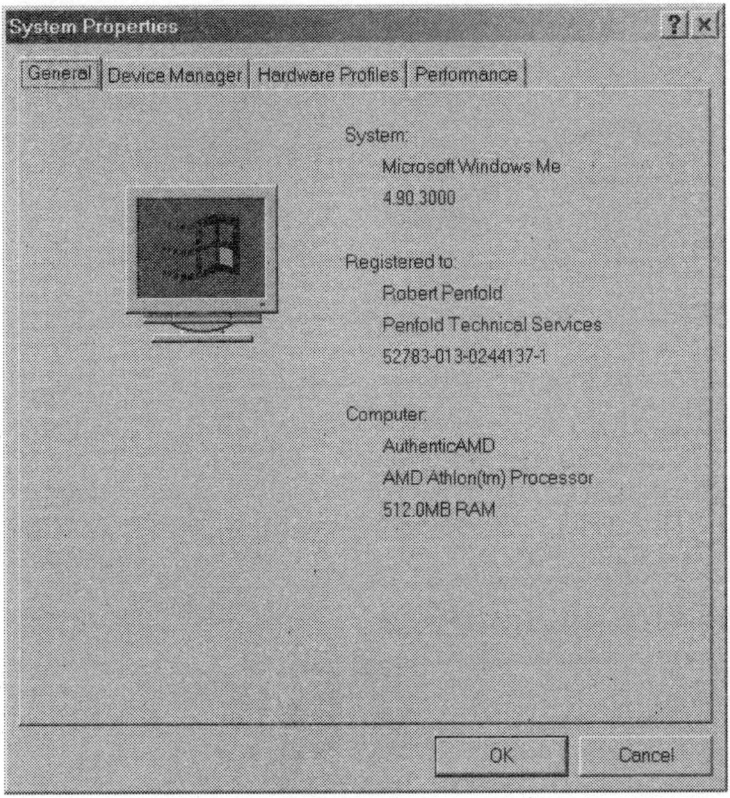

Fig.8.14 The System Properties window

PC it may take several attempts before everything installs correctly, and I assume that in some cases the drivers will only coexist peacefully if they are installed in a certain order.

One piece of hardware that may refuse to install correctly is the USB port. If you are using an early version of Windows 95 it will not have USB support, and the USB port will be unusable unless you upgrade to Windows 98 or later. With Windows 95 OSR2 you will probably find that the USB port has an entry in Device Manager, but that there is an exclamation mark against it, and the port will not work properly.

Again, the only way of getting the USB port to operate properly is to upgrade the operating system to Windows 98 or later. The exclamation

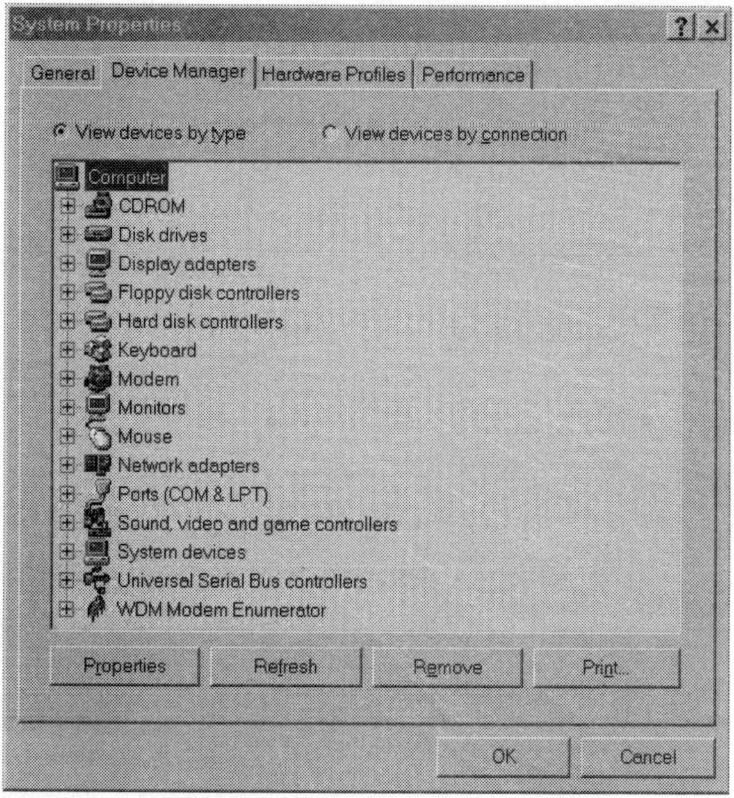

Fig.8.15 The hardware categories listed in Device Manager

mark will then miraculously disappear, and you should find that the USB port functions perfectly. With the final version of Windows 95 (OSR2.1) you might obtain perfect results with the USB port, but there is still a possibility of erratic operation. If USB support is needed it is probably best to upgrade the operating system to Windows 98 or ME.

Problems adjusting

In theory Windows should be able to adjust to suit the new hardware. In practice there is a fair chance that it will refuse to work really well, or at all, with the new hardware. It can be difficult to get Windows 95 to adjust

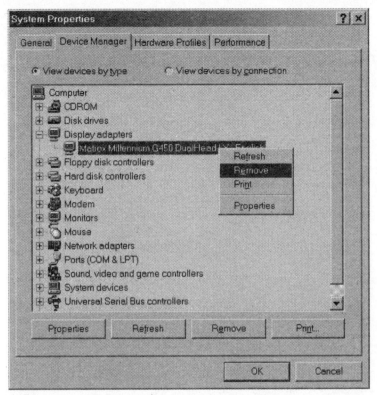

Fig.8.16 Removing the drivers for an item of hardware

to a massive change in the hardware, but later versions of Windows are more accommodating. The chances of success can be increased by uninstalling some items of hardware before starting the upgrade. Ideally, anything that will not be used in the upgraded PC should be uninstalled. This prevents confusion after the upgrade has been completed, when Windows expects to find one set of hardware and actually finds a completely different set. In particular, it can be helpful to uninstall the video card and set up Windows for use with a standard VGA adapter.

Uninstalling hardware from Windows varies slightly from one version to another. A PC running Windows ME is used for this example, but a similar process is used for other versions. The first step is to launch the Windows Control Panel, and one way of doing this is to select Settings from the Start menu followed by Control Panel from the submenu that

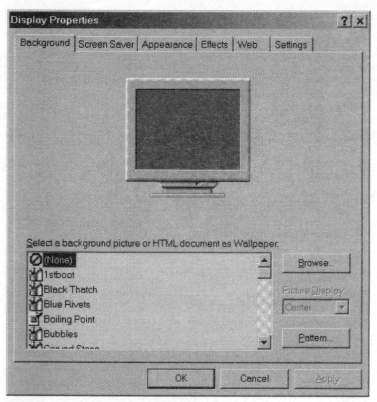

Fig.8.17 The Display Properties window

appears. This produces a window something like Figure 8.13. Scroll down if necessary and then double-click on the System icon. This produces the System Properties window of Figure 8.14, and here the Device Manager tab at the top of the window is operated.

The Device Manager window (Figure 8.15) lists categories for all the installed hardware. It is not possible to uninstall a complete category by selecting it and left-clicking the Remove button. Any attempt to do things this way will simply produce an appropriate error message. The "+" sign at the left end of each entry can be used to expand each one in standard Windows Explorer fashion. Having expanded a category and then selected an individual item, that item can be deleted using the Remove button. Alternatively, right-click on it and select Remove from

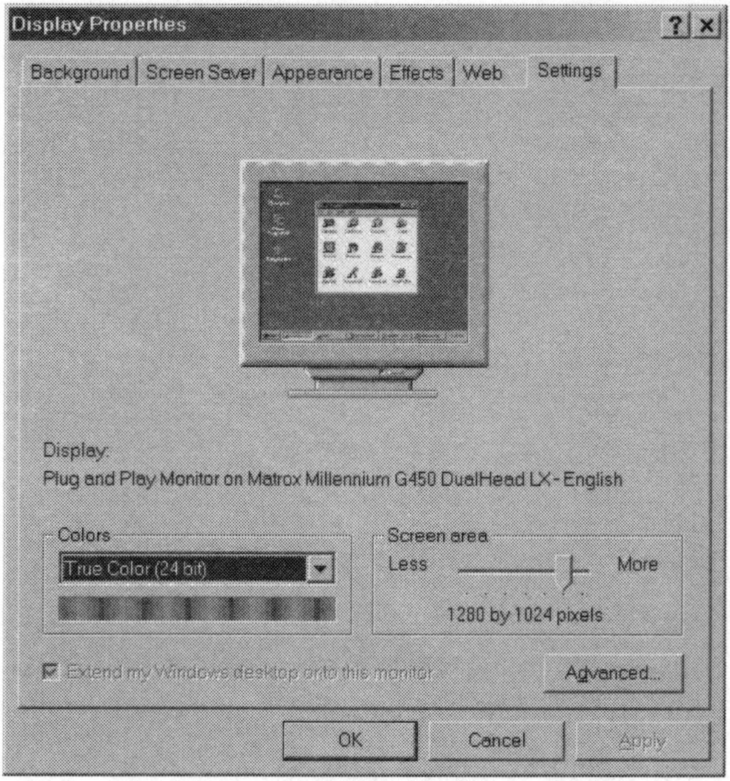

Fig.8.18 At the Settings screen, operate the Advanced button

the popup menu (Figure 8.16). Answer Yes when asked if you are sure you wish to remove that entry.

Any item of hardware can be uninstalled in this way, but there is obviously a risk of making the PC unusable if too much hardware is uninstalled. I suppose that this would not matter too much, since you could simply close down the PC if possible, or switch off if it hangs completely. The upgrade would then be completed, and the old hardware would be uninstalled when the upgraded PC was booted for the first time. Having uninstalled the appropriate hardware it is important not to reboot the computer until the upgrade has been completed. Windows will detect and reinstall the hardware if the computer is started up.

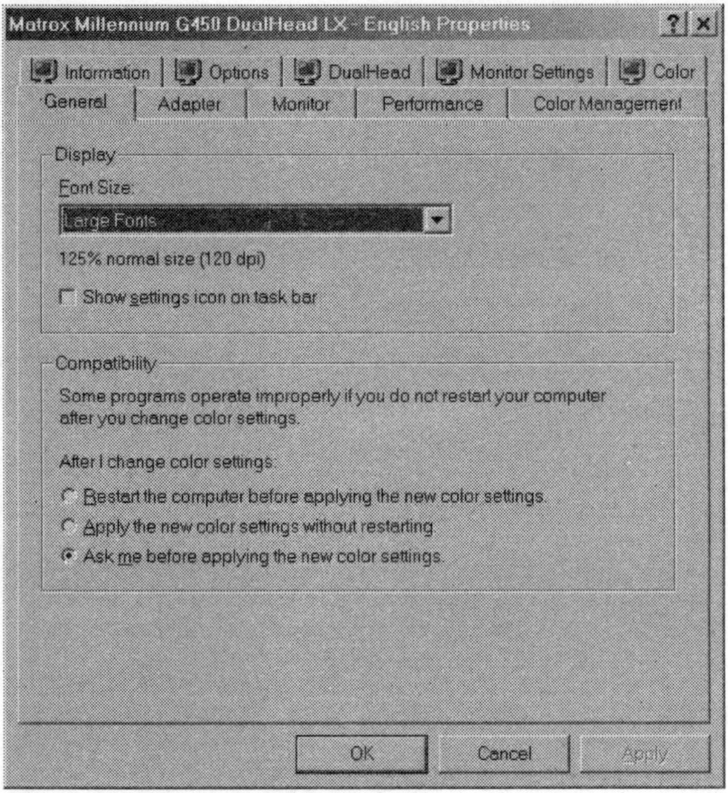

Fig.8.19 Next the Adapter tab is operated

In the case of the video card, the generally recommended method is to switch to a standard VGA adapter rather than simply obliterate the existing one. This can be done by going to the Control Panel and then double-clicking the Display icon. A window like the one of Figure 8.17 will appear, and operating the Settings tab will change it to look like Figure 8.18. The screen resolution and colour depth can be set to 640 by 480 and 16 colours at this stage, but this is not strictly necessary. The system will automatically revert to a basic VGA display when appropriate.

To change the display adapter start by operating the Advanced button, which will bring up a window like the one of Figure 8.19. Operate the Adapter tab to change it to one like Figure 8.20. Operate the Change

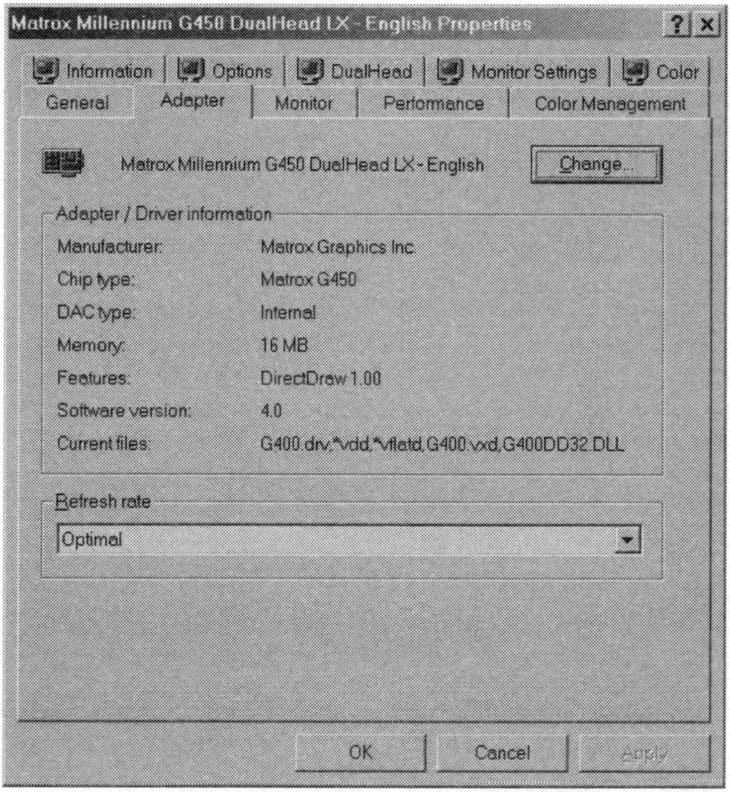

Fig.8.20 Operate the Change button to switch from the listed video card to a different one

button, and then in the next window (Figure 8.21) elect to select the location of the driver. Operate the Next button and at the next window (Figure 8.22), opt to display a list of drivers. Operate the Next button once again, and a window showing a list of available video drivers should be produced (Figure 8.23). The drivers listed will depend on the video cards that have been used in your PC, but one of them should be a standard VGA type. Select this one and then operate the Next button. The necessary driver files should already be present on the hard disc drive, so the installation should be straightforward from there on.

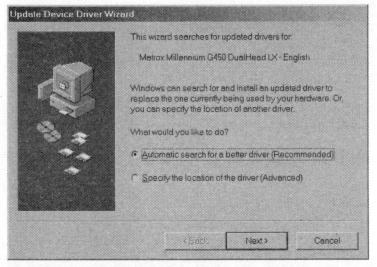

Fig.8.21 *Do not use the default (automatic) option of this screen*

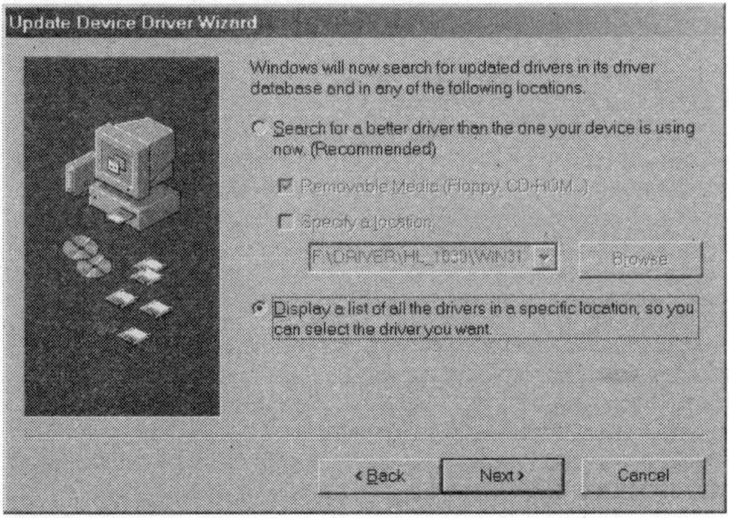

Fig.8.22 *At this screen you must opt to display a list of all the available drivers*

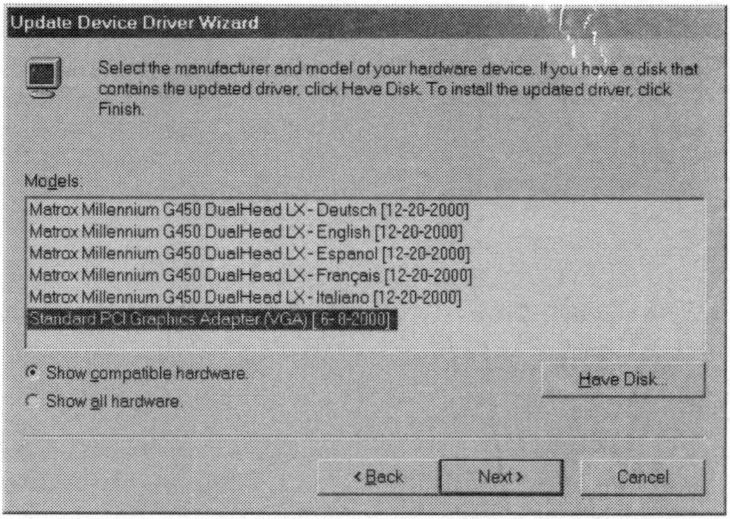

Fig.8.23 Select the Standard VGA option, which will use the existing video card as a very basic VGA type

Reactivation

Once the new drivers have been installed it is possible that some of the software will require product activation, or reactivation as it is in this case. Windows XP is famous for requiring activation followed by reactivation if large changes are made to the hardware, but there are other programs that use the same basic method of copy protection. The most common example is Office XP, but there are others. Changing the motherboard and processor is almost certain to trigger the reactivation routines in any software that uses this method.

The monitoring software will detect the change in the type of processor, the change in the serial number of the processor, and the change in the BIOS. Any changes in the audio, video, and network adapter are also likely to be detected. Various methods of reactivation are used, and in some cases it is just a matter of placing a genuine installation disc in a CD-ROM drive. In other cases it is necessary to reactivate the software online or by making a telephone call to obtain a new activation code. Onscreen instructions should be provided when reactivation is triggered, and there should be no problem provided you are using legitimate software.

Reinstalling Windows

Even with the right preparations it is possible that Windows will fail to adjust to the new hardware correctly. Reinstalling Windows should clear away any problems. Reinstalling Windows onto a new hard disc drive was covered in the previous chapter, and the process is essentially the same when Windows is installed over an existing system. Of course, the hard disc is not reformatted unless you wish to clear away the existing installation and start from scratch.

There are definite advantages in doing things this way, and it does ensure that the PC has a "clean" installation that will work efficiently. However, bear in mind that any data on the hard disc will be lost if it is reformatted. Any important data will therefore have to be backed up before the disc is formatted. With Windows reinstalled on the hard disc it will be necessary to reinstall all the applications and restore you data from the backup device. All this is avoided if you simply reinstall Windows over the original installation. The applications programs should be automatically integrated with the new installation and your data will of course remain intact on the hard disc. Unfortunately, there is no guarantee that this form of reinstallation will clear away any problems with the original one, although it will probably do so in most cases.

If the PC was fitted with a new hard disc drive as part of the upgrade you have what is effectively a new computer, and the operating system will have to be loaded onto the hard disc before it can be used. This process was covered previously in the chapter that deals with upgrading a hard disc drive. Remember to back up any important data so that it can be transferred to the new drive.

Budget upgrades

Many people own PCs that are too old to be of any real use any more, and are not worthy of an expensive upgrade, but they do not wish to simply dump them on the nearest scrap heap. The rapid rate of change in the PC world does provide an alternative in the form of a budget upgrade. Buying the current technology is not necessarily that expensive, particularly if you opt for something less than the fastest up-to-the-minute components. Buying last year's technology is even cheaper, but last year's technology is still quite fast.

We are now reaching the stage where the ultimate in modern PCs is starting to provide overkill for many applications. Game enthusiasts and those who deal with complex 3-D graphics need a very fast computer. For general office applications a fairly modest Pentium PC is usually perfectly adequate, and a computer of this type is even likely to be good enough for things such as 2-D computer aided design (CAD) and basic desktop publishing (DTP).

In essence a budget upgrade is not much different to an upgrade to the latest specification. It will be necessary to replace the motherboard, processor, and memory modules. Other components such as the video card and hard disc drive can optionally be changed as well. The difference is that you buy surplus components that are not exactly new, but have probably never been used. The large mail order companies sometimes have sales of surplus stock, but local computer fairs are probably the best source for items of this type.

Inevitably, some of the items on offer at these fairs are better bargains than are others, and you certainly have to be careful not to buy a "lemon". There is no point in buying something like an ultra-cheap motherboard that only takes old processors that are no longer available, and would not be much better than the one already fitted to the PC. The better buys are often in the form of a motherboard kit. These typically comprise a processor fitted on a suitable motherboard, complete with some memory, a heatsink and a fan. Motherboards that have integrated audio and video are ideal for budget upgrades, since they often cost little more than boards that lack these facilities. For a modest outlay it is often possible to upgrade an old PC to a specification that will run most modern software remarkably well.

Overclocking

Overclocking is sometimes referred to as the "free upgrade", and it is the practice of using electronic components beyond their maximum speed rating. In practice it usually means running the processor beyond its rated maximum frequency, and with modern PCs it usually means running most of the computer beyond its normal operating frequency. Many motherboards have the ability to over-clock the processor, but the manufacturers do not encourage this practice.

The motherboard's instruction manual will usually contain one or two disclaimers, saying something along the lines that the board has the ability to use overclocking, but the manufacturer does not condone this practice. This may seem rather two-faced, but the manufacturer is basically saying that the board has the overclocking facility, but you use

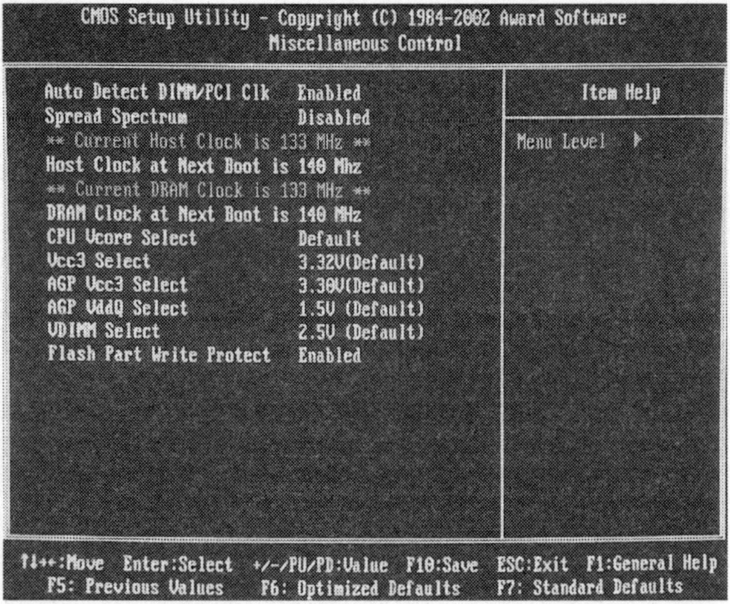

```
        CMOS Setup Utility - Copyright (C) 1984-2002 Award Software
                          Miscellaneous Control

   Auto Detect DIMM/PCI Clk    Enabled              │       Item Help
   Spread Spectrum             Disabled             │
   ** Current Host Clock is 133 MHz **              │  Menu Level  ▶
   Host Clock at Next Boot is 140 Mhz               │
   ** Current DRAM Clock is 133 MHz **              │
   DRAM Clock at Next Boot is 140 MHz               │
   CPU Vcore Select            Default              │
   Vcc3 Select                 3.32V(Default)       │
   AGP Vcc3 Select             3.30V(Default)       │
   AGP VddQ Select             1.5V (Default)       │
   VDIMM Select                2.5V (Default)       │
   Flash Part Write Protect    Enabled              │



   ↑↓→←:Move  Enter:Select  +/-/PU/PD:Value  F10:Save  ESC:Exit  F1:General Help
       F5: Previous Values      F6: Optimized Defaults     F7: Standard Defaults
```

Fig.8.24 This section of the BIOS permits the system frequency to be
altered in one megahertz increments

it at your own risk. Overclocking the motherboard's chipset is unlikely to damage anything, but good reliability can not be guaranteed.

As pointed out previously, most motherboards have the processor's multiplier set automatically. The BIOS detects which version of the processor is installed and sets the appropriate multiplier. The user has no control over the multiplier, and can not overclock the processor by setting a higher multiplier. Some boards use DIP-switches or jumpers to control the multiplier, or have this as an option. With these boards it should be possible to operate the processor at a higher multiplier, but there is obviously no guarantee that it will work.

The other approach to overclocking is to boost the bus frequency of the motherboard. A big advantage of this system is that it boosts the speed of virtually the whole system, and not just the processor. The memory, video card, and just about everything else will be speeded up by boosting the bus frequency. Increasing the clock frequency of the whole system gives a greater boost to performance than boosting the frequency of just the processor by the same amount.

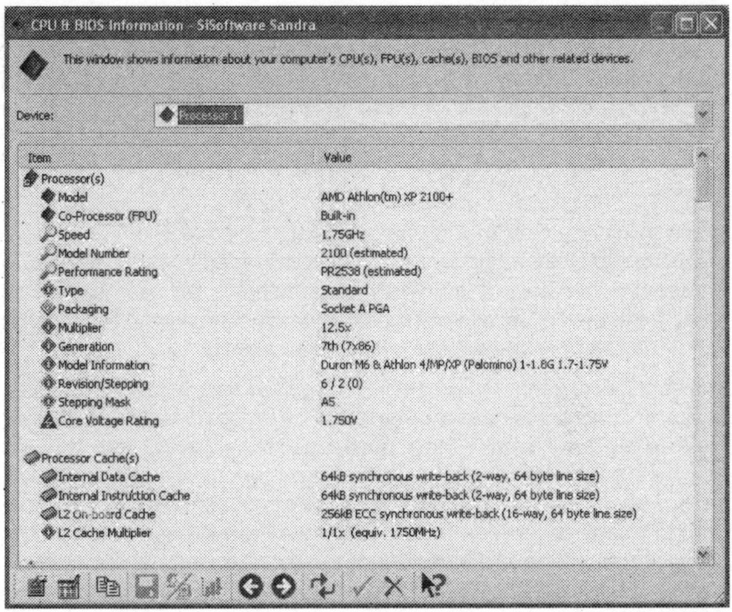

Fig.8.25 Sisoftware Sandra shows that the CPU clock frequency has been duly increased to 1.75 gigahertz

The main pitfall of this system of overclocking is that is boosts the speed of virtually the entire system. As already pointed out, this method has a big advantage if it works, but it is much less likely to work than simply boosting the processor's clock rate. The overclocking will fail to work if any part of the system is unable to handle the higher operating frequency. It is quite likely that even a modest amount of overclocking will result in one of the components failing to work properly.

This type of overclocking is usually achieved via the BIOS Setup program. The PC used for the Athlon XP2000+ processor upgrade has the ability to alter the motherboard bus frequency in one megahertz increments. Before the upgrade it was overclocked by about five percent by having the system bus frequency raised from 133 megahertz to 140 megahertz. With the new processor installed I tried the same thing (Figure 8.24) and this did not seem to compromise stability. The processor still ran quite coolly at about 50 degrees Celsius or so. The relevant section of the Sisoftware Sandra program confirmed that the clock frequency had been increased to 1.75 gigahertz (Figure 8.25).

Whether such a small increase in speed made any noticeable difference in use is another matter. Even with the more demanding applications programs it is unlikely that a change of less than about 10 to 20 percent will be of significance. With the less demanding applications programs it is unlikely that a huge boost in speed would be noticeable. Where things already happen almost instantly there is no real room for improvement.

When trying any overclocking technique you need to bear in mind that the increased clock frequency will produce increased power consumption and heat generation. It is unlikely that any chips will overheat if their clock frequency is increased slightly, and this certainly did not happen when the example system was overclocked slightly.

It is very unlikely that the processor or system as a whole will function properly if their clock rates are increased by a large amount. Therefore, overheating is not a major worry, but if a fault should occur when you are using a component beyond its normal maximum operating frequency it will not be covered by the guarantee. If you experiment with overclocking, you do so entirely at your own risk. You will have to pay to replace any components that fail, whether or not the overclocking had anything to do with the failure.

Points to remember

Upgrading the motherboard and processor is a major undertaking and unlikely to be cheap. On the other hand, with the right PC it can be a very cost effective method of moving up to a PC having a much higher specification.

If the motherboard and processor are upgraded, it will almost certainly be necessary to upgrade the memory as well. They are unlikely to give optimum performance even if the old memory modules can be used with the new motherboard.

Modern motherboards are of the ATX variety. These are incompatible with the AT cases and power supplies used for some older PCs. Note also, that some manufacturers use non-standard cases and power supplies. These are unlikely to be compatible with a standard ATX board.

The new processor will require a matching heatsink and fan. Any heatsink fitted to the old processor is unlikely to be adequate for the new one, and might not fit anyway. The safest option is to buy the retail boxed version of the processor, which should include a suitable heatsink and fan.

A special (80-way) IDE cable is needed in order to obtain full performance from a UDMA66 interface and drive, or later versions of the IDE interface. Most motherboards are supplied with a set of drive cables including an 80-way IDE type.

Do not use a CD-ROM drive, DVD drive, etc., on the same IDE channel as a fast (UDMA66 or later) hard disc drive. To do so could greatly reduce the performance of the hard disc drive.

Changing the motherboard produces substantial changes in the hardware, and Windows requires new drivers for much of this hardware. Windows will detect the changes and start the reconfiguration the first time the upgraded PC is used. The motherboard should be supplied with the necessary drivers for things like integrated audio and the IDE controllers.

It can be helpful to uninstall from Windows any major items of hardware that will not be included in the new PC, such as the video board. This is especially important with Windows 95.

Many motherboards have the ability to use overclocking. In most cases only a small amount of overclocking can be used, if it works at all. If you use overclocking and "cook" the processor it will not be covered by the manufacturer's or retailer's guarantees.

Modems

Hard and soft

A modem used to be a strictly a device for communicating via an ordinary telephone connection. These days broadband is gaining in popularity, and low-cost ADSL services are proving to be very popular. Most users still have ordinary telephone modems though, and these will be covered first. Telephone modems are available in three basic types, which are external serial, external USB, and internal PCI card modems. The serial type has now been largely replaced by USB modems that offer true Plug and Play capability, as do the PCI variety.

Fig.9.1 A software modem uses relatively simple hardware, leaving the software to do most of the work

*Fig.9.2 A hardware modem places little loading on the processor.
All external modems are hardware types incidentally*

Internal modems are offered in two types, which are the software and hardware varieties. These do not look much different (Figure 9.1 and 9.2 respectively), but software modems have relatively simple hardware. They are really just soundcards, and software is used to provide the encoding and decoding. The drivers for a software modem are therefore rather more than normal Windows drivers. There are often two or three sets of drivers, so make sure that all the necessary drivers are installed. A hardware modem uses the hardware to provide the encoding, decoding, and error correction.

Both types of modem are capable of excellent results, but the hardware type tends to be held in higher regard. I suppose that hardware modems are much less demanding on the PC, leaving plenty of processing power for applications programs. Software modems will only work at all with a suitably powerful PC, but the minimum specification is usually quite low by current standards. A 200 megahertz Pentium processor is usually adequate. However, when upgrading an old PC it is probably best to opt for a hardware modem.

Horse to water

Physically installing a modem is usually quite straightforward. Installing the drivers supplied with the modem should not provide any problems either. Getting the modem to do something useful once it is installed is perhaps more troublesome. Installing a modem and actually getting it to work in real-world applications used to be a job that was very difficult, even for experienced computer users. Getting the Internet software installed, set up, and ready for use would often take about half an hour, provided everything went smoothly! It was not surprising if installation ground to a halt half way through the process.

Getting a modem installed and actually using it is not as difficult as it used to be, but things can still go wrong, and occasionally do. A common problem with Windows and modems is that users expect Windows to mind read. It needs full details of your Internet service provider before it can dial the right number, etc. For Internet access a browser is required. This can be the Internet Explorer application that is built into Windows, software provided by your Internet service provider (ISP), or a third-party browser such as Opera. Separate software is needed for other applications such as faxing.

Problems with software provided by an ISP are best sorted out by the customer support department of the ISP. It is likely that the software does not handle things in a standard fashion and that normal modem troubleshooting methods will not work. If the installation software simply sets up Internet Explorer to work with the ISP, then it should be possible to sort out any minor problems yourself.

Modem drivers

Sometimes the modem can be installed without any difficulty, but once installed it fails to work properly. The possibility of a hardware fault can not be ruled out, but it is advisable to check the software side of things before getting the hardware repaired or replaced. Start by looking in Device Manager to see if there are any yellow exclamation marks against the entry for the modem. In the case of an external modem, also check that the modem's port is free of errors.

Where a problem is indicated it is a good idea to try reinstalling the device drivers. The easiest way of doing this is to delete the modem's entry from Device Manager. As pointed out in previous chapters, you can not remove a category from Device Manager, only individual items.

Double-click on the modem's entry to expand it, and then left-click on the modem's entry to select it. Then operate the Remove button followed by the Yes button when you are asked if you are sure that you wish to remove the modem. Alternatively, right-click on the entry and select Remove from the popup menu. The modem's entry in Device Manager will then disappear, as will the Modem category if only one modem was installed.

If at first...

On rebooting the computer, the modem can be reinstalled by carefully following the manufacturer's installation instructions. It is possible that things will not go any better at the second attempt, but if the modem still fails to work, it is worth trying again. This time close down and switch off the computer once the modem has been removed from Device Manager. Physically remove the modem from the PC if it is an internal type, or disconnect it from the PC in the case of an external unit. Then reboot the computer without the modem. Check that the modem is still absent from Device Manager, and if necessary remove it and reboot the PC again.

Once you have established that the modem has been properly uninstalled from Windows, close down Windows and switch off the computer. Refit the modem, switch the computer back on again, and then reinstall the driver software. This should avoid having the old and non-working drivers reactivated. With the device drivers installed from scratch there is a better chance of the reinstallation being successful.

No dialling tone

An error message along the lines of "no dialling tone detected" is not an uncommon problem. Obviously this can occur because there is genuinely no dialling tone present, but this is not necessarily the cause of the problem. It is easy to check this point by picking up the telephone and listening for the usual dialling tone. There is probably a minor problem with the lead from the modem to the telephone wall socket if the dialling tone is present and correct.

Try disconnecting and reconnecting the lead at both the modem and the telephone socket. If an extension lead is in use, disconnect and reconnect this as well. Make sure that all the plugs are properly locked into the sockets. The connectors used for telephones and modems are quick and easy to use, but they are not the toughest of components. Leads tend to get kicked around and tripped over, and the connectors are damaged occasionally. Look carefully at all the connectors and replace any leads that have a seriously damaged plug or socket.

The connection to the telephone socket is via a standard BT plug, but the connection to the modem is by way of a smaller American style telephone plug. Both types of plug are shown in Figure 9.3. The American style plugs and sockets seem to be something less than rigidly standardised,

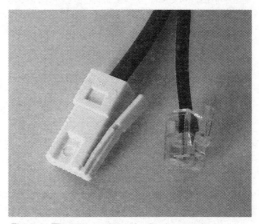

Fig.9.3 The two styles of telephone plug

or perhaps some of them are made to rather low standards. Some plugs do not lock into the sockets properly, while others are difficult to fit into place at all. Unfortunately, a few seem to fit into place perfectly but do not make reliable connections.

When installing a new modem or PC it is normal to use the existing lead to connect the modem to the telephone socket. However, this can give problems and it is safer to make the connection to the modem via the lead supplied with the modem or PC. This should be a good and reliable match for the socket fitted to the modem. On the other hand, if the lead supplied with the modem does not work, try another lead. Mistakes can be made, and it is possible that a lead for a mainland European country or the USA has been supplied instead of a UK lead.

A faulty modem can sometimes result in the telephones on the system failing to work properly. Typically, as soon as the modem is plugged into the wall socket the telephones on the same circuit ring until the modem is disconnected again. This can also be caused by a faulty cable or one of the wrong type. Cables for use in America and Europe will not give the correct set of connections between the modem and socket and will often produce this fault. Once again, it is a matter of using the cable provided with the modem wherever possible and making sure that any

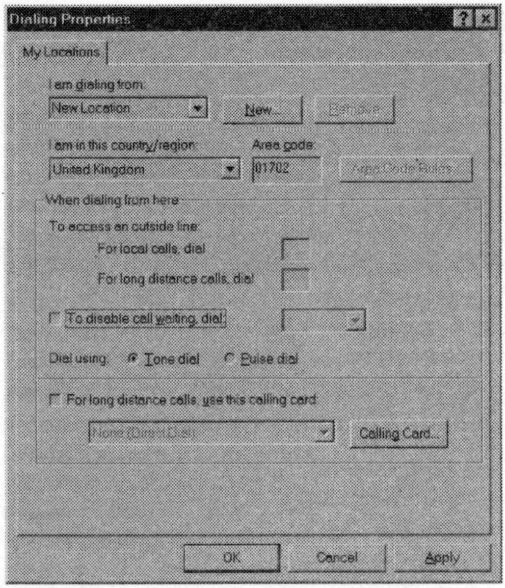

Fig.9.4 *This window enables call waiting to be disabled*

extension cables are of the correct type. Try another cable if the one supplied with the modem seems to be of the wrong type.

Call waiting

The modern telephone system provides all sorts of clever features, but they can give problems when using a modem. This can make it appear as though the modem is faulty when the problem actually resides elsewhere. Call waiting can be troublesome as it can result in an incoming call producing signals on the line that result in the Internet connection being lost, making it seem as though the modem is unreliable. Call waiting can be disabled by dialling the correct code, which is normally *43#. It can be enabled again by dialling the reactivation code, which is usually #43#.

There is a facility in Windows that enables the appropriate code to be dialled prior to the Internet service provider's number being dialled. Select Settings and then Control Panel from the Start menu to launch the Windows Control Panel and then double-click on the Modems icon. In the new window that appears left-click the Dialling Properties button, and another window should popup on the screen (Figure 9.4). Tick the checkbox labelled "To disable call waiting, dial" and then add the appropriate code into the textbox. Operate the Apply and OK buttons to make the changes take effect, and then left-click the OK button to close the Modems Properties window.

Some services, but particularly BT's Call Minder facility, can result in the dialling tone disappearing from time to time. The telephone system still works perfectly, but when someone has left a message the dialling tone becomes intermittent or simply disappears for a while. While this may

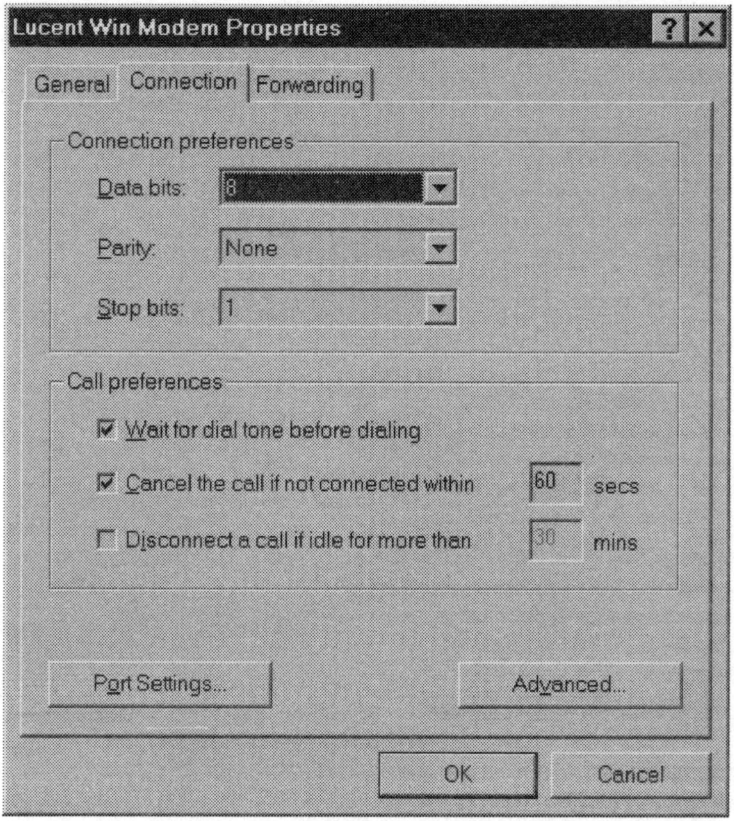

Fig.9.5 The modem can be made to dial the ISP even if no dial tone is detected

not seem to be of any practical importance, it can prevent the modem from dialling your Internet service provider. The modem fails to detect a dialling tone and assumes that there is a fault on the line or it is not connected to the telephone system.

The solution to this problem is to go into the Windows Control Panel, double-click the Modems icon, operate the Properties button in the new window that appears, and then operate the Connection tab. This should give a window like the one of Figure 9.5. Remove the tick in the checkbox labelled "Wait for dialling tone before dialling". The modem will then dial your Internet service provider whether or not a dialling tone is detected.

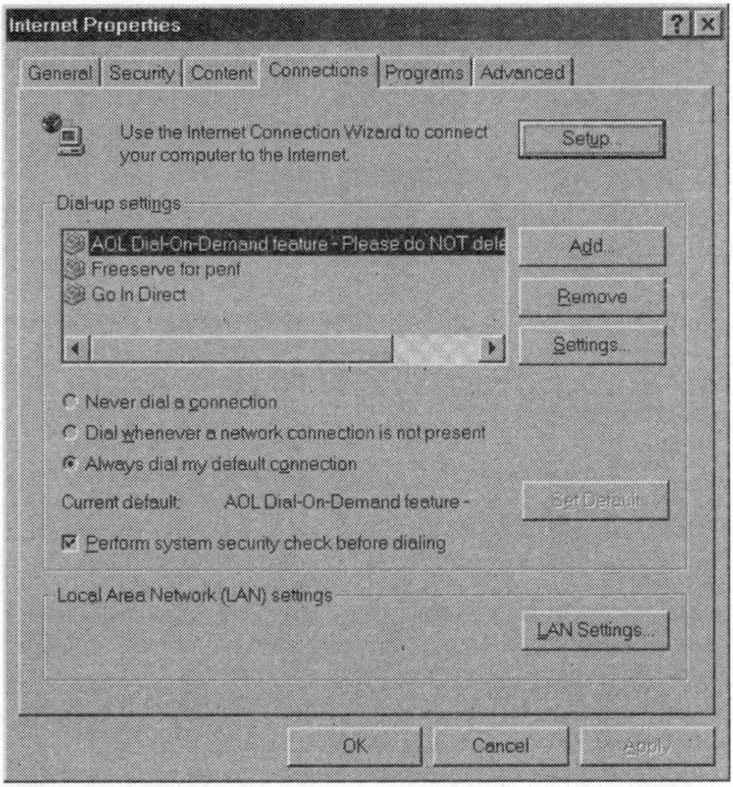

Fig.9.6 The Connections section of the Internet Properties window

More settings

If the modem seems to be working properly, you have made the checks described so far, and connection to the Internet is still problematic, there are still some settings that can be checked. Provided you have signed on to at least one Internet service there should be a default provider for the PC to dial. To check this, go to the Control Panel and double-click on the Internet Options icon and then operate the Connections tab on the window that appears. This should give something like Figure 9.6. To set an entry in the "Dial-up settings" list as the default it is first selected by left-clicking on its entry. Then operate the Set Default button, which should become active when an entry other than the current default is selected.

To check that an entry in the list is set up correctly, select the appropriate entry in the list and then operate the Settings button. This brings up the window of Figure 9.7, where the Properties button is left-clicked in order to produce a window like the one in Figure 9.8. The top section of the window should contain the telephone number of the Internet service provider, and in Figure 9.8 this information is clearly absent. This may look like an error, but in this case it is actually correct. The Internet service provider in this instance is AOL, and this company uses software that has its own database of telephone numbers. Hence no number is needed here, but in most cases the relevant fields of this window should be filled in correctly, as in the example of Figure 9.9. If the number includes an area code that is

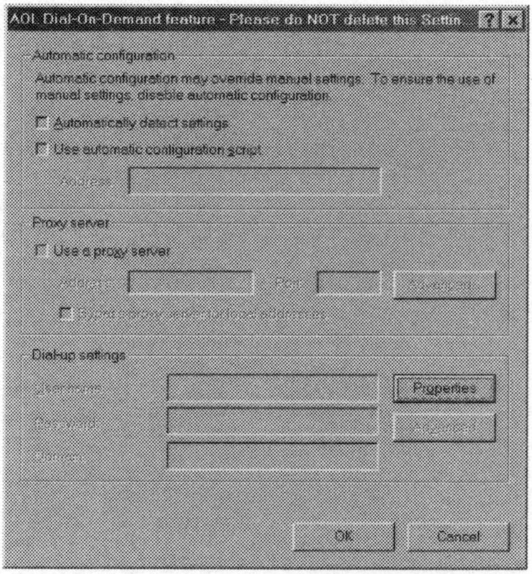

Fig.9.7 Checking the settings for an ISP

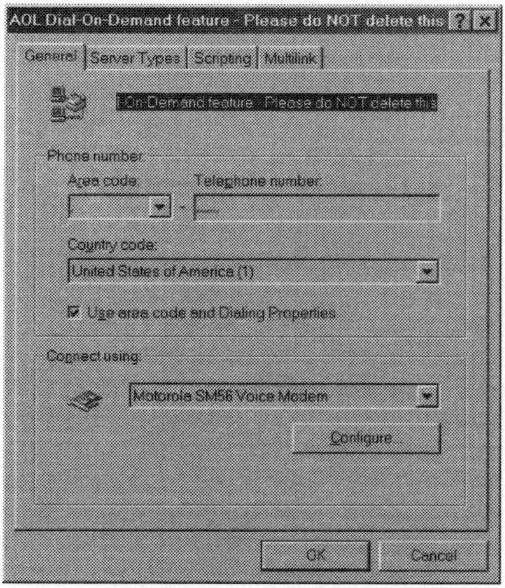

Fig.9.8 Is the telephone number correct?

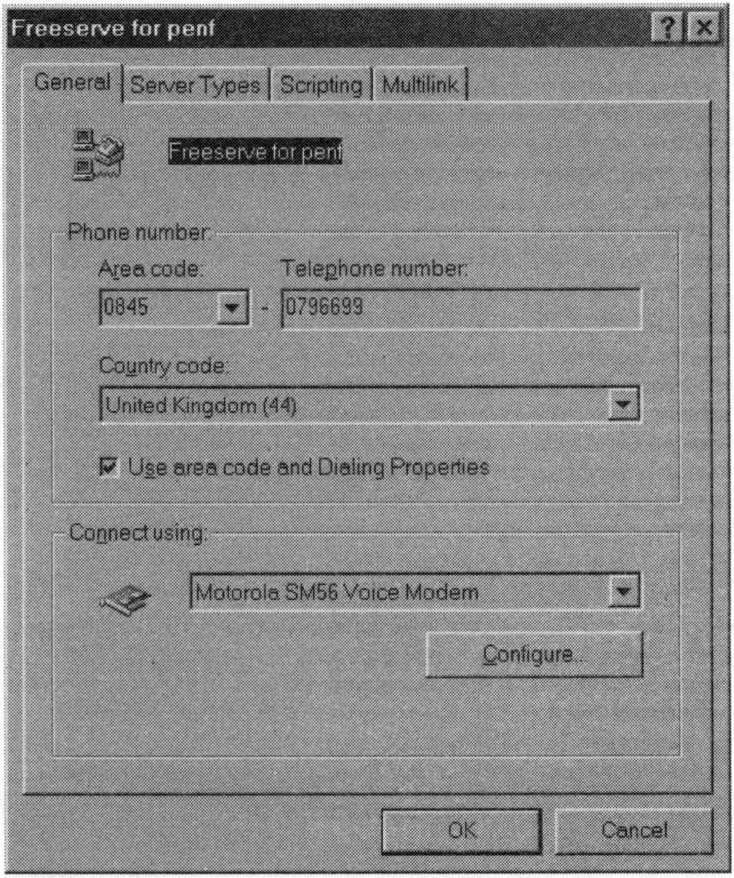

Fig.9.9 With most ISPs the telephone number will be included here

required from you dialling area, make sure that the checkbox is ticked. Also, where appropriate make sure that the correct modem is selected in the menu near the bottom of the window.

Next, try operating the Server Types tab to switch the window to one like Figure 9.10. Incidentally, when using Windows ME these settings are available by selecting the Networking tab. The type of dial-up server should be PPP, and TCP/IP should be selected as the only allowed network protocol. The checkbox that enables software compression is normally checked, but you can try turning off this feature to see if it improves matters.

Windows ME has a Security tab, and left-clicking on this one produces a window like the one in Figure 9.11. This is another case of AOL doing things its own way, so the User name and Password fields are blank in this example. With most Internet service providers the appropriate user name will be shown, but the password field will of course show a series of asterisks rather than the password. If necessary the user name can be edited, and the password can be re-entered if you think that it might be wrong. Note that these are the user name and password issued by your Internet service provider during the sign-up process. They are not any special name and password used to gain initial entry to

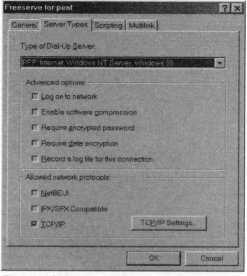

Fig.9.10 Checking the Server Type settings

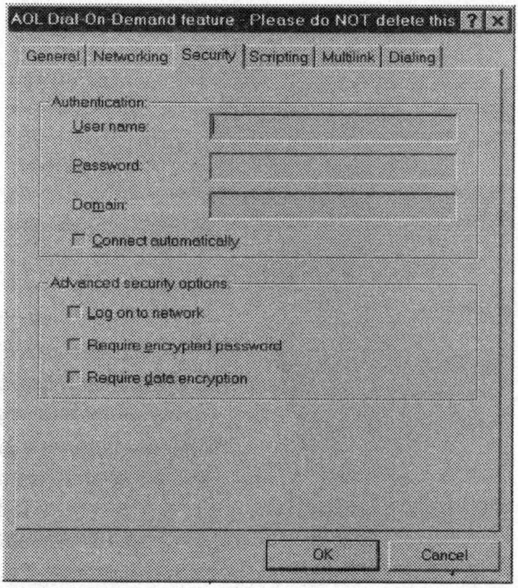

Fig.9.11 Check the user name and password

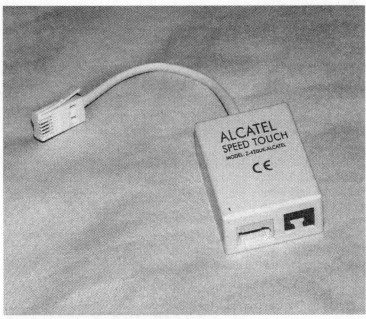

Fig.9.12 A microfilter must be used at each telephone socket when a broadband Internet connection is installed

the system so that the sign-up process can commence. These are only required the first time you access the system, and they are not needed thereafter.

ADSL

Having a broadband Internet connection installed by one of the ISP's engineers is a very easy way to get everything installed. In theory anyway, you simply sit back while it is installed and then start surfing the Internet at high speed. The big drawback is that it tends to be quite costly, and most small business and home users now opt for the do-it-yourself approach. An engineer has to test the line from the telephone exchange to your premises to ensure that the line quality is adequate, and some changes have to be made to your connection to the exchange. The cost of these services is relatively low though.

Fig.9.13 The popular Alcatel Speed Touch ADSL modem

Provided you live close enough to a broadband equipped exchange and the line quality proved to be adequate, you are then ready to install the equipment at your end of the system. First a microfilter (Figure 9.12) must be added at each telephone socket in the house. These are now very cheap and the cost should be quite low even if there are several sockets to contend with. Note that a microfilter is needed at every socket including any where an ADSL modem will not be used.

The purpose of a microfilter is to mix the high frequency broadband signal with the audio signal from the telephones connected to the system. It also ensures that the two types of equipment do not interfere with each other. One socket on the filter takes an ordinary BT telephone plug, and the telephone is plugged into this socket. The other socket is smaller and this is the one that connects to the modem, which should be supplied with a suitable lead. A huge advantage of ADSL is that it can carry the Internet connection while the telephone is in use.

The early ADSL modems were mainly in the form of external USB devices, like the popular Alcatel Speed Touch modem (Figure 9.13). However, these days there are also several internal PCI types, and external types having a standard 10/100 Ethernet port. The internal PCI and external USB types are both installed and set up in more or less standard fashion. Modern versions of Windows have wizards to help with the creation of a

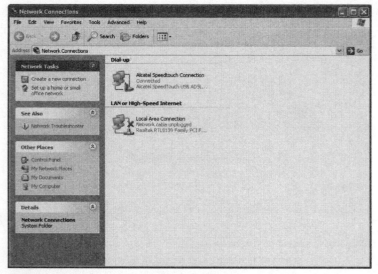

Fig.9.14 The Network Connections window

Fig.9.15 The opening window of the New Connection Wizard

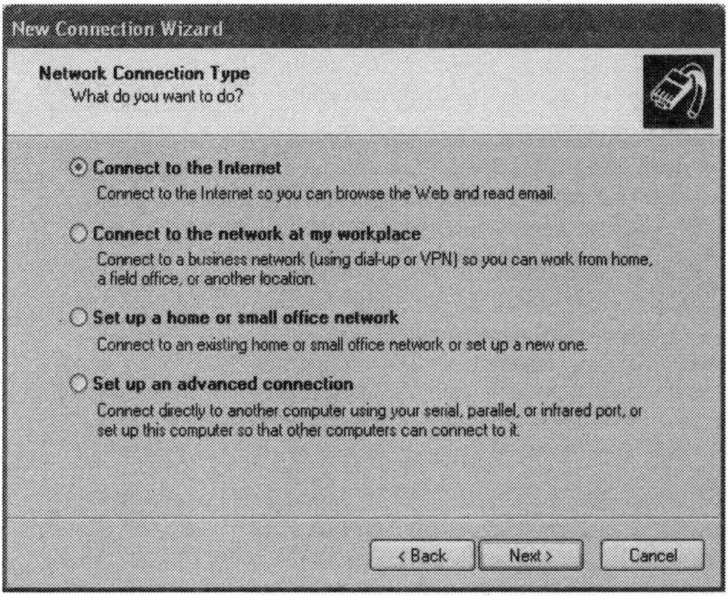

Fig.9.16 Choose the default option (Connect to the Internet)

new Internet connection, and with Windows XP it is the New Connection Wizard that is used. This is accessed by going to the Start menu and then selecting All Programs, Accessories, Communications, and Network Connections. This produces the Network Connections window of Figure 9.14.

Here the existing network and (or) Internet connections are listed. Left-click the Create new connection link near the top left-hand corner of the window, which will launch the New Connection Wizard (Figure 9.15). Then operate the Next button to move on to the first set of options (Figure 9.16). Here the default option, Connect to the Internet, is required. At the next window (Figure 9.17) the bottom option can be used if the ISP has provided a suitable Setup disc, but in most cases the Manual option has to be selected.

Operating the Next button then moves things on to the window of Figure 9.18. On the face of it, either the middle or bottom option should be selected, as these are both for DSL connections. However, most do-it-yourself ADSL connections are actually treated as normal dial-up types.

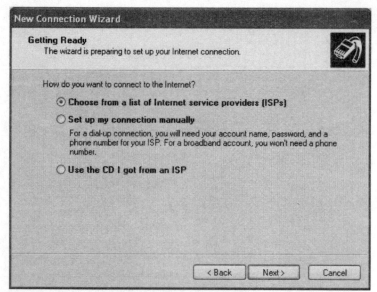

Fig.9.17 Opt to set up the connection manually

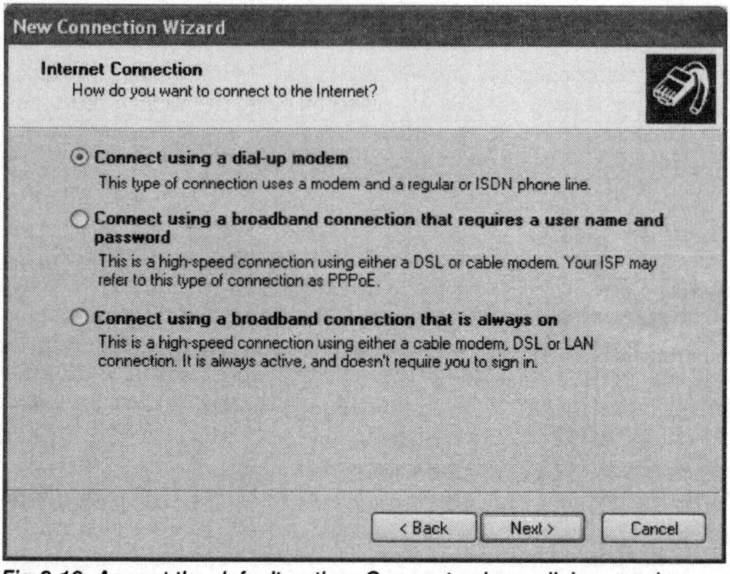

Fig.9.18 Accept the default option, Connect using a dial-up modem

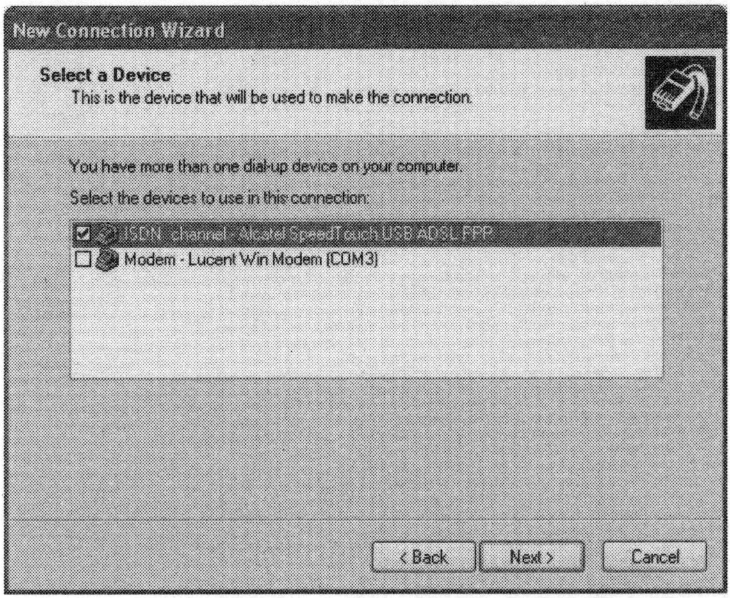

Fig.9.19 Select the appropriate modem, which is the ADSL type

Unless your ISP recommends otherwise, it is therefore the top option that is selected. The next window will look like the one of Figure 9.19 if there is more than one modem installed in the PC. It is a good idea to leave the ordinary modem in place when upgrading to ADSL. It can be used to provide emergency Internet access via a "pay as you go" Internet service, and it will still be needed if faxes have to be sent or received. Anyway, the new connection will obviously use the new ADSL modem, and the appropriate checkbox must be ticked.

A name for the new connection is added in the textbox of the next window (Figure 9.20). This is usually the name of the service provider, but any name can be used here. The next window (Figure 9.21) asks for the ISPs telephone number to be added in the textbox, but with an ADSL connection there is no telephone number. It is probably best to add some random numbers here since the Wizard might be reluctant to move on unless a number is added.

Operating the Next button moves on to the window of Figure 9.22 where your user name and password must be entered. These should have

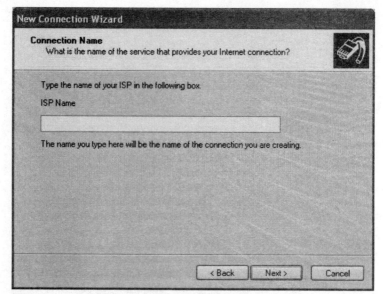

Fig.9.20 Type a name for the connection into the textbox

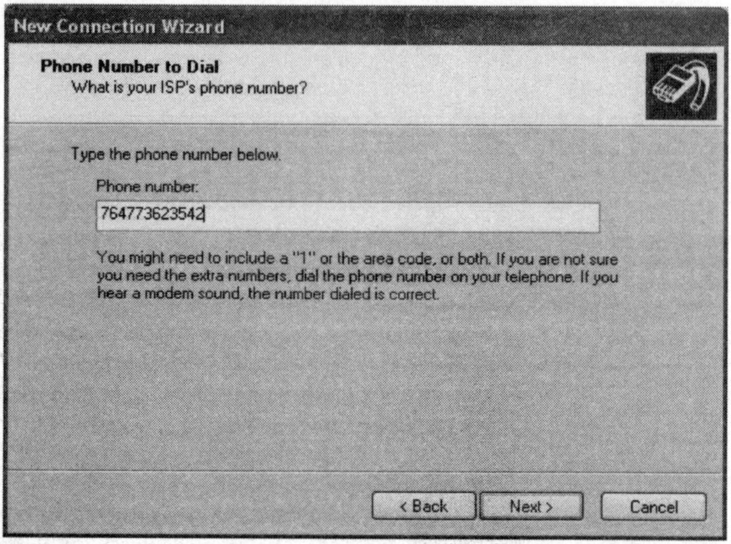

Fig.9.21 The phone number can simply be some random figures

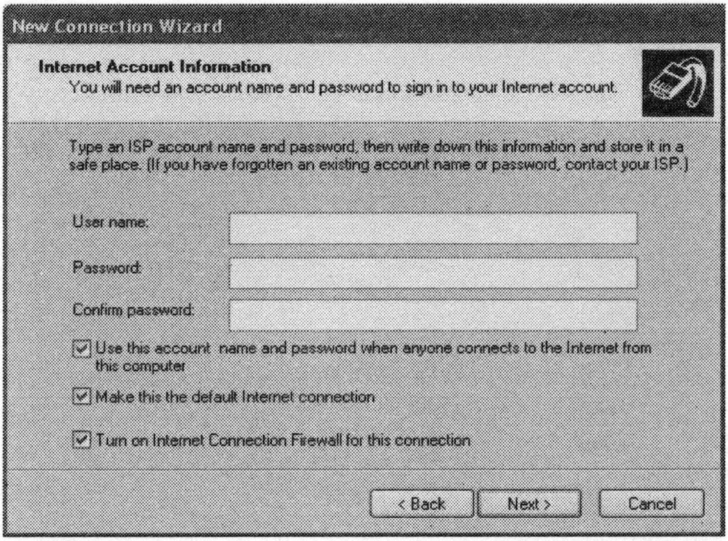

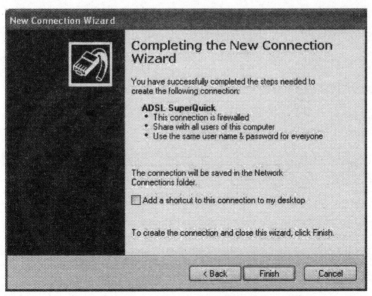

Fig.9.22 Enter the user name and password supplied by your ISP

Fig.9.23 Operate the Finish button to complete the process

Fig.9.24 Use this window to try out the new connection

been supplied to you by your ISP, and it is not possible to produce a dial-up Internet connection without them. The three checkboxes provide useful options, and if necessary the default settings should be amended. Unless firewall software will be used to protect the system from hackers it is advisable to use the built-in firewall protection of Windows XP.

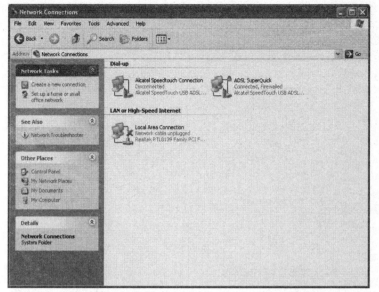

Fig.9.25 An icon for the new connection will appear in the Network Connections window

That more or less completes the creation of the new connection. The next window (Figure 9.23) has a checkbox that gives the option of creating a desktop shortcut to the new connection. Operate the Finish button to create the new Internet connection. A window like the one of Figure 9.24 will then appear. Enter your user name and password and try out the new connection. If you did not opt to have a shortcut placed on the desktop, the new connection can be activated by double-clicking on its icon in the Network Connections window (Figure 9.25). The Windows Copy and Paste facilities can be used to copy this shortcut to the desktop.

Windows ME

The procedure is similar for Windows ME, but you start by double-clicking the My Computer icon on the Windows desktop to produce the window of Figure 9.26. Then left-click the Dial-Up Networking link in the left-hand section of the window to produce the window of Figure 9.27. Double-click the Make New Connection icon to launch the appropriate wizard and start creating the new connection. The procedure is then similar to the one for Windows XP.

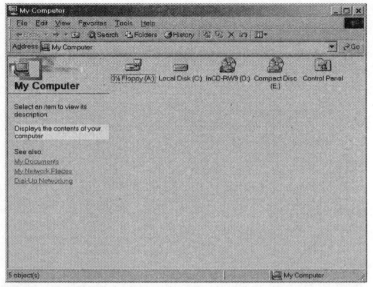

Fig.9.26 The My Computer window gives access to dial-up networking

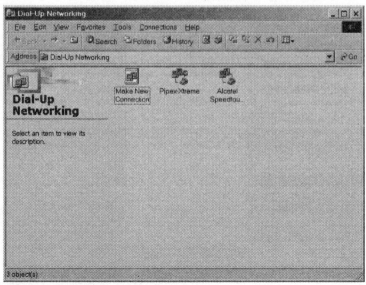

Fig.9.27 The Dial-Up Networking window

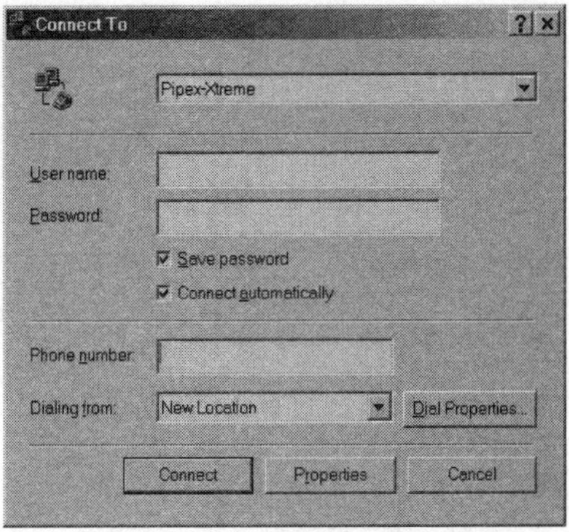

When the new connection has been created, double-click its icon in the Dial-Up Networking window to produce a window like the one of Figure 9.28. Here your user name and password are added, and the appropriate checkbox should be ticked if you wish to save them so that they do not have to be typed in each time a connection is required. The other checkbox is ticked in

Fig.9.28 Enter your user name and password and then try the new connection

order to have programs such as Internet Explorer automatically connect to the Internet when they are launched.

Modem switcher

ADSL modems having a built-in switcher (Figure 9.29) enable several PCs to share an ADSL Internet connection. The rear of the unit has a socket or sockets for connection to the telephone system, and like an ordinary ADSL modem it must be connected via a microfilter. There are typically four inputs (Figure 9.30), and these are standard RJ-45 10/100 Ethernet ports. These days some PCs have built-in LAN ports, but an inexpensive network card is all that is needed for any PC that does not have integral LAN ports.

Setting up this type of Internet connection is inevitably a bit more complicated than dealing with an ordinary ADSL modem. Start by getting the modem/switcher connected to its external power supply and the telephone line via a microfilter. Where appropriate, the LAN cards should be fitted in the PCs and the drivers should be installed. It is best to connect and configure one PC first and then connect and deal with the others one by one. Before starting, make sure that you have all the necessary information.

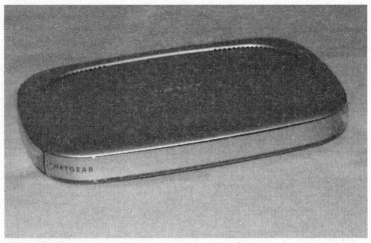

Fig.9.29 This Netgear ADSL modem has four Ethernet inputs

With everything connected up and switched on, check the instruction manual to determine whether the correct indicator lights are switched on. Typically there will be power, network, and Internet lights, plus a test light that switches on initially, but switches off again when the unit has finished its power on self test (POST). It often takes several seconds before the Internet light switches on properly, so do not jump to

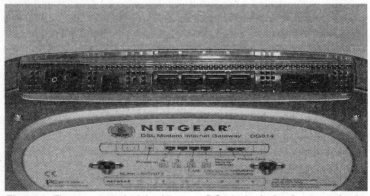

Fig.9.30 The rear panel of the Netgear DG814 includes four standard 10/100 network types

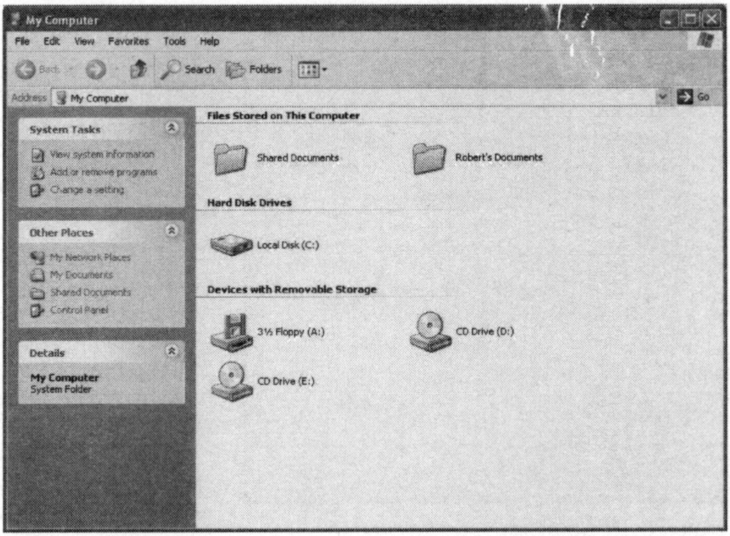

Fig.9.31 Configuration starts at the My Computer window

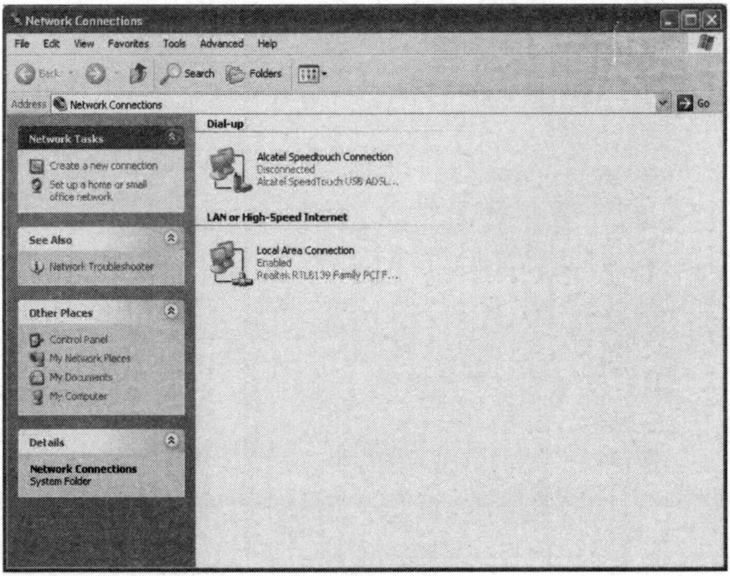

Fig.9.32 The Network Connections window

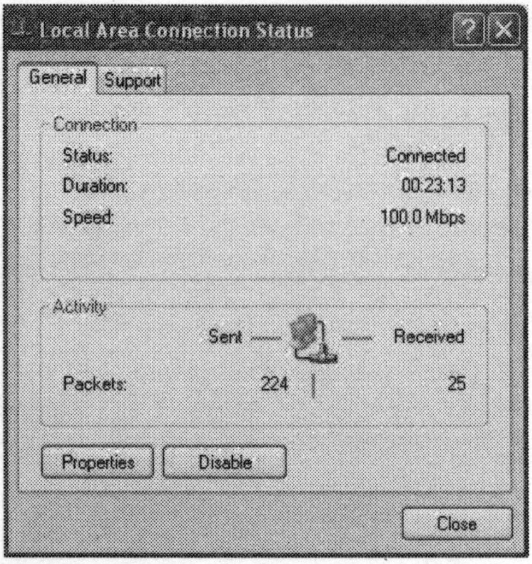

Fig.9.33 Operate the Properties button

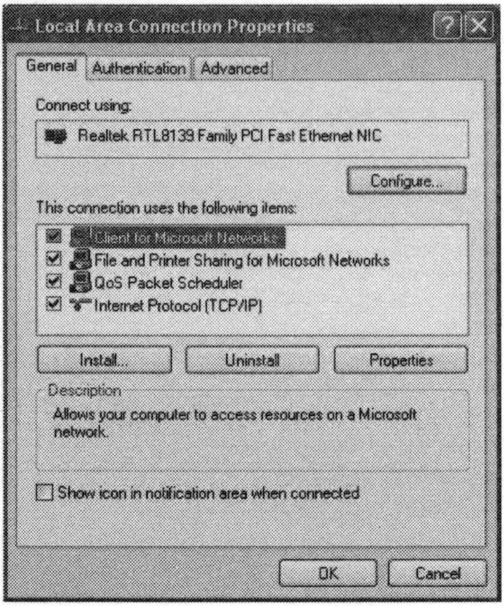

Fig.9.34 Select the network adapter's entry

conclusions about a problem here. Windows can be configured to work with the new modem/switcher when everything is functioning correctly.

Start the configuration by selecting My Computer from the Start menu. In the new window that appears (Figure 9.31) right-click the My Network Places link and select Properties from the popup menu. This produces a new window like the one in Figure 9.32. Double-click the Local Area Network icon, which will produce the new window of Figure 9.33. Then operate the Properties button to produce yet another new window (Figure 9.34). Select the Internet Protocol (TCP/IP) entry and then left-click the Properties button. Yes, another new window will then appear (Figure 9.35). Make sure that the radio buttons for Obtain IP address

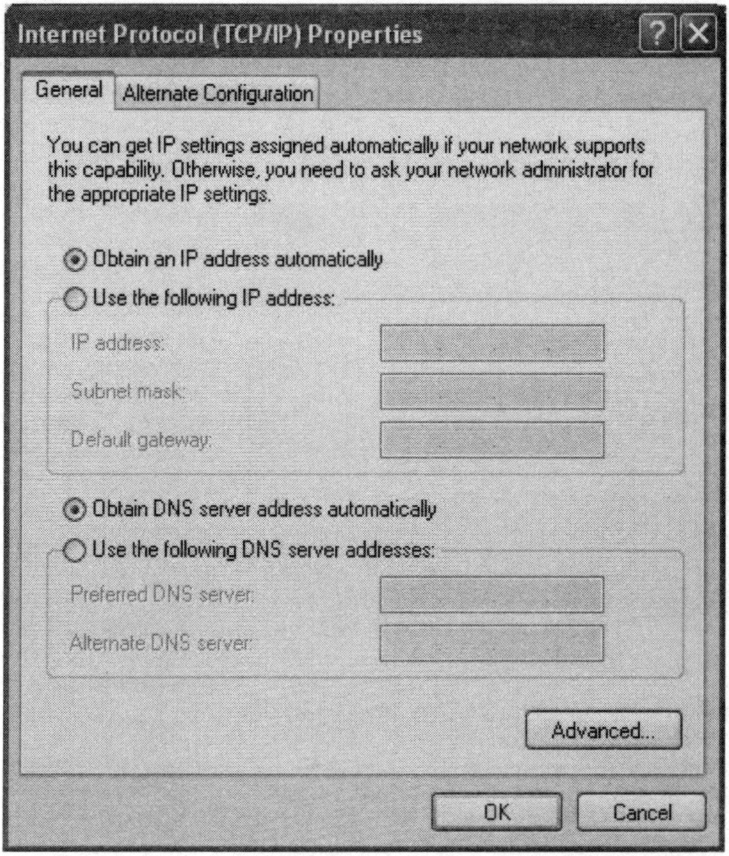

Fig.9.35 Make sure that the radio buttons have these settings

automatically and Obtain DNS server address automatically are both selected. Then operate the OK button, the OK button again, and the Close button to take things back to the Network Connections window. This window and the My Computer window can now be closed as well.

Restarting

In order to move on to the next stage the network must be restarted. This is usually achieved by first switching off the modem/router and then switching it on again a few seconds later. Restart the computer once the panel lights are giving the correct indications. The Netgear DG814 used in this example is configured online, and the next step is to launch a browser and then type in the supplied Internet address. This produces the login window of Figure 9.36 where the user name and password are inserted. Note that these are the ones provided by the modem manufacturer, and not the ones provided by your ISP.

This should bring up the configuration page of Figure 9.37 where the necessary operating parameters are added. Your ISP should be able to help with the settings if you are unsure about something, and there is help available from the right-hand section of the window. In the UK the VPI (Virtual Path Identifier) and VCI (Virtual Channel Identifier) settings are 0 and 38 respectively. If you are unsure about the correct settings and there is an automatic detection facility, this will almost certainly find the correct settings for you.

Fig.9.36 Enter the supplied user name and password

Note that some facilities such as video conferencing might not work unless port forwarding is used. There should be a section dealing with this so that it can be enabled and set up with the correct parameters. The vast majority of web sites and Internet facilities can be used as normal though, so there is no need to worry about port forwarding unless a facility you use fails to work with the new set-up.

More connections

Of course, the whole point of an ADSL modem that has a built-in switcher is that it enables several PCs to share an Internet connection. Although the PCs are all using the same Internet connection, to the users it seems

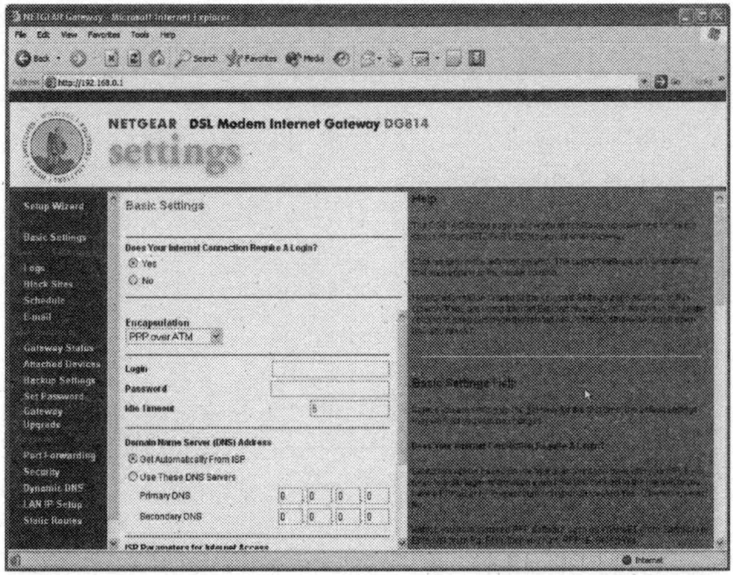

Fig.9.37 The modems's set-up screen. Automatic configuration can be used if you do not feel able to do the job manually

as though they each have their own completely independent Internet connection. Even with four users sharing one modem, the download bandwidth per user is typically well over 100 kilobits per second. This is more than double the bandwidth of an ordinary V90 or V92 telephone modem.

Problems will only be experienced if someone uses the Internet for something that results in large amounts of data being downloaded. Applications of this type include streaming audio and video, and downloading large files. With one PC downloading at several hundred kilobytes per second it will inevitably make the connection run more slowly for other users, although it might still be perfectly usable.

Additional connections are handled in much the same way as the original one. The second computer is wired to the modem using another category 5 Ethernet cable. Note that the cable must be a "straight" type, and not "cross patch" cable (which is used for connecting two PCs together). The original example was for a PC running Windows XP, so a PC running Windows ME will be used to demonstrate the setting up of additional PCs.

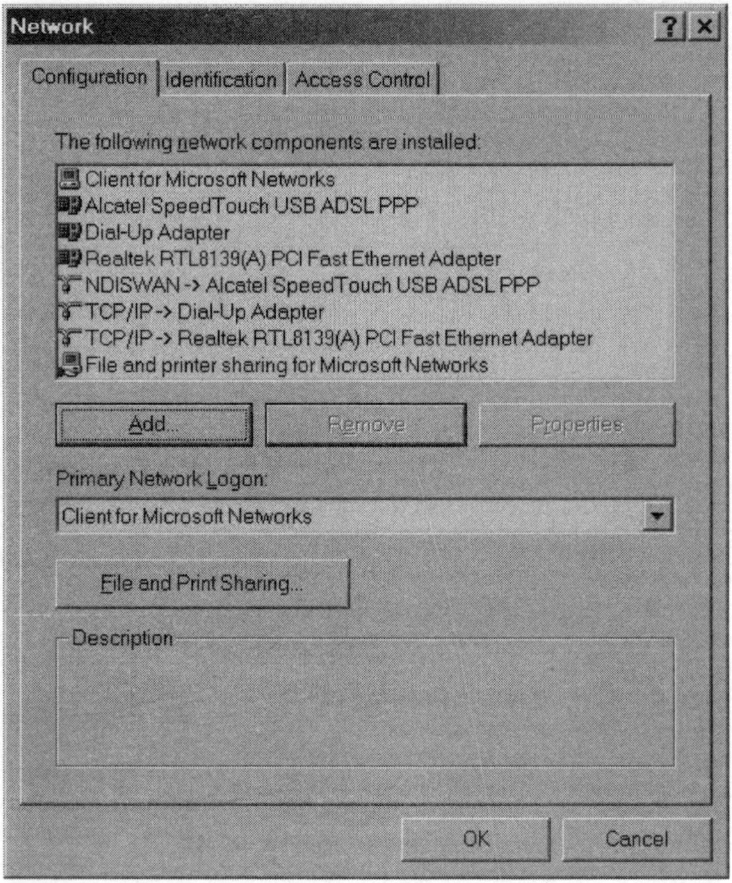

Fig.9.38 The Configuration section of the Network window

Go to the Start menu and choose Settings followed by Control Panel. Next, double-click the Network icon in the Control Panel to bring up the window of Figure 9.38. Operate the Configuration tab if it is not already selected. In the various entries listed there should be a TCP/IP entry for the computer's network card. Select this entry and then left-click the Properties button. This produces the window of Figure 9.39 where the radio button labelled "Obtain an IP address automatically" must be

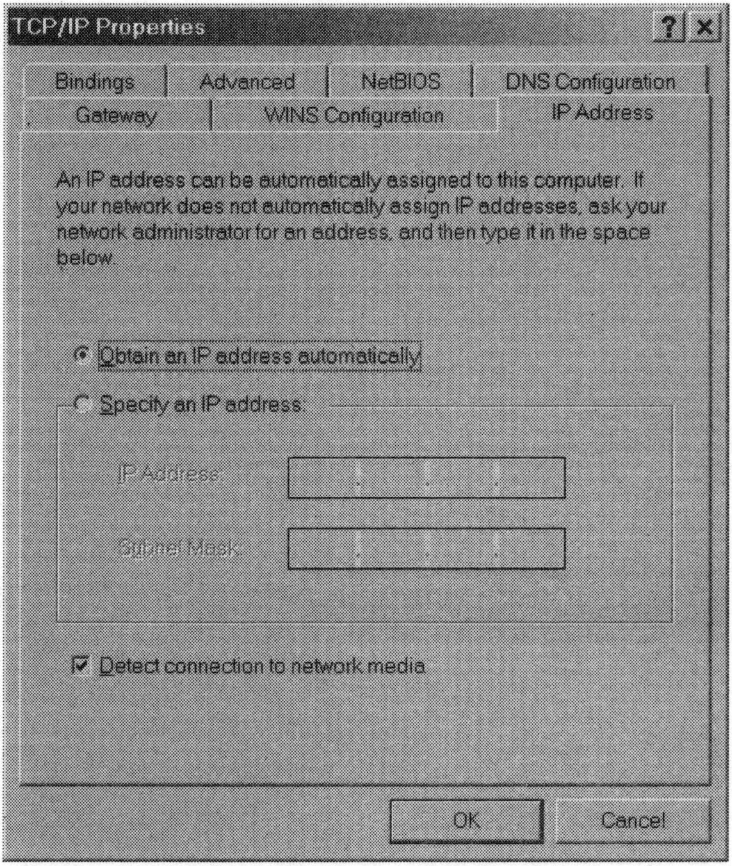

Fig.9.39 Opt to obtain a TCP/IP address automatically

selected. Operate the IP Address tab to switch to the correct section of the TCP/IP Properties window if it does not already look like Figure 9.39.

Next the Gateway tab is operated, and any addresses that are listed must be selected and then deleted using the Remove button. It is likely that none will be listed, as in Figure 9.40. The OK button is then operated followed by the OK button of the previous window so that both windows are closed. This brings up the warning message of Figure 9.41, which

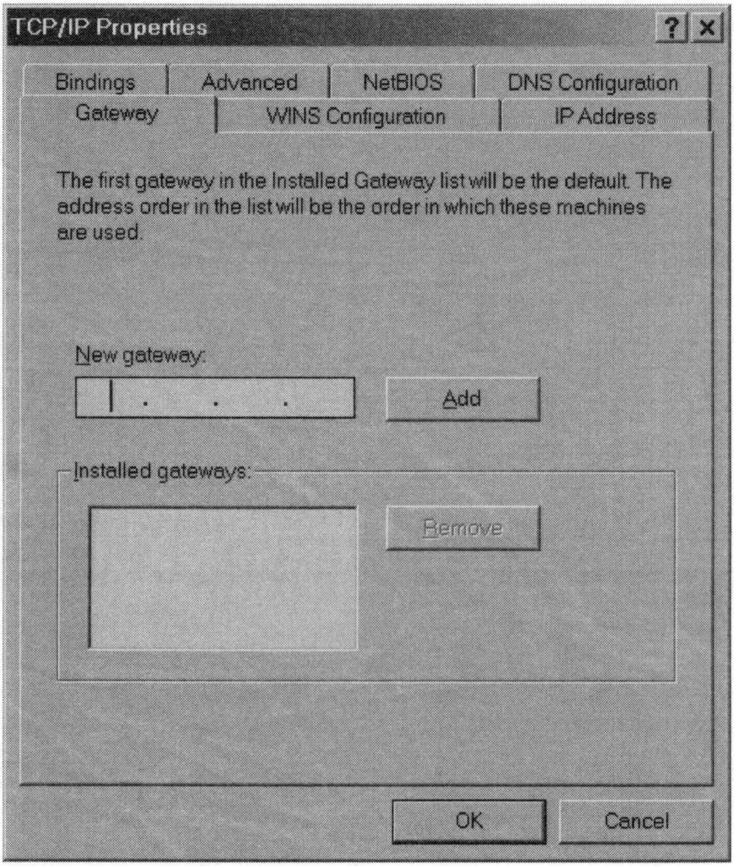

Fig.9.40 Any addresses listed must be deleted

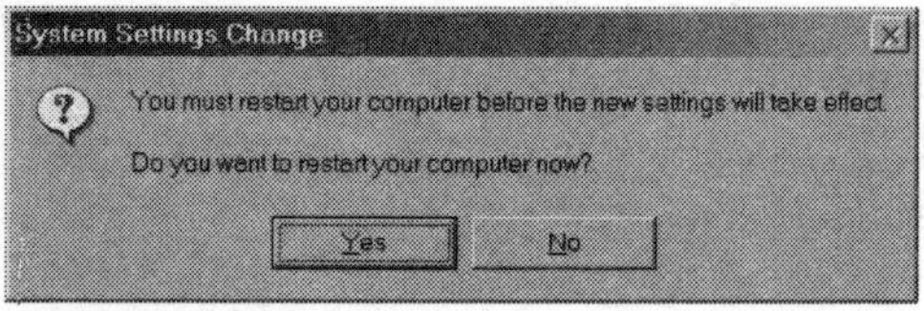

Fig.9.41 Operate the Yes button to restart the computer

explains that the computer must be restarted in order to make the changes take effect. Operate the Yes button to restart the computer. It is then a matter of restarting the network and repeating the

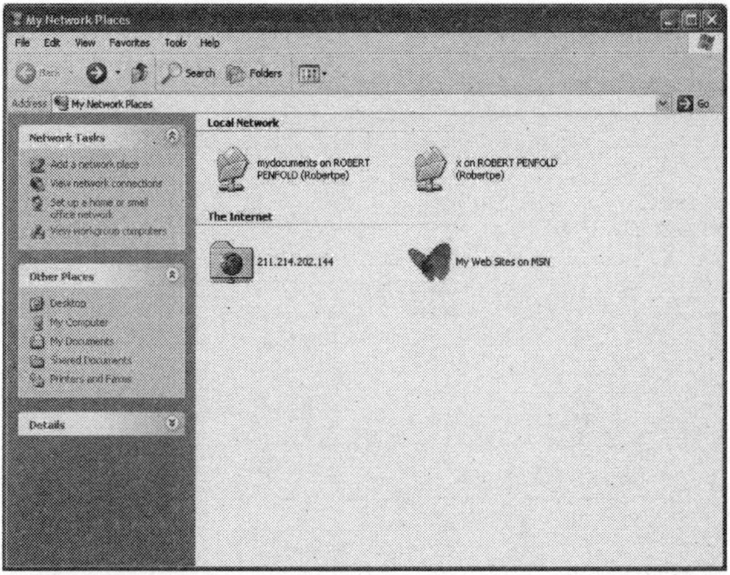

Fig.9.42 It is possible to set up links to files and folders in the other computers in the network

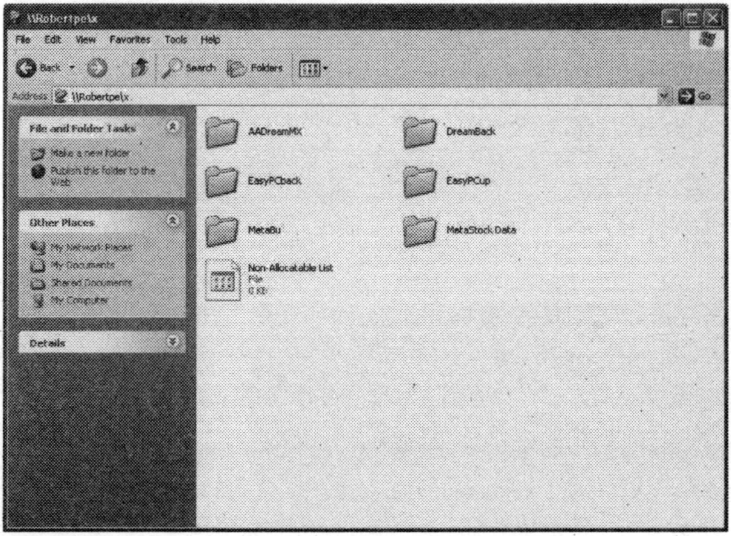

Fig.9.43 These files are on a CD-RW disc in the other PC

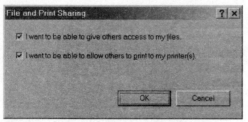

Fig.9.44 The Network window lists the Network components

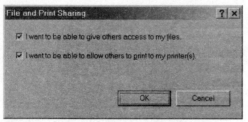

Fig.9.45 Select the required types of sharing

setting-up process that was used for the first computer. This whole procedure is repeated for each additional PC.

With all the PCs set up correctly it should then be possible to

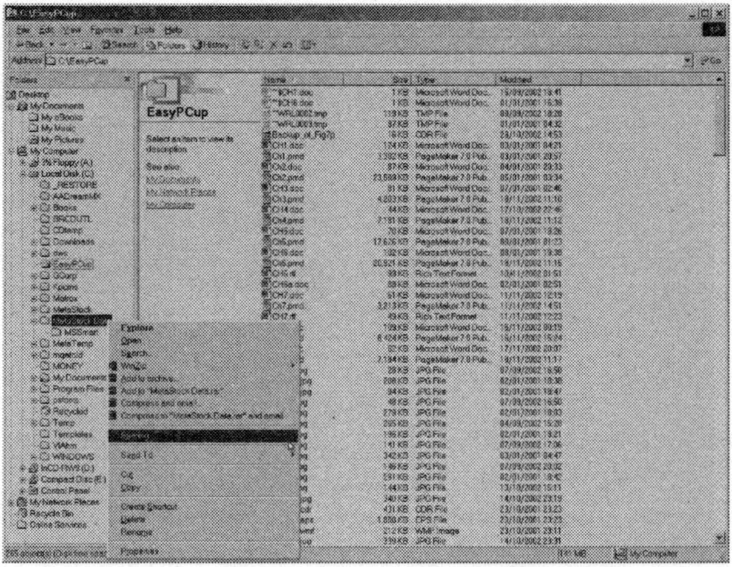

Fig.9.46 Right-click and select sharing from the popup menu

surf the Internet on all of them, with the switcher ensuring that each PC only receives the correct packets of data. This makes the other PCs on the network "invisible" to all the other PCs on the network. However, it is normally possible to use the switcher to network the PCs in standard fashion so that files or directories on one PC can be used by another.

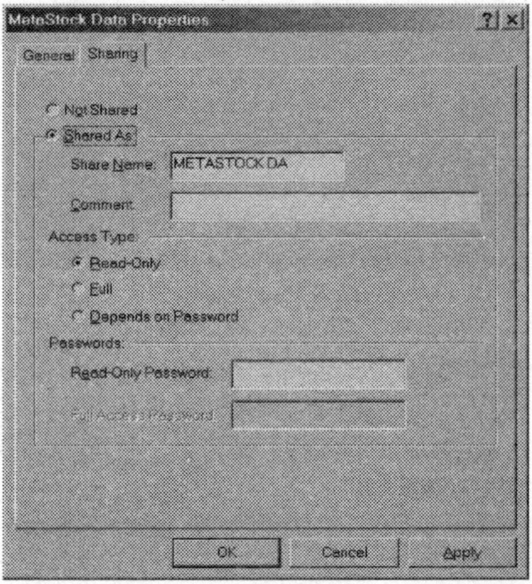

Figure 9.42 shows the My Network Places

Fig.9.47 Operate the Share As button and select the required options

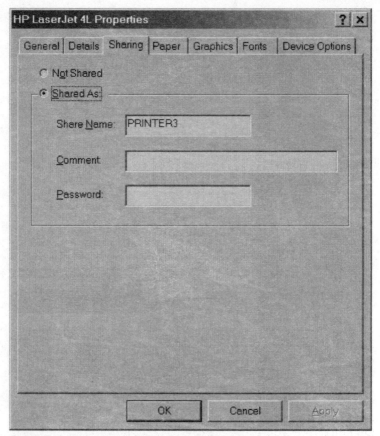

Fig.9.48 Printers can also be shared on the network

window for the PC running Windows XP. The two entries in the Local Network section are actually a directory and a disc on the PC running Windows ME. Double-clicking one of these opens it in the normal way, and Figure 9.43 shows the contents of the accessible disc of the other PC. Of course, it is only necessary to share any files or folders if you wish to do so, and the PCs in the system can remain totally separate if desired.

Sharing files

In order to share files it is first necessary to enable this feature in Windows. Go to the Control Panel and double-click the Network icon to produce the Network window (Figure 9.44). Next, operate the File and Printer Sharing button, which will produce the small window of Figure 9.45. Place a tick in the checkbox for file sharing, and one in the printer sharing checkbox as well if you wish to enable this facility. Then operate the OK button and close both the Network window and the Control Panel.

The next step is to select the files and folders that you wish to share. Launch Windows Explorer and locate a file or directory that you wish to make available to other PCs in the system. Right-click this entry and select Sharing from the popup menu (Figure 9.46). In the new window (Figure 9.47) operate the Share As radio button and then select the type of access required using the lower set of three radio buttons. Add a password if you wish to make the file or directory password protected, or leave this blank if you do not require this facility.

Repeat this process for all the files and folders that are to be made available to other PCs in the system. Then repeat the whole procedure for any other PCs that have files that are to be shared by the system. The sharing system is then ready to use.

A printer can be shared using a similar process. Start by selecting Settings and then Printers from the Start menu. In the new window, right-click the icon for the printer you wish to share and select Sharing from the popup menu. In the new window, operate the Share As radio button and add a password if required. Finish by operating the OK button and closing the Printers window. The system is then ready for use. This general method is used whether the network is via a modem/switcher, two PCs via a cross-patch cable, or via a normal hub, etc.

Points to remember

When upgrading an old PC it is safer to opt for a hardware modem rather than a software type. A hardware modem, unlike the software variety, requires practically no processor time.

Getting the drivers installed for some modems can be tricky. Matters are complicated by the fact that most modems require two or three sets of drivers in order to function properly, and the software modems are worst in this respect.

When a PCI modem or other PCI card fails to install properly and reinstalling the drivers does not improve matters, it is worth totally uninstalling the device and reinstalling it from scratch. Make sure that the manufacturer's installation notes are followed "to the letter" on the second attempt.

Getting the modem physically installed and the drivers loaded are only the first two stages of installation. Further installation is needed in order to surf the Internet. Most ISPs have installation CDs that largely or totally automate this final installation, but it is not too difficult to set up Windows correctly if you have the necessary information.

Where the modem seems to be installed correctly but the Internet connection does not work, look through the Internet and modem settings for any obvious errors. Also, make sure that the user name, password, and connection details are correct. A minor error in any of these will prevent the modem from connecting to the Internet.

Call waiting and other services can give problems with telephone modems, so make sure that the system is set up to deal with anything like this.

It is possible for home or small office users to share an ADSL Internet connection using a combined switcher and modem. This effectively provides each PC with its own Internet connection, but the available bandwidth is shared between the PCs connected to the modem/switcher. Each PC in the system must have a standard Ethernet LAN port.

A combined ADSL modem and switcher should be able to network all the PCs in the system. However, bear in mind that the network connections will not be set up by default. The links have to be set up in Windows, and you can select which files and folders are made available to other computers in the system.

Index

Index